Europe

Regional Studies Series

The Regional Studies Series

Africa
China
Europe
The Subcontinent of India
Japan and Korea
Latin America
The Middle East and North Africa
Russia and the Commonwealth

Europe

Regional Studies Series

Consultant

Michael Kort

GLOBE BOOK COMPANY
A Division of Simon & Schuster
Englewood Cliffs, New Jersey

Michael Kort

Michael Kort is Associate Professor of Social Science in the College of Basic Studies of Boston University. He is the author of *Russia and the Commonwealth* in Globe Book Company's Regional Studies Series (1993), *Eastern Europe Since 1945* (Globe, 1991), *The Soviet Colossus: A History of the U.S.S.R.* (Scribner, 1985), and biographies of Nikita Khrushchev and Mikhail Gorbachev (Franklin Watts, 1989, 1990). He holds a B.A. degree from Johns Hopkins University and M.A. and Ph.D. degrees from New York University.

Executive Editor: Stephen Lewin
Project Editor: Samuel C. Plummer
Art Director: Nancy Sharkey
Cover Designer: Armando Baez
Production Manager: Winston Sukhnanand
Marketing Manager: Elmer Ildefonso

Cover Image: The picture on the cover shows fireworks illuminating the Brandenburg Gate in Berlin, formerly a symbol of a divided Europe, on the occasion of German reunification, October 3, 1990.

Maps: Mapping Specialists, Ltd.
Graphs, Diagrams, and Charts: Keithley and Associates

Photographic acknowledgments appear on page 309.

ISBN 835-90430-x

Printed in the United States of America   4 5 6 7 8 9 10 96 95

CONTENTS

Political Map of Europe

1 *The Land*

For several centuries, Europe was the most powerful and influential region of the world. Europeans created a magnificent culture, and then—by example and by force—they spread it throughout the world.

Today, much of Europe's former power has passed to North America and East Asia. Yet Europe in many ways remains a hub of world influence. Many of the ideas about government and law—and much of the language, food, literature, music, and art—of North America derive from Europe. The same is true in South and Central America, the Caribbean, Australia, and New Zealand. Moreover, Europe has had a great impact on much of Africa and Asia, where European nations once ruled colonial empires.

The geography of Europe has contributed in many ways to the achievements of its people. The natural environment gives many Europeans easy access to the sea and easy access to one another, so that developments in one part of Europe quickly spread to the rest. Many parts of Europe enjoy almost ideal conditions for agriculture, and other parts possess the raw materials needed for industrial development. In addition, Europe's ocean-facing location put adventure—and the riches of the world—within Europeans' grasp when, more than five centuries ago, they reached out to explore the rest of the world.

THE SIZE AND LOCATION OF EUROPE

Europe is a **peninsula**, a land area largely surrounded by water. It juts westward into the Atlantic Ocean from the great land mass of Asia. In the east, Europe includes the western part of Russia, where a range of low hills called the Ural Mountains is usually considered to mark the

1

eastern boundary of Europe and the beginning of Asia. (Until 1991, the European parts of Russia, as well as the nations of Ukraine, Belarus, and Moldova, were parts of the Soviet Union. In 1991, the Soviet Union collapsed, to be replaced by the Commonwealth of Independent States. These eastern nations of Europe are examined in the Globe Regional Studies book *Russia and the Commonwealth* and will not be discussed in detail in this book.)

Only one of the world's continents, Australia, is smaller in area than the continent of Europe. Europe covers about 4 million square miles (10.36 million sq. km.) when Russia, Ukraine, Belarus, and Moldova are included, or about half that area when they are left out. However, the small continent of Europe is relatively crowded. Only Asia is more densely populated than Europe.

Ocean Boundaries. The coasts of oceans and seas make up Europe's other boundaries. On the north lies the Arctic Ocean, on the south the Mediterranean Sea, and on the west the Atlantic Ocean.

A small island in the Mediterranean Sea is seen from the shore of the larger island of Sicily. Southern Europe enjoys a generally warm and pleasant climate.

Compare the coasts of Europe to those of Africa and South America, and notice the contrasts. Europe's coastline is jagged, with countless bays, straits, channels, and inlets. On the other hand, the coastlines of Africa and South America are much smoother. The jagged coastline of Europe extends for 37,887 miles (61,108 km).

Many other peninsulas break off from the bulk of Europe. The two largest of Europe's peninsulas are the Scandinavian peninsula in the north, the location of Norway and Sweden, and the Balkan peninsula in the southeast, occupied by Greece and several other small and medium-sized countries. The "boot" of Italy is yet another peninsula. So is Iberia, the location of Spain and Portugal, in the southwest.

Thousands of small islands and several quite large ones are part of Europe. Europe's largest island is Great Britain, which contains England, Scotland, and Wales. Other large European islands are Iceland and Ireland in the Atlantic Ocean and Sicily, Sardinia, Corsica, and Crete in the Mediterranean Sea.

Because of Europe's jagged coastline, almost every part of Europe lies close to a large body of water. The coastline also has many good harbors. Europeans took naturally to sailing, in part because they seldom had to sail far to reach the next harbor. Consequently, fishing became an important industry.

The Gulf Stream.   The oceans affect the climate of much of Europe. An ocean current called the **Gulf Stream** carries warm water from the Gulf of Mexico all the way across the Atlantic Ocean to the European coasts. One branch of the stream flows just north of Great Britain. Another part carries warm water into the North Sea and south along the coasts of France, Spain, and Portugal. These warm waters bring a moderate climate to much of Europe. For example, they keep the harbors of western Norway ice-free all year, despite Norway's far northern location. Except for its most eastward, interior parts, Europe enjoys a mild, generally humid climate.

EUROPE'S DIVERSE TOPOGRAPHY

A practical way to look at Europe's **topography,** or the shape of the land's surface, is to divide the area into topographic **regions.** A region is an area that shares certain characteristics. Geographers divide Europe into many different kinds of regions for study, such as climate regions, crop regions, language regions—and topographic regions.

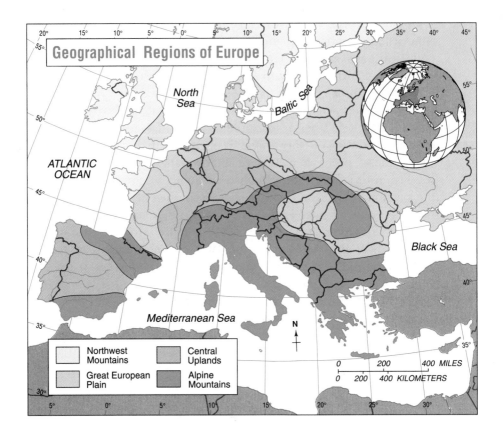

Despite its small size, Europe is extremely diverse, so one could divide it into many small topographic regions. However, geographers generally speak of four main regions: the Northwest Mountains, the Great European Plain, the Central Uplands, and the Alpine Mountains.

The Northwest Mountain Region. The Northwest Mountain region includes Ireland, northern Great Britain, northwest France, Norway, Sweden, northern Finland, and the northwestern corner of Russia. The terrain in the Northwest Mountain region is mostly composed of very old, worn-down mountains, some of the oldest rock formations on earth. The thin soil and steep slopes of the Northwest Mountain region are not good for agriculture, nor are they densely populated.

The Great European Plain. The Great European Plain is a more var-ied region than the Northwest Mountains. Beginning as a narrow ribbon in France, and squeezed to a width of about 50 miles in Belgium, the plain gradually widens through Germany, Poland, Estonia, Latvia, and Lithuania. It stretches far into Russia and Ukraine. The mostly flat or rolling land of the Great European Plain contains some of the world's most fertile farmland. Lakes and swamps make the plain's more northerly parts, such as in Latvia, less suitable for farming.

In its western parts, the plain is densely populated; it is more thinly peopled in its eastern sections. Over the centuries of European history, the Great European Plain has been a major travel route for migrating peoples, for trade, and for the exchange of ideas. Armies have marched across the plain in both directions.

The Central Uplands.   South of the Great European Plain are several areas of hills, low mountains, and small plateaus. These areas are the Central Uplands. The Central Uplands include the high, windswept tableland, or *meseta*, of central Portugal and Spain, the central highlands of France, the central part of Germany, and the western portions of Czechoslovakia.

Many of the hills of the Central Uplands are covered with forests. River valleys often contain fertile soil, although many of the hills are too rocky for farming. Most of Europe's coal deposits are found in the Central Uplands, and large cities grew up there when Europeans began to industrialize.

The Alpine Mountains.   The Alpine Mountains have been described as Europe's "backbone and ribs." The magnificent Alps themselves (the

Two peaks in the Swiss Alps, the Alp Pras Gras (the "Fat Alp") and its neighbor Mont Collon, tower over the shepherds' huts in the foreground.

"backbone") stretch through eight countries: France, Italy, Switzerland, Liechtenstein, Germany, Austria, Slovenia, and Croatia. The highest peak of the Alps is Mont Blanc in France at 15,780 feet (4,807 m.). Other famous Alpine peaks include the Matterhorn and the Jungfrau (YOONG-frow) in Switzerland and the Grossglockner (grohs-GLUHK-nuhr) in Austria. Because the Alps are known for their majestic beauty, tourism is a major industry in each of the Alpine nations. Some of Europe's great rivers, including the Rhine, the Rhône (ROHN), and the Po, begin in Alpine glaciers.

The "ribs" include several mountain chains, beginning in the west with the Sierra Nevada in Spain and the Pyrenees (PIHR-uh-neez) on the French–Spanish border. Other "ribs" of the Alpine Mountains include the Apennines in Italy, the Dinaric Alps stretching from Croatia to Greece, the Balkan Mountains of Bulgaria, the Transylvanian Alps of Romania, and the Carpathian Mountains of Czechoslovakia, Poland, Romania, and Ukraine.

For centuries the Alpine mountain system was a mighty barrier between the European plains and southern Europe. However, the barrier was never complete, because many passes and river valleys provide ways to cross the mountains. In the south, the Apennines made communication among different parts of Italy difficult, as did the Pyrenees between France and Spain.

EUROPE'S WATERWAYS

A favorite excursion in Europe is a boat trip on the Rhine River as it winds its way through the Rhine Gorge just above Bonn, Germany. While their boats move along with or against the swift current of the river, tourists can sit in the sunshine and marvel at the beauties of medieval castles and steeply terraced vineyards on the cliffs above them.

The Rhine has an even more important role in the economy of Europe than as a tourist attraction. From the mouth of the Rhine in the Netherlands on the North Sea, oceangoing ships can travel upstream as far as Cologne (kuh-LOHN). River barges, loaded with farm products, coal, iron ore, and manufactured goods, can travel even farther, all the way to Basel, Switzerland, which is 700 miles (1,130 km.) inland.

The Rhine is a major part of Europe's vast river-based transportation network. Europeans ship large quantities of goods by river because it is cheaper than shipping by rail or truck. Besides the Rhine, many other European rivers provide transportation, access to the sea, water

Barges on the Rhine River in Germany pass one of the river's famous castles. Terraced vineyards can be seen on the river's opposite bank.

for agriculture, and power to make electricity. These include the Thames (TEMZ) in England, the Rhône in France, the Elbe in Germany, and the Danube in central and southeastern Europe.

Rivers of Northern Europe. Northern Europe has many rivers, but few are important arteries of transport. The rivers of Norway, Sweden, and Finland carry melting snows from inland mountains to the sea. They allowed loggers of the 1800s to float their logs to sawmills. Nowadays, many are dammed to produced electricity. Finland and the Baltic countries have many lakes that allow travel by boat.

Rivers of Western Europe. The Thames is a relatively short river, running about 200 miles (about 325 km.) from the central part of Great Britain to the North Sea. However, the Thames is very important because it allows oceangoing ships to reach London, one of the world's busiest ports and Britain's capital.

Although France has many rivers, most of them cannot be used for any distance by oceangoing ships. However, the French have linked their rivers by canals to the great Rhine system. The chief of France's many rivers are the Seine (SEN), the Loire (LWAHR), the Garonne (gah-RUHN), and the Rhône.

7

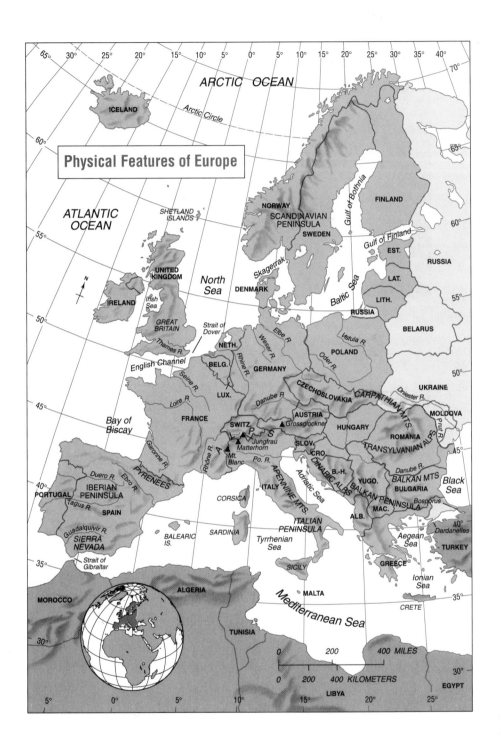

Physical Features of Europe

ARCTIC OCEAN

Arctic Circle

ICELAND

ATLANTIC OCEAN

SHETLAND ISLANDS

NORWAY

SCANDINAVIAN PENINSULA

SWEDEN

FINLAND

Gulf of Bothnia

Gulf of Finland

EST.

RUSSIA

LAT.

UNITED KINGDOM

North Sea

DENMARK

Skagerrak

Baltic Sea

LITH.

RUSSIA

IRELAND

Irish Sea

GREAT BRITAIN

Strait of Dover

Elbe R.

Weser R.

Vistula R.

BELARUS

Thames R.

NETH.

POLAND

Oder R.

English Channel

BELG.

Rhine R.

GERMANY

UKRAINE

Seine R.

LUX.

Danube R.

CZECHOSLOVAKIA

CARPATHIAN MTS.

Dniester R.

MOLDOVA

Loire R.

FRANCE

AUSTRIA

HUNGARY

ROMANIA

Prut R.

Bay of Biscay

SWITZ.

Grossglockner

A L P S

Jungfrau

Matterhorn

SLOV.

CRO.

TRANSYLVANIAN ALPS

Garonne R.

Mt. Blanc

Rhône R.

Po. R.

APENNINE MTS.

DINARIC ALPS

B.-H.

YUGO.

Danube R.

BALKAN MTS.

BULGARIA

Black Sea

PYRENEES

Duero R.

Ebro R.

IBERIAN PENINSULA

ITALY

Adriatic Sea

BALKAN PENINSULA

Bosporus

PORTUGAL

CORSICA

MAC.

Tagus R.

SPAIN

BALEARIC IS.

SARDINIA

ITALIAN PENINSULA

Tyrrhenian Sea

ALB.

Aegean Sea

Dardanelles

TURKEY

Guadalquivir R.

SIERRA NEVADA

Strait of Gibraltar

SICILY

GREECE

Ionian Sea

CRETE

MOROCCO

ALGERIA

MALTA

Mediterranean Sea

TUNISIA

0   200   400 MILES

0   200   400 KILOMETERS

LIBYA

EGYPT

8

The Seine is a slow-moving river of northwestern France that empties into the English Channel at Le Havre (luh HAHV-ruh). The Seine and its many tributaries drain the entire Paris Basin, the largest agricultural region of France. Oceangoing vessels can reach Rouen on the Seine. Rouen is France's second most important port, after Marseilles.

The Loire is France's longest river, rising in central France and flowing north and then west before reaching the Atlantic Ocean at Saint-Nazaire, a ship-building center. Shipping can reach the seaport of Nantes, about 30 miles inland, only at high tide. The valley of the Loire is famous for its vineyards and its beautiful *châteaux*, or castles.

The Garonne rises on the slopes of Pyrenees. It joins with the Dordogne River a few miles north of Bordeaux (bawr-DOH) to form the Gironde estuary. An **estuary** is the wide part of a river where the tides meet and influence the river's current.

The Rhône rises in the Swiss Alps and flows mainly southward to the Mediterranean Sea. Navigable for about 300 miles (440 km.), it flows through Lyon, France's third largest city, and is connected by a canal near its mouth to Marseilles, France's second largest city and its major port.

Rivers of Central Europe. The rivers of Germany and Poland have contributed in many ways to the growth of industry. Although the mouth of the Rhine is in the Netherlands, the Rhine flows through Germany for most of its length. In addition, in northern Germany the Elbe (EHL-buh), the Spree (SHPRAY), and the short but important Weser (VAY-zuhr) are useful navigable rivers. Between Germany and Poland lie the Oder and Neisse (NEYE-suh) rivers, and through central Poland flows the Vistula (VISS-tyoo-luh). All of those rivers head generally northward.

The great Danube, which begins in southern Germany, takes a different direction—south and east. The Danube is the longest river in Europe outside Russia. It rises in Germany's Black Forest. After flowing 1,750 miles (2,820 km.), it finally empties into the Black Sea, along the way having formed the boundary between Czechoslovakia and Hungary, Croatia and Yugoslavia, Yugoslavia and Romania, and Romania and Bulgaria. The Danube touches the territory of more nations than any other river in the world. The Danube's historic role as a boundary reduces its commercial usefulness, because shipping has to cross so many political frontiers. Its mouth at the Black Sea is also relatively isolated for shipping to other parts of the world.

The Rivers of Southern Europe. The Danube is one of many rivers that lend their charms to Southern Europe. Its tributaries are important waterways for the southern Slav states.

Italy's chief river is the Po. Rising in the snow-clad Alps, it flows southward and eastward across northern Italy, emptying into the Adriatic Sea south of Venice. Vessels can travel as far inland as Turin, a major industrial city. Farther south, the Tiber River flows westward through Rome to the Tyrrhenian (tih-REE-nee-uhn) Sea. Only the 20-mile stretch from Rome to the sea is navigable.

The Tagus River is the longest river on the Iberian Peninsula and neatly divides its western half. Rising in east central Spain about 80 miles north of Madrid, the Tagus empties into the Atlantic Ocean at Portugal's capital, Lisbon (LIHZ-buhn). The Tagus is navigable for about 100 miles. A much shorter river, the Guadalquivir (gwah-duhl-KWIV-uhr), is more important economically because of the fertility it brings to the oases along its path through southern Spain to the Atlantic.

Canals. Europeans improved their river systems by building large systems of **navigation canals**. A navigation canal is an artificial waterway for use by ships and other vessels.

Canals can shorten journeys. By using the Canal du Midi in France, vessels can pass from the Mediterranean Sea to the Bay of Biscay. Without the canal, ships would have to travel all the way around the Iberian Peninsula. In Germany, about 90,000 vessels use the Nord-Ostsee, or Kiel, Canal every year to move between the Baltic and North seas. Another canal, the Mittelland Canal, crosses Germany from east to west, intersecting the Oder, the Elbe, and the Weser rivers as they flow northward. Connecting the Rhine and Danube river systems is the Main-Danube Canal in southern Germany. Canals also are important in the Netherlands, where 20 percent of the nation's freight moves on them. Canals link France to the German river and canal system.

Europeans continue to improve their canals with the latest technology. For example, boats on the Brussels-Charleroi Canal in Belgium enter a steel tank at the locks at Ronquières. The tank moves on rails up a steep slope, raising the boats 220 feet (60 meters) in only 20 minutes.

Ports. In Europe, the large number of good ports makes trade easier with other parts of the world. Much French and German shipping moves through the port of Rotterdam, in the Netherlands, at the mouth of the Rhine River. Rotterdam, in fact, is the busiest port in the world. Germany also uses ports at Hamburg and Bremen for its shipping.

10

Ports on the Mediterranean Sea are less important than they once were. However, the Mediterranean Sea itself remains important, since many ships cross it on their way to or from Egypt's Suez Canal, which links the Mediterranean to the Indian Ocean. For almost 300 years, Great Britain has maintained a fortress at Gibraltar to help it protect Mediterranean shipping. Gibraltar, on the coast of Spain, commands the narrow entrance to the Mediterranean from the Atlantic. A narrow waterway of this sort is called a **strait**.

In the east, the straits between the Mediterranean and the Black Sea are also closely guarded. Ships passing from the Mediterranean to the Black Sea must use two straits—the Dardanelles and the Bosporus—that go through Turkish territory. Control of those passages has often been important in wartime. The Dardanelles and the Bosporus are part of the dividing line between Europe and Asia.

THE CLIMATES OF EUROPE

Just as the small continent of Europe has many different kinds of topography, so it also enjoys a diversity of climates.

The sea and its winds give much of Europe a mild **maritime** climate, with moderate temperatures and much rainfall in all seasons. In the eastern sections of Europe, however, where the sea is far away, the climate is **continental**. Winters are long and cold and summers are hot, as in the Middle West of the United States. Rainfall is moderate to scarce, often less than 20 inches a year.

Lands along the shores of the Mediterranean Sea share a climate called **Mediterranean**. Summers are warm and dry. Most of the rainfall occurs during the mild winters.

Small parts of northern Europe experience colder climates. Areas with a **subarctic** climate have short, cool summers and long, cold winters. Even farther north, some small portions of northernmost Europe are in the **polar** climatic region. There it is cold all the time, even in summer. In each of these northern climate zones, rainfall is scarce.

NATURAL RESOURCES

Most parts of Europe have been blessed with a variety of **natural resources**. Natural resources are the many parts of the environment that people can use to improve their lives. Fertile soil is a natural

Cornstalks are stacked on a farm near Gerona, Spain. The hillsides in the background are terraced to conserve water and prevent erosion.

resource that allows farmers to grow abundant crops. Fuels, such as coal and oil, are valuable natural resources.

Europe's excellent waterways allow Europeans to reach the available resources and take them to market. In addition, the rivers and oceans of Europe yield many resources themselves. The waters are home to numerous different species of fish, an important natural resource for many nations. For example, fish make up 75 percent of Iceland's exports. Rivers and oceans can also provide energy resources. Powerful rivers can be tapped to produce electricity. Under the North Sea lie vast fields of petroleum and natural gas.

Soil and Plant Resources. Like people everywhere, Europeans depend on the land for plant resources such as food and timber. Many factors affect the crops and trees that a country or region can produce. Some soils are rich, others poor. Some regions get plenty of rain, others tend to be dry. Some climates offer sunny summers and mild winters, others rainy summers and snowy winters.

The best soils—in Europe as elsewhere—tend to collect in broad river valleys, where floods or winds leave rich deposits. One of Europe's prime agricultural areas is the Po River valley of northern Italy. There, farmers produce wheat, vegetables, citrus fruits, olives, and grapes for wine. Another area of rich soils lies in the hills and valleys of central Germany. Around Leipzig (LEYEP-sihg), winds have piled up dust from the Great European Plain, helping to create excellent farming soils.

Agricultural land is a much prized resource in the Netherlands, where much of it has been painstakingly claimed from the sea. In order to reclaim this land, the Dutch must first dam off a portion of the ocean. Then they pump the water out of the area behind the dam, while bringing in soil to fill it. The land is kept dry by a system of drainage canals and pumping stations. The Dutch say, "God created the world, but the Dutch created Holland."

Careful cropping practices have helped Europeans to make use of many areas of much poorer soil. European farmers have long rotated row crops (such as peas and turnips) with grass crops, resting the soil altogether in some years by letting it lie fallow (tilled but unplanted). Germans helped to pioneer the use of chemical fertilizers to restore the value of worn-out soils. On steep hillsides, such as the slopes of France's Rhône Valley, wine growers have carefully built terraces to keep rains from washing the soil away.

Where soil is too thin or hilly for growing crops, farmers may graze sheep, cattle, and other animals. For example, sheep grazing is common on the hills of Wales, Scotland, and Northern Ireland. Wool from such sheep became the basis for the early textile industries of the British Isles.

Grassland regions of Ireland, France, Hungary, and other countries are noted for dairy-cattle raising. The milk is used not only for drinking but also to make such products as yogurt and cheese. Bulgaria is one of many countries noted for its yogurt, created by culturing milk with bacteria until it becomes semisolid. European cheeses are prized the world over. Because the flavor and texture of cheese depend not only on what the cattle eat but on how the milk is processed, hundreds of kinds of cheeses are available. Europe's fine cheeses include Cheddar and Cheshire from England, Roquefort and Brie from France, Parmesan and Gorgonzola from Italy, Edam from the Netherlands, Havarti from Denmark, Limburger from Belgium, Emmental ("Swiss") from Switzerland, Feta from Greece, and hundreds more.

The crops of European countries depend on the local climate as well as the local soil. In the cooler regions of the north, underground crops like potatoes and turnips do well, as do cabbages, beets, and peas. Some Dutch growers specialize in another cool-weather crop, flower bulbs. Northern orchards produce crops such as apples and pears. The warmer, drier regions of central and southern Europe are suited to crops such as tomatoes, eggplants, peppers, and tobacco. Bulgaria is famed for its roses, which are widely used in perfume-making. Olives and citrus fruits can be grown even on dusty hillsides in countries like Portugal, Italy, and Greece, although often the farmer must supply water through irrigation. Europe's grain crops range from wheat, corn, and rice (mainly in the center and south) to barley, rye, and buckwheat in the north.

Plant resources also include forests, which are important to many European countries. Sweden, Norway, and Finland are among the world's leading exporters of lumber, wood pulp, and paper products. Most other European countries also have forests that supply local needs and sometimes also products for export. The trees range from pines and birches in northern reaches to olives and cork trees in the south. Forests are also highly prized as resort areas, from the ski slopes of Alpine countries to the fishing streams of Poland and Czechoslovakia.

Resources Related to Water.   Water benefits us in many ways. When it falls as rain, it nourishes crops and fills rivers and reservoirs. If rivers collect enough water, the water can be trapped by dams and used to turn giant turbines that produce hydroelectricity. Hydroelectricity is electricity that is generated by moving water. Moreover, when water flows in rivers or collects in oceans, it provides a highway for travel and for transporting goods.

The rivers of England provided the power that first cranked up the Industrial Revolution in the late 1700s and early 1800s. Water from the rivers turned large wheels and gears that powered the machinery of early textile mills. Other countries later applied the same principles to their industries.

More recently, countries like Norway, Sweden, Switzerland, Austria, and Italy took advantage of their swift-running mountain streams to create hydroelectric power. Cheap hydroelectric power made it possible for Norway to become a major producer of aluminum. (The production of aluminum requires large amounts of electricity.) Nations like Sweden, Switzerland, and Austria use hydroelectric power to manufacture small, high-quality instruments and tools. The Alpine nations have specialized in light industry in part because of the difficulty of shipping heavy goods on narrow, often treacherous mountain roads.

The busy ports of Europe are testimony to the importance of the oceans and seas that lap at the coasts. Only a handful of European countries—Austria, Czechoslovakia, Hungary, Switzerland, Luxembourg, and a few "mini-states"—are **landlocked,** or totally enclosed by land. European ports such as Rotterdam have industries

Fishing boats unload their catch of sardines at Portimão, Portugal. Many of Portugal's people live in small fishing villages like this one.

that process raw materials brought by ship (coffee beans from Latin America, chocolate from Africa) and turn them into high-quality consumer goods. Moreover, such port cities as Glasgow (GLAZ-goh) in Scotland, Gdansk (guh-DAHNSK) in Poland, and Piraeus (peye-REE-uhs) in Greece have long been centers of shipbuilding.

Most coastal countries of Europe have large fishing industries. French, British, and Portuguese fishing boats ply the North Atlantic as far as the coasts of North America. The North Sea, the Baltic, and the Mediterranean supply fish to nations such as Denmark, Sweden, Greece, and Italy. Fishing boats from Poland circle the globe, as do whaling vessels from Norway, Iceland, and other countries. However, efforts to protect the declining whale population have hurt the whaling industry in recent years.

The fresh-water resources of Europe tend to be most abundant in the north and west, where moist air masses from the Atlantic Ocean bring frequent rains, and mild or cold weather holds down evaporation. Farther inland and farther south, rain is often sparse and evaporation is high. In the far south, irrigation becomes essential to farming.

Mineral Fuels.   The leading **mineral fuels**, also called **fossil fuels**, are coal, oil, and natural gas. Europe possesses all three. It was abundant

15

CASE STUDY:

Life on a North Sea Oil Rig

The discovery of oil beneath the North Sea has meant new resources for the United Kingdom and an important source of income for economically depressed Britain. Workers willingly endure the hardships of life on the isolated, dangerous oil rigs for the high pay.

[The flotel, where the workers live is] a giant catamaran—a coffee table as big as a football field and four stories high, mounted on two submarines. The accommodation is arranged in three decks: two-berth and four-berth cabins for five hundred men, a big mess hall, a coffee shop that stays open round the clock, a cinema and two smaller TV rooms, a little gymnasium, separate rest area and coffee room for the field's helicopter pilots . . . a corridor of offices, a radio room, a machinery room and various workshops and stores, and a glass-fronted box . . . where the captain steers the vessel when it is under way. . . .

Work on an offshore installation is unremitting. The regular, basic shift is from six o'clock to six o'clock, and it is worked with a minimum of breaks. . . . By the end of the minimum twelve-hour day—or night, depending on the shift—no one has any energy for anything more taxing than a game of billiards or a movie before bed. . . . Depending on the company that employs them, workers spend, at best, half their time away from their families. . . .

Without . . . live television or current newspapers—the latest are rarely less than a couple of days old—food is the only form of relaxation, apart from videotapes, and the mess hall is the only place where people pause to talk a little before weariness and digestion engulf them.

A. Alvarez. *The New Yorker*, January 20, 1986.

1. Why do you suppose that shifts are so long and breaks are short on the oil rigs?
2. What do you find attractive about life on the flotel? What do you find unpleasant?

16

supplies of coal in the Midlands region that allowed Britain to move from water power to coal power as the Industrial Revolution picked up speed. For more than a century, Britain's miners dug out coal at a feverish pace. Now most of Britain's easily mined coal is gone, and most of its mines have shut down.

Europe's main coal field runs from northeastern France and western Germany northwestward through Belgium to England and Wales. Massive coal deposits and handy waterways have made the Ruhr (ROOR) Valley the most important center of German industry. Other significant deposits of coal occur in the Saar region of western Germany, in the Silesia region of Poland, and in Spain.

Until the 1960s, the main oilfields of Europe lay in Romania, while deposits of natural gas seemed to be concentrated in France. Then vast reserves of oil and gas were discovered under the North Sea. Britain (especially Scotland) and Norway developed large oil industries, and Denmark tapped underwater reserves of natural gas. More underwater supplies of gas and oil have been sought off Ireland and Albania.

Uranium, used as a fuel in nuclear reactors, occurs in Czechoslovakia and a few other European countries. However, quantities are limited.

Other Minerals. For as long as we have records, Europeans have made use of mineral resources that lie on or below the earth's surface. Copper mining began in Spain as early as 2400 B.C. Tin deposits in Germany and Czechoslovakia allowed Europe to enter the bronze age about 1500 B.C. By late Roman times, as many as 40,000 miners were dredging gold, silver, lead, copper, and other minerals from the hills and mountains of Spain.

Today iron is one of the most valued minerals, a key ingredient of the steel used in making machinery and in providing the skeletons of large buildings. Iron is especially valuable when it occurs near coal, as it does in Spain, in northeastern France, in Germany's Ruhr Valley, in Luxembourg, and in Poland. Sweden is a major exporter of iron, and many European countries have lesser deposits.

European nations contain a variety of metals used to make **alloys**. An alloy is a blend of two metals, like copper and tin which, when melted together, form bronze. Various metals can be blended with iron to make different alloys of steel. These metals include chromium (from Albania and Finland), tungsten (from Portugal, Spain, France, and Sweden), tantalum (from Portugal), and molybdenum (from Finland and

Norway). However, European supplies of these metals are much smaller than those found elsewhere in the world.

Bauxite, the chief ore used in making aluminum, gets its name from the southern French village of Les Baux, where it was first found in 1821. Hungary is one of the world's leading producers of bauxite.

LAND USE

At one time, almost all Europeans were farmers. Now only a small fraction of Europeans live on farms, and most people reside in metropolitan areas. The percentage of the population living in cities is as high as 90 percent in Britain and 95 percent in Belgium.

European cities have not lost as much population to surrounding areas as have many United States cities. The center of a European city is the main business district, filled with business offices, shops, government buildings, and the homes of the wealthy. Other residential areas radiate outward from the central district, divided by income groups. Remoter suburbs are usually served by railroads, which carry commuters into city centers. Europeans work hard to avoid suburban sprawl and to maintain open land and farms near the cities.

Northern, central, and western Europe are more urbanized and also more industrialized than eastern and southern Europe. One important reason is that the Industrial Revolution began in the north and west, near supplies of iron, coal, and water power. By the early 1900s, industry had spread to Italy, Czechoslovakia, Slovenia, and Croatia. But many other countries did not begin to industrialize until after World War II. Under centralized Communist control, nations like Poland, Hungary, and Yugoslavia built up heavy industry in the postwar years. Spain, Portugal, and Greece also industrialized during this period.

A second factor favoring the more rapid industrialization of northern, central, and western Europe was easy access to the Atlantic Ocean and to overseas empires. Nations like Britain, France, Germany, Belgium, and the Netherlands drew on the resources of distant colonies in building up their industries.

Still another factor favoring the north, center, and west was a better mix of natural resources. Sweden, for example, was able to export large quantities of forest products and iron ore to earn the money to invest in industry. Much of southern Europe, on the other hand, had only skimpy mineral resources, with only Spain possessing significant supplies of coal and iron.

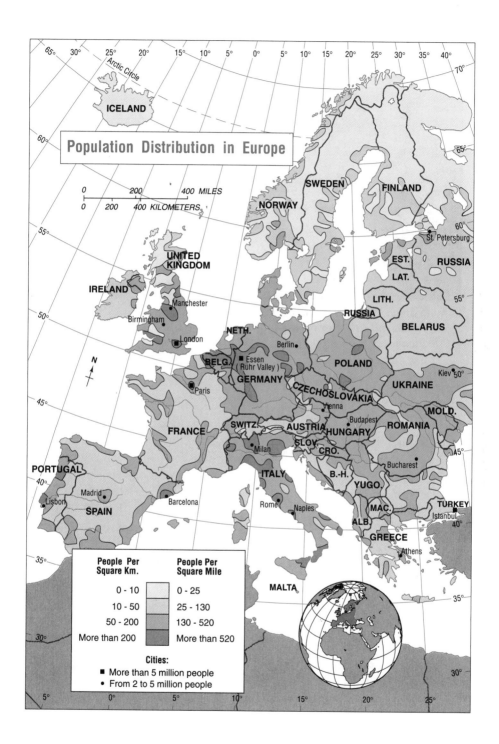

Population Distribution in Europe

People Per Square Km.	People Per Square Mile
0 - 10	0 - 25
10 - 50	25 - 130
50 - 200	130 - 520
More than 200	More than 520

Cities:
- More than 5 million people
- From 2 to 5 million people

19

*With about 29,000 people living in an area of less than
one square mile, the tiny nation of Monaco on the
Mediterranean is the most densely populated in Europe.*

POPULATION DISTRIBUTION

Some 500 million people—slightly more than 9 percent of the world's
population—live in Europe west of Russia, Ukraine, Belarus, and
Moldova. With the exception of Albania, where the population is growing rapidly, Europe's nations have been gaining population very slowly.

Parts of Europe are among the most densely populated regions on
earth. Dense settlements extend from the Netherlands through the
Ruhr Valley to Munich (MYOO-nihk), Germany. The Netherlands and
tiny Monaco (MAHN-uh-koh), on the Mediterranean, are two of the
most crowded nations in the world. Another very crowded part of
Europe is the southern British Isles. Parts of France, Italy, and Spain are
densely populated—for example, almost half of Italy's people live in or
near the basin of the Po River. But in the Alps, the highlands of Spain,
the most northern reaches of Scandinavia, the Baltic nations, and
Iceland, there are few people.

London is Europe's largest city, with more than 9 million residents.
About two dozen additional European cities have populations of 1 mil-
lion or more. Among the biggest are Manchester (4 million); Berlin,
Madrid, and Athens (between 3 and 4 million); and Rome, Birmingham,
Paris, Budapest, and Bucharest (between 2 and 3 million).

REVIEWING THE CHAPTER

I. Building Your Vocabulary

In your notebook, write the correct term that matches each definition.

peninsula	region	natural resources
meseta	topography	navigation canal

1. an area that shares certain characteristics

2. a human-made waterway

3. a land area almost completely surrounded by water, with a narrow link to a larger land area

4. the high tableland of central Spain

5. parts of the environment that people can use to improve their lives

6. the shape of the land's surface

II. Understanding the Facts

In your notebook, write the numbers from 1 to 5. Write the letter of the correct answer to each question next to its number.

1. What geographical feature is commonly accepted as the eastern boundary of the continent of Europe?
   a. Black Sea   **b.** Danube River   **c.** Ural Mountains

2. Which geographic feature most strongly affects the climate of most of Europe?
   a. location near the sea   **b.** large plain   **c.** mountain ranges

3. Which of the following is part of Europe's Alpine "backbone"?
   a. Pyrenees   **b.** Carpathians   **c.** Mont Blanc

4. Which is the cheapest way to ship coal or grain in most of Europe?
   a. by water   **b.** by truck   **c.** by rail

5. Which is Europe's largest port?
   a. London   **b.** Rotterdam   **c.** Marseilles

III. Thinking It Through

In your notebook, write the numbers from 1 to 5. Write the letter of the correct conclusion to each sentence next to its number.

1. The geographic feature that encouraged Europeans to explore other parts of the world was Europe's:
   a. need for food.
   b. easy access to the sea.
   c. absence of mountains.
   d. need for coal and iron ore.

2. The topographic feature that has the strongest connection to Europe's food production is the:
   a. Central Upland.
   b. Great European Plain.
   c. Alpine Mountains.
   d. Northwest Mountains.

3. The areas of Europe that are the most developed and industrialized include the:
   a. south and center.
   b. center and west.
   c. west and south.
   d. center and south.

4. Sweden and Switzerland are alike in that:
   a. both nations have outlets on the North Sea.
   b. both nations are in the Alps.
   c. both nations specialize in producing finely tooled products.
   d. both nations are landlocked.

5. The areas that industrialized first benefited especially from their supplies of
   a. oil.   b. water.   c. coal.   d. gold.

DEVELOPING CRITICAL THINKING SKILLS

1. Explain why Europe's rivers are an important resource.

2. Why are the seas of southern Europe strategically important?

3. Explain how natural resources contributed to the development of industrialization in Germany's Ruhr Valley.

4. Explain why the southern part of Europe is not so densely populated as the north.

INTERPRETING A MAP

Use the maps on facing page 1 and on page 8 to help you answer the following questions.

1. Locate Belgium. Describe its topography.

2. Which of the following nations is the most mountainous?
   a. Germany   b. Poland   c. Czechoslovakia

3. Name Europe's Alpine nations—the nations in which the Alps are located.

4. Belgium, the Netherlands, and Luxembourg are called the "Low Countries" because of their location on a coastal plain. Name three contiguous nations of northern Europe that might also be called "Low Countries."

ENRICHMENT AND EXPLORATION

1. Find out about the location, physical features, population, and major products (if any) of the smallest nations in Europe: Andorra, Liechtenstein, Malta, Monaco, San Marino, and Vatican City.

2. Fill in an outline map of Europe by showing the major locations of the following resources: coal, oil, forests, bauxite, hydroelectric power, iron. Use a symbol to represent each resource and draw a key explaining the symbols.

3. The political map of Europe was redrawn in the early 1990s. Find a political map of Europe in an encyclopedia or atlas that was published before 1990. Compare a map of Europe from that source to the political map of Europe facing page 1 of this text. List at least five differences between the maps.

4. In 1992, the Winter Olympics were held in several villages in the French Alps. Use an almanac or other source to find out where other Winter Olympics have been held. What special problems does finding a site for the winter games present to planners?

EUROPE'S BEGINNINGS
8000 B.C.–A.D. 1054

8000 B.C.	Beginning of Neolithic period in Europe
2850–2360 B.C.	*Earliest Mesopotamian Civilization*
2600 B.C.	Rise of Minoan civilization
1400 B.C.	Rise of Mycenaean civilization
1100–800 B.C.	Dark Age in Greek world
594 B.C.	Solon's reforms in Athens
509 B.C.	Establishment of the Roman Republic
490–479 B.C.	The Persian Wars
480–404 B.C.	Greek Golden Age
462 B.C.	Beginning of direct democracy in Athens
449 B.C.	Law of the Twelve Tables in Rome
431–404 B.C.	Peloponnesian War
323–30 B.C.	Hellenistic Age
206 B.C.–A.D. 221	*Han Dynasty in China*
27 B. C.–A.D. 180	Pax Romana
A.D. 29	Crucifixion of Jesus
A.D. 34-64	Saint Paul's missionary activities
A.D. 399–900	*Mayan Classic Period in Guatemala*
A.D. 313	Edict of Milan
A.D. 350	*Axum conquers Kush.*
A.D. 330	Constantinople becomes capital of Roman Empire.
A.D. 392	Christianity becomes the state religion of the Roman Empire.
A.D. 476	End of Roman Empire in the West
A.D. 732	Battle of Tours
A.D. 768–814	Reign of Charlemagne
A.D. 1054	Split between Roman Catholic and Eastern Orthodox churches

2 Europe's Beginnings

Europe's first great civilizations were those of the Minoans, the Greeks, and the Romans. Yet thousands of years before they came on the scene, other cultures flourished in Europe.

EARLY EUROPEAN CULTURES

The earliest Europeans are shrouded in mystery. We know very little about who these people were, where they came from, or what they felt and thought. The only clues we have are the objects they left behind. Based on such evidence, archaeologists have identified several different periods among prehistoric European cultures.

The Neolithic Period. Neolithic (nee-oh-LITH-ihk) means "New Stone." The Neolithic period is called a *Stone Age* because the tools that survive from that period are made of stone. It is called *New Stone Age* because important new tools, and new uses for older tools, were introduced at this time. In the earlier **Paleolithic** (pay-lee-oh-LITH-ihk) (Old Stone) period, people had survived by hunting and by gathering wildgrowing foods. The Neolithic period marked nothing less than the introduction of agriculture and a settled way of life in Europe.

How the knowledge of agriculture was acquired is unknown. It may have been discovered locally, or it may have been learned from Africa and the Middle East. Because of the kinds of crops that were grown and the kinds of animals that were tamed, scholars think it likely that early European agriculture was learned from other peoples. This spread of knowledge from one culture to another is called **cultural diffusion**.

Because cultural diffusion can be a slow process, the Neolithic period did not occur at the same time in all parts of Europe. In the warmer, southeastern parts, farming seems to have developed around 8000 B.C.

In the colder, more mountainous, more remote parts, it appeared about 3,000 years later. In all the sites so far discovered, distinctively shaped and decorated pots have been found, which give clues to the ways people lived. Many of these **prehistoric** cultures (cultures that existed before written records) have been given names based on the kinds of pottery that have been found.

The most spectacular remains from Europe's Neolithic cultures are the **megaliths** (MEG-uh-liths), or giant stone monuments, that still rest upright in many parts of Switzerland, France, the British Isles, and Spain. Scholars agree that these huge stones once marked holy places where people came to bury their dead and to attend religious ceremonies.

The most famous of all Neolithic monuments is Stonehenge, in southern England. Here megaliths are arranged in a circular pattern. The arrangement has led some to believe that this monument was not only a burial ground and religious shrine, but also an astronomical observatory. Whatever its purpose, the level of human effort and organization required to build Stonehenge was remarkable. Many of the stones, some weighing nearly 50 tons (45 metric tons), were hauled to Stonehenge from mountains many miles away.

Many of the megaliths of Stonehenge are still upright and in place. Scholars believe that the stones once were arranged to form two concentric circles.

The Bronze Age.   The next major period was the Bronze Age. Like the New Stone Age, the Bronze Age occurred at different times in different places. Its name refers to the development of **metallurgy**, or the knowledge and use of metals. The earliest evidence of a European metal-using culture has been found in the Balkan Peninsula. Copper tools from this area are some of the earliest in the world, dating from about 5000 B.C. Even more remarkably, recent discoveries suggest that the people of this area were the first anywhere in the world to work with gold. For these reasons, archaeologists speculate that metal-working was invented here rather than learned through cultural diffusion.

During the Bronze Age, successive waves of migrating people swept over the European continent. These newcomers, including the Balts, the Celts, the Italics, the Greeks, the Germans, and the Slavs, are the ancestors of most modern Europeans. No one is sure of their original homeland, though it seems likely to have been somewhere in eastern Europe. What is sure is that their languages can be traced to a common tongue, which linguists call Indo-European.

In spite of archaeological finds and linguistic detective work, the prehistoric Europeans remain shadows from a distant past—with one notable exception. In 1991 hikers near the Austrian–Italian border found a 4,000-year-old male corpse nearly buried in an Alpine glacier. The extremely well-preserved body was clothed in sewn leather garments, which had been stuffed with straw for warmth, and one hand still clutched a copper-headed axe.

ANCIENT GREECE

The first great European civilization, the Greek, arose in southeastern Europe, the part of Europe nearest to the Middle East and North Africa. Greek civilization drew on two earlier civilizations, the Minoan and the Mycenaean. These, in turn, had learned much from earlier cultures in Egypt and the Middle East.

The Minoans.   The Minoans (mihn-OH-uhnz) were a people whose civilization arose between 2600 and 1200 B.C. on the island of Crete. They were not Greek, for they did not speak a Greek language, but their influence on later Greek culture was considerable.

The Minoan culture was highly developed. Its elaborate and beautifully decorated palaces were unearthed by archaeologist Sir Arthur Evans in 1900. Greek legends of a later age told of a powerful king,

Minos, who ruled Crete and its environs. The civilization disappeared rather suddenly, perhaps destroyed by a massive earthquake and tidal wave that wiped out a neighboring island.

The Mycenaeans. Judging from archaeological evidence, the Minoans were invaded and conquered at one point in their history by a group from mainland Greece called the Mycenaeans (mye-suh-NEE-uhns). The Mycenaeans were the descendants of an early Greek-speaking people who had migrated to the Greek peninsula about 3000 B.C. and mixed with the pre-Greek population they found there. Their civilization reached its peak from 1400 to 1230 B.C. Many of its remains, from palaces to arts and crafts and tablets containing a written language, reflect contact with the Minoans.

The Mycenaeans also left to the Greeks who followed them an oral tradition of a war fought with Troy, a city in Asia Minor (present-day Turkey). Tales of that conflict were passed from generation to generation and form the basis for two great epics, the *Iliad* and the *Odyssey*, composed by the Greek poet Homer nearly 500 years later.

The Rise of the Hellenes. No one knows exactly why the Mycenaean civilization was destroyed. What is known from archaeological evidence is that between 1100 and 800 B.C., the Greek world passed through a "dark age." During this time of confusion, much of Mycenaean civilization was lost, including the knowledge of reading and writing. Waves of Indo-European peoples migrated to Greece from the north. One group, the Dorians, settled in the peninsula called the Peloponnesus (pel-uh-puh-NEE-suhs). Another group, the Ionians, settled first in Attica, where the city of Athens (ATH-uhnz) is located, and later spread onto the islands of the Aegean (i-JEE-uhn) Sea and the coastlines of Asia Minor. The Dorians, the Ionians, and other Greek-speaking peoples all referred to themselves as **Hellenes**. As a result, their common civilization is called the **Hellenic** (hell-EN-ihk) culture.

About 800 B.C. the Hellenes experienced a great cultural explosion. Reading and writing were rediscovered, populations increased, city-building and colonization took place, and overseas trade expanded. With wealth came the time and means to develop the arts and sciences and to refine the craft of governing well.

The City-State. The political basis for this newly energized civilization was the **city-state**. Hundreds of these political units developed throughout the Greek world. The city-state was neither a city nor a state in the modern sense. In area it was more like a county, being composed of a town and the farmland surrounding it. The city-state of Athens, one of the largest, covered about 1,000 square miles (about 2,600 square km.). At its peak it contained a population of only 150,000, and of these only about 30,000 adult males were citizens. The rest—women, children, foreigners, and slaves—had no political rights.

The citizens of the city-state often knew one another personally or were related by blood. This closeness encouraged a sense of patriotism and civic responsibility. As classical scholar H.D. Kitto has remarked, the city-state "was a living community, based on kinship, real or assumed—a kind of extended family, turning as much as possible of life into family life."

At first, the city-states were ruled by kings. In time, groups of landowning nobles became more powerful and gained control of the governments, thus creating rule by **aristocracy** (nobles, taken as a group). Frequently the middle and lower classes became dissatisfied with government by and for those privileged by virtue of their birth. A leader who could play on the discontent of these groups was sometimes able to seize control by force. These leaders, called **tyrants**, sometimes did bring about reforms after taking office. Many of them, however, became obsessed with power and forgot the people who had given it to them. As a result, the tyrant was often overthrown in favor of **oligarchy** (AHL-uh-gar-kee), or rule by a few wealthy citizens.

The Dawn of Democracy. In some city-states, there was a move toward a completely new form of government called **democracy**, or government by all citizens. (Only free, native-born men were citizens. Women, foreign-born men, and slaves were excluded.) In Athens, the new political order began in 594 B.C. when a wise lawgiver named Solon introduced a group of reforms that paved the way for democracy. Operating on the principle of justice for all, Solon wrote laws that everyone could see and understand. He allowed all classes of free men, even the poorest, to sit in the assembly, one of several legislative bodies.

Following in Solon's steps was another statesman, Cleisthenes (KLEYES-thuh-neez), who increased the powers of the assembly. He also developed a system called **ostracism** (AHS-truh-sihz-uhm), in which potential tyrants were banished from the city for a ten-year period by means of a popular vote.

By 462 B.C., the power of the aristocrats was broken. The Athenian government became a **direct democracy**, in which all free male Athenians, not their elected representatives, made the laws. All duties

*The Parthenon, a temple built to honor the goddess
Athena, stands atop the Acropolis, or central hill, in
Athens. It was built between 447 and 442 B.C.*

of government, including military service, were considered the patriotic
responsibility of ordinary citizens.

The Persian Wars and the Golden Age.   Somewhat earlier, in 490
B.C., Athenians had been forced to defend their infant democracy
against the powerful King Darius (duh-REYE-uhs) of Persia, who sent
his army across the Aegean Sea to conquer the Greek mainland.
Though badly outnumbered, the Athenians defeated the invaders at the
battle of Marathon. Ten years later Persian troops under King Xerxes
(ZURK-seez) I, son of Darius, returned. An alliance of Greek city-states
was formed to oppose them. The Persians dealt a stunning blow to a
small Greek force that fought bravely to the death in a mountain pass
north of Athens. Then they swept on towards the city and set it afire.
Defiantly, the Greek navy cornered the Persian fleet in the Bay of
Salamis and sank about half its ships. The following year, in 479 B.C.,
the Greek army defeated Persia's land forces as well.

  With peace came Athens' Golden Age, sometimes called the Age of
Pericles (PEHR-ih-kleez) in honor of the gifted statesman and military
commander of that name. Under his leadership, democracy flourished,
as did drama, sculpture, architecture, and literature. The Golden Age
was also an age of Athenian leadership. After the Persian retreat, more
than 150 city-states joined with one another in a mutual security organi-

zation called the Delian League. Athens, with its superior navy, assumed leadership of the league.

The Peloponnesian War.   In time Athens took advantage of its powerful position to demand **tribute** (regular payments of money) from many of the other city-states. As hatred of the common Persian foe declined, fear of Athenian domination grew. In 431 B.C., this fear erupted in full-scale war between Athens and another city-state, Sparta. Because Sparta is located in the Peloponnesus, this conflict is known as the **Peloponnesian War.**

Sparta represented an entirely different approach to government and life. While Athens was a democracy, in Sparta the government controlled all aspects of life. While Athenians valued freedom, government by law, and the dignity of the individual, Spartans valued strict obedience and self-discipline.

The war between Athens and Sparta dragged on for 27 years. At one point a plague swept through Athens, killing Pericles and one third of the population. Later the Athenians lost 50,000 of their soldiers and 200 of their ships in an ill-fated military expedition. Finally, in 404 B.C., as Sparta's superior land forces breached the city walls, the weakened and demoralized Athenians surrendered. The Spartans left their once-powerful neighbors with only a handful of ships, a war-ravaged city, and a casualty list that included most of their able leaders. Greece's Golden Age had come to an abrupt end.

THE TRIUMPH OF REASON

The creative outpouring of the Golden Age was founded on two basic attitudes. At that time, these were found nowhere but in Greece. One was a dedication to **rational** thought, or thinking based on logical reasoning. The other was belief in the worth and dignity of the individual.

Greek Philosophy.   Previous civilizations throughout the world tended to view the universe as ruled by powerful and mysterious forces. The Greeks, however, came to believe that it was possible for human beings to understand the world and to exercise some control over it. Many scholars believe that it was the Greek political system that helped to make this new outlook possible. Leaders like Solon had developed laws

CASE STUDY:

In Praise of Democracy

At the outset of the war between Athens and Sparta, the great statesman and orator Pericles delivered an address in honor of Athenians who
had died in battle. In it he eloquently described the Athenian political
ideal.

> We call our constitution a democracy, because with us power is in
> the hands, not of a minority, but of the whole people.
>
> In private matters everyone is equal before the law. In public
> affairs, when it is a question of putting power and responsibility into
> the hands of one man rather than another, what counts is not rank or
> money, but the ability to do the job well. No one is kept out of
> politics because he is poor. And just as our political life is free and
> open, so we are free and tolerant in our day-to-day lives. We do not
> get into a state with our next-door neighbour if he enjoys himself in
> his own way, nor do we give him the kind of black looks which,
> though they do no real harm, still do hurt people's feelings.
>
> We obey those whom we have appointed to positions of authority,
> and we obey the laws, especially those which are for the protection of
> the oppressed. . . .
>
> Here each one of us is interested not only in his own affairs, but in
> the affairs of the state as well. Everyone is well informed on general
> politics. And if we find a man who takes no interest in politics, we do
> not say that he is minding his own business; we say that he has no
> business here at all. Each one of us takes part in our decisions on
> policy and in discussion of them, since we consider that thought and
> action should go together. . . .
>
> This, then, is the kind of city for which these men, who could not
> bear the thought of losing her, nobly fought and nobly died.

Rex Warner. *Athens at War: From* The History of the Peloponnesian War *of Thucydides.*
New York: Dutton, 1971

1. In Pericles' view what is the basic principle underlying the Athenian
   legal system?

2. What responsibilities of citizenship does Pericles describe?

3. Why was Pericles describing the Athenian political system during a
   funeral address?

to govern human affairs. This may have inspired others to reflect that the universe might also be subject to laws—predictable and understandable natural laws. If that was true, then human beings could use reason to discover nature's laws, and also the laws underlying human thinking and conduct. Using reason in this way is called **philosophy**.

The true beginning of science occurred with the invention of philosophy by the Greeks in the 500s B.C. The earliest philosophers tried to discover the basic nature of matter. Another group of thinkers called **Sophists** applied reason to understanding the nature of people and society. They also advocated liberty and condemned slavery.

The three most famous Greek philosophers were Socrates (SAHK-ruh-teez), Plato (PLAYT-oh), and Aristotle (AR-uhs-taht-uhl). Socrates' chief concern was to help his students discover their own value systems. He did this by subjecting students to rigorous questioning and cross-examination, a technique ever since called the **Socratic method**. His student Plato wrote down the teachings of Socrates, but Plato also developed his own views about nature, ideas, and politics. Aristotle was the leading expert of his day—and for the next thousand years—in most fields of knowledge, including physics, biology, zoology, botany, and

Socrates believed that evil arises from ignorance. He taught how to overcome ignorance by a process of honest and thoughtful questioning. "The unexamined life," he is reported to have said, "is not worth living."

other disciplines. He was interested also in the nature of the good life and how to achieve it. "Nothing in excess" was the key to his approach. In political theory he was equally rational and moderate, putting his trust in the city-state and law.

The spirit of rationality also inspired another Greek invention: the study of history. Before the Golden Age, deeds of kings and heroes had been the subject of myth or legend, but not of rational investigation. When Herodotus (huh-RAHD-uh-tus), known to later generations as "the father of history," wrote an account of the Persian Wars, he sought the cause of the conflict not in the whims of the gods but in the human events preceding it. His successor, Thucydides (thoo-SID-uh-deez), refined the writing of history by examining the social forces and human decisions behind the Peloponnesian War.

Greek Drama, Architecture, and Art.   Drama was another invention of the Greek mind. Its roots lay in religious festivals that featured music, dance, and a chorus that chanted poetry. When one chorus member, Thespis, stepped out of the group and began to speak alone, drama was born. The focus had shifted from ritual to an exciting depiction of individual human beings.

The three great dramatists of the Golden Age were Aeschylus (ES-kuh-luhs), Sophocles (SAHF-uh-kleez), and Euripides (yoo-RIP-uh-deez). Their plays are **tragedies,** in which noble heroes come to grief, sometimes through fate but more often through a fatal character flaw like pride, stubbornness, or passion. Toward the end of the Golden Age, comedy was born in the plays of Aristophanes (ar-ih-STOF-uh-neez). His plays ridicule politicians, intellectuals, and government policies.

The Golden Age was also the high point in Greek artistic achievement. Here again, the ideals of rationalism reached their finest expression. Greek temples, such as the Parthenon (PAHR-thuh-nahn) in Athens, were built in accordance with strict laws of balance and proportion. This classical style has continued to influence Western architecture, most notably in such monuments as the Lincoln Memorial in Washington.

Greek sculpture was realistic, based on a careful observation of human anatomy. Yet at the same time it portrayed ideal people rather than real ones. Sculptors such as Praxiteles (prak-SIT-uh-leez) and Phidias (FID-ee-uhs) created beautiful bodies in stone, free of human flaws. In doing so, they celebrated the worth and excellence of human beings.

34

The Olympic Games.   Individual excellence was part of the appeal of the Olympic Games, another Greek creation. To Greeks of the Golden Age, physical fitness was almost as important as a rational mind. In fact, they believed that the two went hand in hand. The games, however, were far more than an exhibit of athletic ability. Like our modern Olympics, they were commercial ventures, opportunities to meet people from other places, and chances for demonstrating pride in one's city-state.

Like other Hellenic institutions, the Olympic Games were only for men. Women could not even attend, much less take part.

Daily Life.   In a Greek household, the husband was the head of the family. The wife managed the household and did most of the work, unless the family was wealthy enough to own slaves. Women had few rights, and for the most part, their lives were controlled by their fathers or husbands. People married when they were in their teens, usually to partners who had been chosen by their parents.

In general, only the sons of citizens went to school. Boys learned the basic subjects of reading, writing, and arithmetic, plus music and athletics. If they continued their education, they would specialize in either philosophy, rhetoric (public speaking), medicine, or law. Some girls learned to read at home, but their main education was learning how to run a household.

Because Greece's climate is mild, most daily activities took place outdoors. As a result, houses tended to be small and simple. The most important pastime of most Greeks, men and women, was attending and participating in religious festivals. Most men also took part in athletics.

THE HELLENISTIC AGE

After the Peloponnesian War, the Greek city-states became increasingly weak and disunited. It was not long before they fell under the domination of the Macedonians (mas-uh-DOH-nee-uhnz), a people from a mountainous area north of Greece.

After subduing the Greek mainland, the Macedonians' king, Philip, turned eastward. He hoped to wrest the city-states along the coast of Asia Minor from Persian control. But he was assassinated before he could achieve his goal, and the task fell to his son, Alexander.

Alexander the Great in battle against the Persians. This picture is a mosaic, *a design made by fitting together small pieces of stone and colored glass.*

Alexander the Great.   Alexander was superbly qualified to carry out his father's plan. Although only 21 years old, he was a strong, handsome man and a natural leader. Through his teacher, the great Athenian philosopher Aristotle, he had been exposed to the best of Greek culture, including the heroic epics of Homer. Such legends must have inspired the young man to his own dreams of glory—dreams far exceeding those of his father.

In 334 B.C., Alexander led an army of 35,000 into Asia Minor and swept like a hurricane down the coast, capturing city after city. He continued on the heels of the Persian troops through Syria, Egypt, and Mesopotamia, eventually chasing them into their own country and burning their capital.

Alexander continued his push through Asia, crossing through present-day Afghanistan into northern India, where he defeated the local king. By this time his men were weary of foreign adventures and longed to return home. Yielding to their pleas, Alexander turned back. In 323 B.C., halfway back to Greece, he fell sick and died at the age of 32.

After Alexander's death, his immense empire was divided among three of his generals. Their descendants continued to rule for the next 300 years. This period, from 323 B.C. to 30 B.C., is called the **Hellenistic** (hel-uh-NIS-tik) Age. (The word *Hellenistic* distinguishes this culture from the *Hellenic,* the earlier Greek culture.)

The Hellenistic World. The Hellenistic world that Alexander's generals inherited was a world-state containing hundreds of nationalities scattered over a huge area. Yet in each of these far-flung cities there was now an overlay of Greek culture. The architecture was Greek. The common language was Greek. The education and lifestyle of the upper classes were Greek. These similarities made it easy for people to travel and trade with one another, and as a result economic activity flourished.

Some aspects of the Hellenistic world were quite different from the older Greek culture, most notably the repressive governments of the ruling monarchs. Instead of enjoying a sense of civic pride and community closeness, the subjects of the Hellenistic monarchies often felt oppressed by a large and impersonal world.

The center of learning in the Hellenistic era was Alexandria, Egypt, which attracted many scholars to its state-supported museum and library. Thinkers there tended to divide their knowledge of the natural world into various scientific disciplines. Building on the discoveries of earlier civilizations, Euclid (YOO-kluhd) systematized the study of geometry, while Archimedes (ahr-kuh-MEE-deez) helped to systematize physics and mathematics. To **systematize** is to arrange existing knowledge into a system. Eratosthenes (ehr-uh-TAHS-thuh-neez), an Alexandria geographer, made the first measurement of the earth's circumference. Doctors advanced healing skills and gained a knowledge of anatomy and physiology that was hardly improved upon for 2,000 years.

Reacting to some of the problems of the times, philosophers tried to understand how people could best achieve happiness in a complicated, competitive world. The most important philosophy of the times was **Stoicism** (STOH-uh-siz-uhm). At its core was the belief that people should take what happens to them without complaining. Another important Stoic (STOH-ik) belief was the idea that since all human beings are able to reason, they are all members of the same "city of humanity" and thus basically equal.

ROME

In the second and first centuries B.C., the Hellenistic kingdoms were taken over one by one by the Roman Empire. The Roman culture had begun some 500 years earlier in a small city-state in Italy.

The Roman Republic. In 509 B.C., Rome won its independence from the Etruscans (ee-TRUS-kuhnz), a people who at one time had ruled much of central Italy. The Romans then established a **republic**, a form of government in which the citizens elect their leaders. In Rome, the elected leaders formed a group called the **Senate**. The Senate, in turn, made the laws and appointed the government administrators.

At first, most of the power lay in the hands of the wealthy aristocrats known as **patricians**. Over the next 200 years, however, the common people, called the **plebeians** (plee-BEE-uhnz), were able to expand their civil rights significantly. Early in the fifth century B.C., they gained representation in a governing body called the Assembly of Tribes. In 449 B.C., they forced the Senate to establish the first Roman legal code. A **code** in this sense is a body of laws organized and arranged for easy use. This code, carved on 12 bronze tablets, or tables, was called the Law of the Twelve Tables. The law applied only to Roman citizens, who did not include women, foreigners, and slaves. Despite this limitation, it contained two important principles of justice. One principle was equality before the law, the idea that all citizens should be treated equally. The second principle was the idea that a citizen should be considered innocent of any crime until it was proved in court that he was guilty.

From City-State to Empire.   From the sixth to the second centuries B.C., Rome grew from a small city-state into an empire. The superbly organized Roman **legions**, army units composed of citizens, first united the Italian peninsula. Then they moved on to conquer lands bordering the Mediterranean Sea. The first was Carthage, a powerful city-state in North Africa in what is now Tunisia. Next were the Hellenistic kingdoms that surrounded the eastern Mediterranean, the last of which, Egypt, fell to Rome in 30 B.C.

As Rome expanded, the old form of government proved unsuited to ruling over conquered peoples. In the first century B.C., the republic weakened and eventually collapsed, a victim of class tensions, poor leadership, and civil war.

In these difficult times, only military leaders seemed to offer any hope of restoring order. One of these, a general named Julius Caesar (SEE-zuhr), attempted to rescue Rome by imposing a dictatorship in 49 B.C. His efforts were doomed when some members of the Senate, jealous of his success and fearing that he intended to make himself king, assassinated him on the Ides of March (March 15), 44 B.C.

After Caesar's death, the stage was set for a new act in Rome's history. The major player was Octavian, a nephew of Caesar's who became ruler in 27 B.C. Octavian was an **absolute** monarch, one whose rule was not limited by any other persons or government bodies. However, he shrewdly avoided taking the title of king. Instead, he dubbed himself *Augustus*, meaning "the revered one," and *Caesar*, in honor of his uncle.

The reforms that took place under the brilliant statesmanship of Augustus led to the longest period of peace the ancient world had ever known. This time span of more than 200 years (27 B.C.–A.D. 180) is called the **Pax Romana**, the Latin term for "Roman peace." It survived the excesses of several of Augustus's heirs—notorious emperors such as Caligula (kuh-LIG-yoo-luh) and Nero (NIHR-oh)—and went on to thrive under leaders known as the "five good emperors" (A.D. 96-180). Rather than passing the throne on to a son, each of these men, except the last, chose a successor on the basis of proved ability and then "adopted" him.

Augustus Caesar's reign brought an end to more than 100 years of civil war in Rome. It also brought prosperity to the largest empire the world had yet seen.

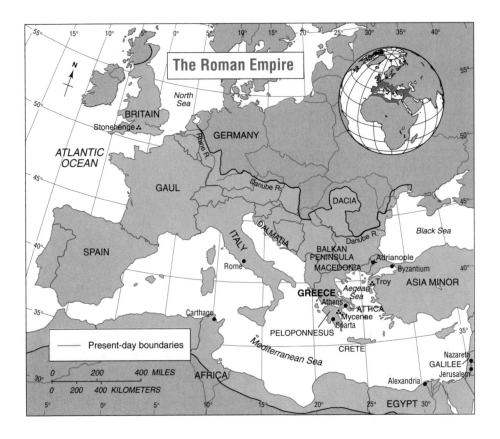

The Roman Empire

During this period, the Roman empire reached its greatest extent. It included all of Europe as far as the Rhine and Danube rivers (see map, above), plus Dacia (present-day Romania) north of the Danube and much of the island of Great Britain. In Africa it took in Egypt and all of the Mediterranean coast. In Asia it stretched as far east as Mesopotamia (present-day Iraq) and included all of Asia Minor (present-day Turkey).

Roman administrators excelled at finding practical solutions to global problems. The military, in addition to defending the empire's borders, built thousands of miles of paved roads across three continents and set up a speedy, efficient postal service. They policed the highways and the sea lanes to rid them of bandits and pirates and thus made possible a worldwide trading network. A wide variety of goods traveled back and forth as far north as Gaul (present-day France) and Britain, as far south as Egypt and Kush in Africa, and as far east as India and China. The result was an unparalleled period of prosperity.

Life in the Roman Empire. Generally speaking, the subjects of the Roman empire were treated fairly by Roman administrators. They benefited greatly from the Roman concept of international justice. This **Law of Nations** combined Roman civil law with legal traditions of the Greeks and with ideas about human equality borrowed from Stoicism. Under this code, an individual was judged not as a Greek, an Egyptian, or a Briton, but—first and foremost—as a Roman. With expected behavior clearly written out, the different nationalities were accorded significant, if limited, human rights.

The *Pax Romana* brought prosperity, so that most people in the Roman empire lived well. Well-to-do people in the cities and towns lived in houses built around large courtyards. People spent most of their waking hours in the courtyards, for the rooms surrounding them usually were small and without windows. Because oil for lamps was expensive and the light from lamps dim, most people arose at dawn and went to bed at dusk. The last meal of the day began in late afternoon.

Poorer people, especially in the large cities like Rome and Alexandria, generally lived in apartment buildings that were from three to five stories tall. On holidays, which were frequent, they escaped from their cramped homes to the outdoor arenas that were part of every city. In Rome itself, they might go to the Colosseum, a huge arena where professional fighters called **gladiators** (GLAD-ee-ayt-uhrz) fought to the death, sometimes against wild animals and sometimes against one another. On other days they might go to chariot races at the Circus Maximus, a racetrack that held about 250,000 spectators. For a more restful time, they could go to one of the lavish public baths, where Romans exercised, bathed, and met with friends.

The Classical Heritage. The culture of the Roman Empire—its art, architecture, literature, philosophy, scientific thought—was borrowed largely from the Greeks. The Romans made it their mission during the years of empire to adopt most of Greece's art and philosophy, adapting them and passing them on to the rest of the world as the **Greco-Roman,** or **classical,** heritage.

The Romans' own unique contribution lay in their genius for organization. During the glory days of the *Pax Romana*, the emperor and his civil servants were able to govern, in an orderly and just manner, an empire ranging over three continents and containing some 70 million people. Centuries later, Roman techniques were still studied and imitated by leaders of other European powers.

CHRISTIANITY AND ROME

At the time that Augustus was laying the foundations for the *Pax Romana*, a seemingly ordinary event occurred that was to have profound effects within the empire, the rest of Europe, and the entire Western world. A baby named Jesus was born into a Jewish family from Nazareth, a village in the Roman province of Galilee.

The Life and Death of Jesus. When he was about 30, Jesus began to teach, telling his followers that the kingdom of God was about to appear on Earth. To be saved, he said, people needed a moral transformation involving repentance, right living, and a loving heart.

Although Jesus saw himself as part of the ancient Hebrew tradition, some Jewish leaders were deeply disturbed by what they considered his disregard of Hebrew law. Roman authorities also saw him as a threat, possibly suspecting him of being a **Zealot**, one of a Jewish sect that urged armed revolt against the emperor. (A **sect** is a smaller group or organization within a religion.) About A.D. 29 Jesus was tried by a Roman court in Jerusalem and put to death by crucifixion, a cruel means of execution frequently used by the Romans.

The **disciples**, or followers, of Jesus believed that on the third day after he died and was buried, he was raised from the dead. They interpreted this event as evidence that Jesus was the Son of God, who had come to earth to save all human beings. They believed that he was the **Messiah** (or, in Greek, **Christos**), the savior promised by Hebrew prophets. They saw their duty now as spreading this "good news," or **Gospel**, to others.

Those who carried the Gospel to the rest of the world were called **apostles**. Foremost of these missionaries was Paul, who more than any other person was responsible for changing Christianity from a Jewish sect into a world religion. A Greek-speaking Jew from Tarsus in Asia Minor, Paul came to believe that it was possible for all people, Jew and gentile (non-Jew) alike, to have eternal life in the kingdom of God. To those gentiles who were attracted to the Jewish concept of a single God, but had reservations about some Jewish rules of behavior, Paul was prepared to say that Jewish law had been replaced by the teachings of Jesus. During the years of his missionary activities, A.D. 34–64, he succeeded in making Christianity attractive to many in the the Greco-Roman world.

At first, Roman officials viewed Christianity as a minor irritation and did not interfere with the movement. But as the numbers of

Christians grew, the government began to see them as traitors, and the mood of tolerance changed to one of persecution.

The first large-scale murder of Christians was ordered in 64 A.D. by the emperor Nero, who ordered Christians—young and old, male and female—into a circus arena filled with wild beasts. Later emperors used Christians as scapegoats for many of the social and economic problems of the empire. A **scapegoat** is a person or group that is blamed for conditions caused by others. Christian martyrs were imprisoned, beaten, starved, burned alive, and crucified.

ROME IN DECLINE

By A.D. 180, the *Pax Romana* had come to an end, and Rome began a slow decline that continued for the next 300 years. Contributing to its many woes were military chaos, economic and social disorders, and the threat of invasion.

The Army in Disarray. During the republic and the early empire, Rome's all-citizen army had been famous for its patriotism, organization, and loyalty. Now, however, the quality of recruits declined dramatically. Troops consisting largely of **mercenaries**, or hired foreign soldiers, fought solely for money, terrorized civilians, and engaged in plots to overthrow the emperor.

The results were **anarchy** (complete absence of government) and civil war. The army selected emperors and helped them stay in power or removed them at will. During one 50-year period, 26 emperors came and went, none of them lasting more than two years. All but two were killed by their own troops.

Taking advantage of the military chaos were Germanic nations from the northern and eastern parts of Europe, who were able to break through the empire's border defenses for the first time. As a result of their looting raids, cities were burned, people robbed, and farms laid waste.

In order to find money to pay the troops in the face of these disasters, emperors resorted to raising taxes, confiscating goods and property, and forcing peasants into virtual slavery. When these measures proved insufficient, the amount of silver in coins was reduced, making it possible to mint more coins. Instead of solving the problem, this policy caused runaway **inflation** (increase in prices). Many people then returned to a **barter** system, in which goods and services were exchanged without using money. The empire's economic system collapsed.

Further challenging the quality of life were two great epidemics, possibly the first appearance of bubonic plague. Nearly 20 million people died, almost a third of the total population of the empire.

In reaction to these grave economic and social woes, many people retreated to huge, fortress-like estates in the countryside, where they lived simple, self-sufficient lives far away from the dangers of the city. This movement was more severe in the western parts of the empire, particularly in Gaul (present-day France), than in the eastern parts. It was this mass movement from the city to the countryside that began the period known as the Early Middle Ages, or "Dark" Ages, in Europe.

Attempts at Reform.   Two emperors, Diocletian (deye-oh-KLEE-shuhn) (A.D. 284–305) and Constantine (KAHN-stuhn-teen) (A.D. 306–337), attempted to remedy these problems by reorganizing the government. Diocletian created a highly **centralized** monarchy that had many elements of a police state. (To centralize is to concentrate power in one person or place.) To better control the huge empire and to guard against military mutiny, he divided the empire into eastern and western parts. An emperor ruled in each part. Constantine continued this policy of separation. In A.D. 330 he moved the capital to Byzantium (bih-ZAN-tee-uhm), on the Bosporus where Europe meets Asia. He renamed the city Constantinople (kahn-stan-tuh-NOH-puhl) in honor of himself. (Today, it is called Istanbul [is-tahn-BOOL]).

For a time it seemed as if order might be restored. One result, however, was that the division between eastern and western parts gradually became permanent. This development left the poorer, less populated western half in a vulnerable position, with fewer troops and little money with which to pay them.

The Germanic Invasions.   Toward the end of the fourth century, the problem of guarding the frontier became critical. The Huns, a Mongol people from central Asia, rode into eastern Europe, causing a Germanic nation called the Visigoths to flee in terror before them. Yielding to pressure, the emperor in A.D. 376 allowed the Visigoths to cross the border near Constantinople. Within two years, the Visigoths brought the Roman army to its knees at the battle of Adrianople, one of the most devastating defeats in the history of the empire.

From this time onward, successive waves of Germanic tribes swept through the western half of the empire in search of riches, farmlands, and safety from the Huns. Angles, Saxons, and Jutes overran the Roman province of Britain. Visigoths, Ostrogoths, Vandals, Franks, Lombards, and many other Germanic nations moved throughout western Europe, and some even crossed from Spain to Africa. In 410 Rome itself was attacked by Visigoths and again in 455 by Vandals. Finally, in A.D. 476, the emperor in Rome was overthrown and replaced by the leader of one of the Germanic nations. With this act, Roman rule came to an end in the western part of the empire.

THE BYZANTINE EMPIRE

After 476, western Europe sank into deeper decline. Its cities grew smaller. Its once-vital civilization was largely forgotten, except for what was kept alive by the Roman Catholic Church. But the richer, more populous eastern branch of the empire remained strong. With a seemingly endless supply of gold and silver, its leaders financed large military forces. These armies defended the empire. They even won back some of the lands in the western Mediterranean that the Germanic invaders had claimed, although in most cases only temporarily.

The eastern capital at Constantinople became the center of a vibrant trading network. It formed the nucleus of an empire that has come to be called the **Byzantine** (BIZ-uhn-teen) Empire, after Byzantium, the earlier Greek city that Constantinople replaced.

The Byzantine civilization came from three different sources. Its language, literature, and customs were Greek. Its laws and form of government were Roman. Its religion was Christianity. The official acceptance of this faith, once considered subversive, was largely due to Constantinople's founder, the emperor Constantine.

Christianity Victorious. For the first 300 years of Christianity's existence, its followers had endured terrible persecutions. Most Christians stood fast, however, and by the example of their courage won new converts to their faith.

As the numbers of Christians continued to grow, it eventually seemed wise for the government to try to win their support. Constantine, the first emperor to convert to Christianity, issued the **Edict** (an order or decree) of Milan in A.D. 313, which granted tolera-

Constantine, the first Roman emperor to become a Christian, shifted the center of Roman power to his new capital of Constantinople in the east.

tion to Christians. Almost 70 years later, in A.D. 392, the emperor Theodosius I made Christianity the state religion and declared the worship of the old Roman gods illegal.

During the first few centuries of the Byzantine Empire, many differences developed between the eastern church and the church in Rome. They quarreled over types of ceremonies, dates for holidays, activities of priests, and the power of the emperor. In 1054 the two branches split permanently. The western branch, with the pope as its spiritual head, became known as the Roman Catholic Church. The eastern branch became the Eastern (Greek) Orthodox Church, with the patriarch of Constantinople as its religious leader.

The Byzantine Heritage.   Over its thousand-year history, the Byzantine Empire had a significant impact on European history. It helped block Muslims in their push toward Europe. It preserved Greek literature, philosophy, science, and mathematics. Under its most famous emperor, Justinian (A.D. 527–565), all the laws of the Roman Empire were collected and assembled in one large document. In time the Justinian Code, as this collection is called, became the basis for the modern legal codes of most of Europe and Latin America. Justinian was married to Theodora, a remarkable person in her own right. On one occasion she saved Justinian's throne by persuading him to stay and fight a rebellion, when he had been ready to flee.

THE EMPIRE OF CHARLEMAGNE

While the Byzantine emperors were ruling over their empire in the East, the western part of the former empire sank into confusion for several centuries. Finally, in the late 700s A.D., a king of the Franks named Charlemagne (SHAHR-luh-mayn), meaning "Charles the Great," led the conquest of a sizable part of Europe. The Franks were a Germanic nation who had settled in what is now Belgium and northern France. Although Charlemagne's empire lasted only a short time after his reign (768–814), its accomplishments in this short amount of time mirrored many of those of the Byzantine Empire.

Charlemagne's ancestors, the founders of the Carolingian (kar-uh-LIN-jee-uhn) dynasty, had already gained control over a large part of central Europe. Pepin II, founder of the line, had become ruler of the Franks. His son, Charles Martel ("Charles the Hammer"), consolidated this position by subduing other Frankish nobles and rival tribes. Charles is best remembered, however, for stopping the advance of the Muslims into Europe at the battle of Tours in 732. His son, Pepin the Short, invaded Italy and defeated the Lombards, who had settled there. The devout Pepin's donation of part of this territory to the Roman Catholic Church made the pope ruler of an area that became known as the **Papal States**.

Charlemagne continued the policy of expanding the Frankish kingdom by adding the Lombard kingdom, Bavaria, and Saxony. Toward the end of his reign he conquered an area called the Spanish March, which became an important buffer zone protecting the Christian Franks against the Muslims in Spain.

On Christmas Day in the year 800, the pope crowned Charlemagne emperor of the Romans, acknowledging his position in a Christian empire. His empire, however, was but a pale shadow of the earlier Roman empire. Charlemagne and his palace staff lacked the knowledge and experience to effectively administer such a large and diverse area. His principal success in this regard was the creation of an inspection team of royal messengers who traveled through the various counties to prevent the nobles from undermining his authority.

Charlemagne believed that part of his duty as a Christian lay in making sure that the clergy could pass on the writings and teachings of the church. To achieve this end, he gathered the best scholars in Europe to establish a school in his palace. This enterprise, which enlightened an otherwise culturally darkened era, is known as the

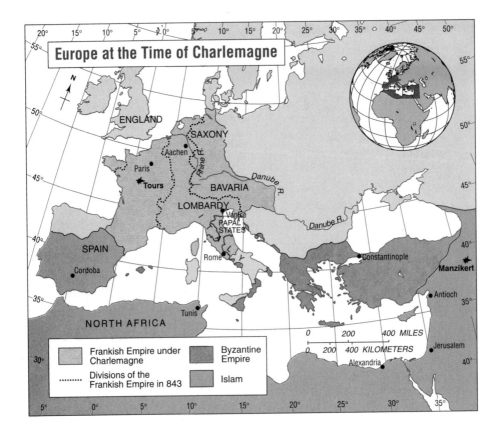

Europe at the Time of Charlemagne

Frankish Empire under Charlemagne	Byzantine Empire
Divisions of the Frankish Empire in 843	Islam

Carolingian Renaissance (ren-uh-SAHNS). (*Renaissance* is the French word for *rebirth*. The term was first applied to the period in European history from about 1350 to 1600 [pages 69–73]. Later historians came to apply it to other, similar movements, such as the one in Charlemagne's time.) Not only were clergy and the royal family taught to read and write, but ancient religious and classical texts were carefully preserved and copied. Thus was the spirit of learning preserved through the dark years following the collapse of Rome.

Charlemagne's empire rested more on his personality than on a sound administrative or economic base. After his death, his son, Louis the Pious, proved unable to control either the Frankish nobles or his own rebellious sons. After Louis' death, the empire was divided into three kingdoms. This division formed the basis for the future boundaries of France, Germany, and a long-disputed region between those two countries.

REVIEWING THE CHAPTER

I. Building Your Vocabulary

In your notebook write the correct term that matches the definition.

mercenary	ostracism	Hellene
Solon	megalith	patrician

1. a soldier who serves mainly for wages

2. temporary banishment by popular vote

3. a wise Athenian lawgiver

4. a word meaning Greek

5. a wealthy Roman aristocrat

II. Understanding the Facts

In your notebook, write the numbers from 1 to 6. Write the letter of the correct answer next to its number.

1. What major development took place during the Neolithic period?
   a. agriculture   b. metallurgy   c. astronomy

2. Where did the Dorian Greeks settle?
   a. Crete   b. Peloponnesus   c. Attica

3. Who is known as "the father of history"?
   a. Herodotus.   b.Thucydides   c. Euclid

4. What form of government did the early Romans establish?
   a. an oligarchy   b. a republic   c. a democracy

5. Which city became the center of culture during the Hellenistic Age?
   a. Constantinople   b. Sparta   c. Alexandria

6. How many years did the *Pax Romana* last?
   a. 1000   b. 24   c. 200

III. Thinking It Through

In your notebook, write the numbers from 1 to 5. Write the letter of the correct answer next to its number.

1. A major motive for the Germanic invasions was:
   a. the need to recover lost territory.
   b. a fear of the Huns.
   c. the desire to spread Christianity.

2. At the end of the Peloponnesian War:
   a. Athens' dominance as a world power came to an end.
   b. Athens' civilization suddenly flowered.
   c. Athens' cultural influence came to an end.

3. Both Charlemagne and the Byzantine emperors:
   a. ruled empires that lasted 1,000 years.
   b. were emperors at Constantinople.
   c. preserved learning during a period of cultural decline.

4. Which of the following statements is not true of the Law of the Twelve Tables?
   a. It represented an improvement in the rights of plebeians.
   b. It represented an improvement in the rights of all Romans.
   c. Its underlying principles were equality before the law and innocence until proven guilty.

5. One of the effects of Alexander's conquests was:
   a. to spread Greek culture through much of Europe and the Middle East.
   b. to spread democracy through much of Europe and the Middle East.
   c. to limit trade through much of Europe and the Middle East.

DEVELOPING CRITICAL THINKING SKILLS

1. How did the size and makeup of the Athenian city-state's population contribute to the development of a direct democracy?

2. Compare the Hellenistic Age with the Hellenic era that preceded it.

3. Discuss reasons why the *Pax Romana* is regarded as one of the finest periods in history.

4. Describe some of the military and economic reasons for the decline of the Roman Empire.

INTERPRETING A MAP

Study the map of the Roman Empire on page 40. Using the map and information that you have gained from this chapter, answer the following questions.

1. On what three continents were Roman provinces located?

2. How is the importance of the Mediterranean Sea demonstrated by this map?

3. What natural features of Europe helped to protect the Empire's borders against Germanic peoples?

4. What political problems did Diocletian and Constantine hope to solve by dividing the Empire?

ENRICHMENT AND EXPLORATION

1. Working in small groups and using library resources, collect information about the archaeological remains at Crete, Mycenae, Troy, Athens, Delphi, and Olympia. In a classroom presentation, describe each site and give details about its discovery, condition, restoration, etc. Supplement your presentation with drawings or pictures.

2. Consult library resources to identify the three basic styles of Greek architecture: Dorian, Ionian, and Corinthian. Demonstrate these styles by preparing a drawing of three columns with their distinctive capitals and bases. Display the drawing on the class bulletin board. Label each column with the name of its style.

3. In a written and illustrated report, describe Roman military life in the days of the republic. By consulting the library catalog, locate books that describe how the army was organized, how it fought, and what weapons it used. Include a description of the major campaigns that helped transform the city-state of Rome into an empire.

4. Locate photographs of American and European buildings and monuments influenced by the classical style. Make a bulletin board display. Carefully label the name and location of each item.

THE MIDDLE AGES AND THE RENAISSANCE

c. 840–1600

c. 840s	The height of the Viking attacks
c. 890	Magyars invade central Europe.
962	Otto I crowned first Holy Roman Emperor.
1066	Norman conquest of England
1071	Capture of Jerusalem by Turks Battle of Manzikert
1096	Start of the First Crusade
1099	Capture of Jerusalem by Crusaders
1187	Recapture of Jerusalem by Saladin
1204	Sack of Constantinople by Crusaders
1215	Signing of the Magna Carta
1337	*Mongol invasion of Russia*
1337–1453	The Hundred Years' War
1347	Arrival of Black Death in Sicily
1350–1600	The Renaissance
1368	*Ming Dynasty begins in China.*
1429	Joan of Arc leads liberation of Orléans.
1438	*Inca rule in Peru*
c. 1445	Gutenberg invents movable metal type.
1453	English are driven out of France, except Calais. Ottoman Turks take Constantinople, ending the Byzantine Empire.
1492	Expulsion of Jews and Muslims from Spain First Voyage of Columbus
1501	*First African slaves in Spanish colonies in America.*
1512	Michelangelo finishes painting ceiling of the Sistine Chapel.
1600	Shakespeare begins his most successful decade as a playwright.

3 The Middle Ages and the Renaissance

Europe as we know it today arose slowly out of the ashes of Charlemagne's Empire. This period—indeed, the entire time from Rome's collapse until the 1500s—is now called the **Middle Ages**. The name *Middle Ages* was coined by writers at the end of the period. These writers thought of the Greco-Roman civilization as one high point of civilization and of their own era, the Renaissance, as another. The centuries between they dismissed as the "Middle" or "Dark" Ages. Historians today see those centuries, not as one long dark age, but as a rich and varied period in which the Greco-Roman legacy blended with Christianity and old Germanic customs to produce a unique civilization. The term **medieval** (mee-DEE-vuhl) means having to do with the Middle Ages.

THE VIKING AGE

After Charlemagne's empire was divided in A.D. 843, the effectiveness of governments broke down. By A.D. 900, there were few well-organized governments left. Few governments could protect people and property, while new invaders battered Europe on all sides. From North Africa in the south came Muslims who raided Italy and the Mediterranean coasts of Spain and France. From the east came Magyar (MAG-yahr) horsemen who raided parts of Germany and France before settling on the plains of the Danube River (present-day Hungary). Most fearsome of all were the Vikings, or Northmen, ferocious raiders from Scandinavia.

Masters of the Sea. The Vikings were sea warriors. Their long, graceful boats were lightweight and flexible, so that they could be sailed in rough seas without breaking. These qualities also allowed the boats to

To assure a safe voyage to the land of the dead, wealthy Vikings were sometimes buried in ships. This Viking ship was found in such a grave in Norway.

sail in shallow water, so that they could be brought upriver or dragged onto beaches in areas without natural harbors. These boats enabled the Vikings to stage surprise attacks all along Europe's coastline.

The Vikings who sailed these ships to the farthest reaches of Europe were skilled and fearless in battle. They began to raid European communities in the 700s, motivated partly by the need for new land on which to settle their growing population. By either killing or conquering the inhabitants of a given region, they were able to establish their own colonies around the Gulf of Finland, along the Dutch coast, and on islands north of Great Britain.

During the 800s and 900s, the Vikings extended their colonies into Russia, Ireland, Iceland, and Greenland. From Greenland, they continued westward and settled briefly along the coast of North America. They also settled in parts of England and in a part of France that came to be known as Normandy, meaning "Northmen's Land." The descendants of the Vikings who colonized Normandy were known as Normans.

Not all Viking raids were conducted in order to gain new lands. Many attacks were carried out for the purpose of seizing jewels and precious metals. To satisfy this appetite for plunder, whole villages were burned, ports destroyed, churches looted, and inhabitants slaughtered. Other raids kidnapped the local people in order to sell them as slaves in the Middle East.

In time, the Vikings adopted Christianity, ended their raids, and settled down in Scandinavia. Those who had settled in other countries adopted many of the cultural traits of the peoples they conquered. Descendants of these settlers, such as William the Conqueror (see page 61), became great and respected leaders.

FEUDALISM AND THE MANORIAL SYSTEM

The vicious attacks of raiders destroyed town life in much of medieval Europe. In search of protection, people retreated to the estates of lords, who were able to mobilize groups of knights to help defend their lands. It was out of these local efforts to provide some order and security that the institution of **feudalism** (FYOOD-uhl-iz-uhm) developed.

Fiefs and Fealty. Feudalism differed from region to region. However, it always was based on the granting of land, called a **fief** (FEEF), in return for military service. In addition, feudal relationships always required **fealty** (FEE-uhl-tee), or loyalty.

In practice, feudal relationships worked something like this. In a solemn ceremony, a noble pledged an oath of fealty to a great lord, an action that made him the great lord's **vassal**. In return, the great lord granted his vassal a fief—land that he could use, but did not own. The vassal was then honor-bound to perform certain services for his lord. These included providing a specific number of days of military duty each year and offering the hospitality of his castle when the lord came to visit. The great lord, in return, was honor-bound to perform other types of service, such as protecting the vassal's fief from invaders or settling his legal disputes.

As feudalism evolved over the years, kings emerged at the top of the feudal system. A king distributed fiefs to the lesser lords, who thus became the king's vassals. These vassals, in turn, took portions of their fiefs and redistributed them as smaller fiefs to other nobles, who then became their vassals. In this way, all members of the ruling class became part of a great web of give-and-take.

The Manorial System. Economic activity under feudalism was based on the **manorial** (muh-NOR-ee-uhl) system. This system did not involve a world-wide trading network nor even a city market. It did not even involve much money, since land, the basic commodity, was neither bought nor sold. Under the manorial system, almost all production, distribution, and consumption of goods and services took place within the lord's manor. The manor contained the noble's castle, as well as fields, woods, pastures, a free-standing oven, a mill, a wine press, and a church. It also included a village where the farm workers and their families, or **peasants**, lived. Some of these peasants were free men and women. Many, however, were **serfs**, persons who were not free to move away from the manor.

Between lord and peasant there existed a complex system of give-and-take, just as there was between lord and vassal. The lord gave the peasant protection and the right to cultivate the land. The peasant gave the lord a portion of the crops and a specified number of days of labor each year. All the work on a manor was performed by the peasants, from farming to road building and from cooking to dressmaking. As one historian has observed, "Manorialism . . . presupposed an unchanging social order—clergy who prayed, lords who fought, and peasants who toiled."

The lives of the peasants were hard and unpredictable. Poor crops or warfare between local lords could mean starvation and death. Almost everything peasants owned or produced was taxed by their lord and the church, so that saving anything was difficult. Primitive farming technology resulted in small crops. Over the centuries, much of the farmland became exhausted and no longer fertile. Men, women, and children worked together to cultivate their lands, usually from dawn until dusk. They lived in simple one-room huts with their livestock, slept on straw mattresses, and often ate only black bread.

The community that clustered around a lord's manor was very close-knit. Since travel was dangerous, most peasants never ventured more than ten miles from their homes. Most people knew one another all of their lives, and strangers were subjects of intense curiosity and suspicion. Most people were uneducated and knew little about the outside world. Though they worked very hard, peasants also celebrated many holidays, often based on pre-Christian traditions, such as Mayday and harvest festivals.

Women in the Middle Ages. Warfare was frequent in the Middle Ages, and most warriors were men. Even among the nobility, women therefore had a lower status compared to their male counterparts. Marriage was mainly a business contract between families, and a woman expected to be controlled by her father, husband, or eldest son. The education of a noblewoman usually consisted of learning practical skills, such as cooking, sewing, and weaving.

However, since life in feudal society was clustered around the manor, a noblewoman had many responsibilities. Her primary role was to manage the household, which was often very large. She was responsible for the well-being of everyone in the house and, by extension, everyone on the manor. Many of these women practiced traditional medicine and were very skilled at it.

Since travel in the Middle Ages was dangerous, guests often stayed for extended visits. Social life came to depend on a highly developed code of hospitality. Because a noblewoman was responsible for caring for guests, a generous and gracious hostess was in a position to enhance her family's reputation. The woman of the house also arranged for the guests' entertainment. Often they hired **troubadours**, wandering poets and singers, often of noble birth, who sang the praises of beautiful, generous, and wise noblewomen. The portraits of noblewomen that these troubadours spread, especially their messages of respect and protection, contributed to a gradual improvement in the status of women.

The Legacy of Feudalism.   Feudalism became outmoded during the 14th and 15th centuries, when kings took more power into their own hands. To later generations, it left the idea that government and its citizens have a set of mutual rights and duties. Feudalism's cultural legacy includes castle architecture and **chivalry** (SHIH-vuhl-fee), the knights' strict code of behavior. Chivalry helped to shape our own definitions of sportsmanship, duty, honor, and loyalty.

THE MEDIEVAL CHURCH

In medieval Europe, the most important organization was the Roman Catholic Church. By giving to much of Europe a common religious and cultural outlook, the church also brought meaning, purpose, and order to the lives of medieval people. Because the church used and preserved Rome's Latin language and alphabet, the countries where it held sway are referred to as **Latin Christendom.**

The Church as a Spiritual Force.   Central to the importance of the church was the medieval view of the world. The vast majority of people believed that happiness existed only in heaven. Going to heaven was not certain, however. Also possible was damnation in hell, which was pictured in vivid detail in the religious art of the era. Life, as one poet wrote, was "a hard and weary journey toward the eternal home for which we look; or, if we neglect our salvation, an equally pleasureless way to eternal death."

What, then, was the path to salvation in heaven? It was to understand and follow God's will as it had been revealed in church doctrine. God's will could be learned solely from the teachings of the clergy, the ordained priests of the church. It was this spiritual function of the church—to act as intermediary between the individual and God—on which all its other functions rested.

If the promise of salvation was great, the threat of damnation was even greater. Damnation was certain for anyone that the church had **excommunicated**. An excommunicated person was barred from attending church and participating in the **sacraments**, the rituals necessary to guarantee salvation. The church used this powerful weapon against those who defied its authority and rejected its beliefs.

Political Function. In order to administer the church, its early leaders devised a church **hierarchy** (HEYE-uhr-ahr-kee), or system of officials in graded ranks. At the top was the bishop of Rome, who came to be

Medieval churches were richly decorated with statues and other carvings. This is a view of the entrance to the great cathedral at Chartres in France.

known as the **pope**. He and his administrators in Rome were known as the **papacy** (PAY-puh-see). Below the pope were archbishops, and below them were bishops. At the bottom were the parish priests.

Somewhat outside of this hierarchy were members of religious orders: monks, nuns, canons, and friars. Mostly, they lived in monasteries with other members of their order. A **monastery** is a residence for people who have withdrawn from the world for religious reasons.

The church claimed authority not only within its own organization, but over **secular** (SEK-yuh-luhr), or nonchurch, governments as well. As individual European kings began to gain power, the church often attempted to maintain power over them. It would do so by supporting feudal vassals in quarrels with their king, releasing the vassals from their oaths of fealty to the king. Another weapon that popes sometimes used against kings was the threat of excommunication.

Economic Power.   Besides its political strength, the medieval church held awesome economic power. It was the largest landholder in Europe, with the papacy itself administering vast estates, timberlands, and mines. In addition, the church collected such large amounts of money that it became the leading financial institution in Europe. It received regular revenue from a **tithe**, a tax amounting to a tenth of a person's income. Often it sold appointments to positions within the hierarchy, as well as official pardons for sins. In time, reformers, both within and outside the church, would attempt to correct these excesses.

Social and Cultural Functions.   Although the church was sometimes accused of greed, it should be remembered that the medieval church needed large resources. In the Middle Ages, the church performed many of the functions that in the modern world we expect from other organizations.

Monasteries, for example, developed a tradition of learning and teaching. Monks copied by hand the works of classical authors and early Christian writers. Monastic schools taught reading and writing to boys who planned to become monks, while parish or cathedral schools instructed boys who planned to be parish priests.

The church also brought beauty and dignity into lives that otherwise lacked these qualities. In soaring Gothic cathedrals, such as Notre Dame (NOH-truh DAHM)(Our Lady) of Paris, worshipers could rest beneath lofty ceilings and gaze at magnificent stained glass windows.

Anti-Semitism.   During the Middle Ages, the concept of religious freedom was unknown, and tolerance was not seen as a virtue. **Anti-Semitism**, or discrimination against Jews—the only visible non-Christian minority in most of European society—was common. Part of this antagonism was aimed at the Jews for refusing to embrace Christianity. Another part of it was aimed at their role as moneylenders. What anti-Semites refused to recognize was that non-Christians often were prevented from owning land or entering other professions. Thus Jews were forced to turn to a line of work forbidden to Christians, that of lending money at interest.

Throughout the Middle Ages and beyond, European Jews were isolated in ghettos, pressured to renounce their religion, banished from their homelands, and massacred. In spite of such persecutions, most Jews kept their faith. The scholars among them translated many of their ancient biblical and legal texts and developed a medieval Hebrew literature and philosophy.

THE STRUGGLE FOR POLITICAL UNITY

By the end of the 1000s, Europe had entered a period of vitality and expansion known as the High Middle Ages. New agricultural methods increased the production of food and helped to raise birth rates.

Growth of the Towns.   In the High Middle Ages, the number of people living in walled towns began to grow. As trade between towns increased, the need to produce goods increased, and small industries were created. In towns, people found work as craftspeople, laborers, and shopkeepers. Many people worked at home in small family businesses.

As the towns grew, merchants and craftspeople organized into trade associations called **guilds**. International trade revived, giving rise to great fairs where people gathered from all parts of Europe. Doctors, lawyers, and merchant bankers formed a professional elite. These townspeople formed an entirely new social group, called the **middle class** because its status was not so high as that of the nobles but higher than that of the peasants.

The middle class had more opportunities to acquire wealth and status than did their peasant cousins in the country. They also had more holidays and amusements. Townspeople participated in festivals and pageants, which often were sponsored by local guilds. They enjoyed religious and secular plays, mock battles, wrestling, and bear-baiting. They heard ballads and songs that brought news from other parts of the world, and joined rowdy processions through the streets of the town.

Life in the towns also had disadvantages. Townspeople started work early and usually went to bed when it got dark, because tallow for candles was expensive. Streets were dangerous because there were many thieves, and most people carried knives. Towns became crowded as more people lived inside the limits of the town wall, and they became even more filthy. People just threw their garbage and waste water on the street, usually first calling out a warning to people walking by. Because of these conditions, towns were breeding grounds for disease. The only escape from epidemics was to flee to the countryside.

The English Monarchy. During the High Middle Ages, European monarchs tried to consolidate power and unify their kingdoms. The kings of England and France were successful in these attempts. Other countries, including Germany, Italy, and Spain, remained divided.

The foundation of English unity was laid in 1066 as a result of the Norman Conquest. In that year, Duke William of Normandy invaded England and, at the battle of Hastings, defeated an English army and killed their king. William, known ever since as "the Conqueror," took the English throne for himself. Seeing land as the key to power, William the Conqueror kept a sixth of the English land for himself. The rest he divided among his Norman nobles. To further strengthen his control, he dispatched his own royal agents, called **sheriffs,** to administer the counties. In order to introduce a more efficient tax system, he ordered a complete census, known as the *Domesday Book*, which listed every landowner in the kingdom.

One of William's successors, Henry I (1100–1135), added to national unity by creating a legal system common to all. Prior to this time, England had conflicting traditions, including old Anglo-Saxon laws, Norman feudal laws, canon (church) laws, and various commercial laws. Under Henry, all cases were tried in a king's court, with the decisions written down so that they could be used as precedents in later cases. This **common law** is the basis of the English and the U.S. legal systems.

At the same time that the Norman kings were shaping a strong monarchy, the seeds of future democratic institutions were also being planted. In 1215 a group of angry barons forced King John to sign a document called **Magna Carta,** which guaranteed certain rights to them. Later generations have seen Magna Carta as the first step toward guaranteeing the rights of all citizens. In addition, a council composed of different classes of society was convened to advise the king on policy matters. Gradually the townspeople came to meet separately from the knights, so that the council divided into two groups. These groups, which later came to be called the House of Lords and the House of Commons, were the beginnings of the English Parliament.

France and Germany. French monarchs, starting with Louis VI in the 1100s, were also able to unify the country by wresting power from the nobility. However, they consolidated their power more slowly than did the English kings. Over a 200-year period, they extended control over pockets of land through warfare and marriages. Under France's best-loved monarch, the pious and merciful Louis IX (1226–1270), laws were issued for all of France, thus stimulating political unity. To make justice the same throughout the kingdom, a king's court called the *parlement* was introduced. Since decisions made in the traditional feudal courts could now be appealed to the *parlement*, the local lords no longer had the final word.

In Germany, a completely different situation developed. After Charlemagne's empire collapsed, Germany fragmented into small land units controlled by local dukes. A king was elected out of this nobility, but in reality he had little more power than the rest. One such king, Otto the Great (936–973), was determined to assert control. He entered into an agreement with church officials, who supplied him with fighting troops and administrators. With this help, he marched into Italy to help protect the pope against his Italian enemies. In 962, the pope reciprocated by crowning Otto emperor.

Otto's empire gradually came to be referred to as the "Holy Roman Empire." The name suggested not only Charlemagne's empire but also that of the ancient Romans themselves. In fact, the empire was mainly German-speaking Europe (present-day Germany, Austria, and Switzerland) plus the Netherlands and parts of present-day Italy, France, and Czechoslovakia.

Otto's alliance with the papacy did not last long, nor did the German monarchs who succeeded him fulfill the rich promise of their title. Over several centuries, emperors and popes plotted, maneuvered, and battled, each side determined to gain control over the other. This bitter struggle, in which the balance of power shifted back and forth between the two contestants, gave the real advantage to the German dukes. They retained and gained strength, partly because the papacy supported them against the emperor, partly because the emperor gave most of his time and energy to his struggle with the pope.

Otto the Great, founder of the Holy Roman Empire, as portrayed in a sculpture in the cathedral of Magdeburg, Germany

Italy and Spain. Italy and Spain also remained divided throughout the Middle Ages. Portions of the Italian peninsula changed hands frequently as allies of the emperor and of the pope struggled over them. In Spain, Christians in 1248 won a decisive victory over the Muslims who had occupied the peninsula since the 600s. A small and weakened Islamic kingdom remained in Granada until 1492, when the Spanish succeeded in driving the last Muslims from Spain.

THE CRUSADES

During the 600s, when Muslims first settled in Spain, other followers of the Prophet Muhammad were consolidating an empire that stretched across North Africa and the Middle East. The empire included Palestine, the region where Jesus had lived and preached, and the city of Jerusalem, where he was crucified.

Seljuks and Crusaders. For centuries, Muslims had allowed Europeans to visit Christian sites in Jerusalem. This tolerance disappeared, however, with the appearance of the Seljuks, a Turkish people from Central Asia, in 1071. Recent converts to Islam, the Seljuks captured Jerusalem from other Muslims. The hospitality once accorded Christian visitors was withdrawn. Also in 1071, the Turks defeated the Byzantines at the battle of Manzikert. Fearing future Turkish victories and further erosion of his once-great empire, the Byzantine emperor appealed to Latin Christendom for help.

CASE STUDY:
A Perfect Gentle Knight

In his *Canterbury Tales*, the great English poet Geoffrey Chaucer (1340–1400) describes the ideal medieval knight. His description lists the qualities that a feudal society considered most desirable in its warrior class.

> There was a Knight, a most distinguished man,
> Who from the day on which he first began
> To ride abroad had followed chivalry,
> Truth, honor, generousness and courtesy.
> He had done nobly in his sovereign's war
> And ridden into battle, no man more,
> As well in Christian as in heathen places,
> And ever honored for his noble graces . . .
> In fifteen mortal battles he had been
> And jousted for our faith at Tramissene
> Thrice in the lists*, and always killed his man.
> This same distinguished knight had led the van
> Once with the Bey** of Balat, doing work
> For him against another heathen Turk;
> He was of sovereign value in all eyes.
> And though so much distinguished, he was wise
> And in his bearing modest as a maid.
> He never yet a boorish thing had said
> In all his life to any, come what might;
> He was a true, a perfect gentle-knight.

*   combat tournaments
** a Turkish title of respect

The Canterbury Tales, by Geoffrey Chaucer. Translated by Nevill Coghill. Baltimore: Penguin, 1971.

1. Where and with whom has the knight fought?

2. What words suggest that Chaucer shared a commonly held medieval prejudice against non-Christians?

3. Compare Chaucer's ideals of gentlemanly behavior with our own.

In 1095, Pope Urban II responded by calling for volunteers, first to help the Byzantine empire, then to recapture Jerusalem from the Turks. With his plea "God wills it!" ringing in their ears, thousands of Europeans started on a Christian military expedition called a **crusade**. Additional crusades were to continue for the next two centuries.

Causes of the Crusades. These two centuries of bloodshed and foreign adventure were not caused solely by the Byzantines' plea for help. Historians pinpoint a number of political, economic, and spiritual reasons for the Crusades.

One reason was the opportunity provided for Latin Christendom to regain control over Muslim-held lands. By extension, the Crusades were also seen as the means by which the Roman Catholic Church might gain domination over the Byzantine empire's Greek Orthodox Church.

Economically, the Crusades gave Europe's expanding population a way of satisfying an appetite for more land. In a very real sense, the crusading knights were medieval pioneers, bent on settling a new country. For those who did not find land, there was always the possibility of "liberating" the riches of a vanquished foe. For the seafaring merchants of such Italian cities as Venice (VEN-is) and Genoa (JEN-uh-wuh), the Crusades were a way of opening more trade routes to Asia.

Beyond these practical considerations, the Crusades appealed to real spiritual concerns. The knights who answered the pope's call saw themselves as pilgrims engaged in a holy war. They believed that participation in a crusade was a way of receiving pardon for their sins. Hence, the appeal of going on a crusade was irresistible to many. It combined the adventure of a lifetime with the lure of land and plunder, the opportunity for glory, and—ultimately—the promise of salvation.

The Campaigns. Those in the forefront of the First Crusade were bands of poorly armed pilgrims—common folk whose enthusiasm had been kindled by two evangelical orators known as Peter the Hermit and Walter the Penniless. Many members of these ragtag bands were killed by Magyars on their way east. The rest were massacred by Muslims after arriving in Asia Minor.

A year later, the main army of knights arrived in Asia Minor. They marched south to Antioch (AN-tee-ahk), then proceeded to Jerusalem. In 1099, they captured Jerusalem after a long and bloody siege in which thousands of Jewish and Islamic men, women, and children were killed. As a result of this victory, the knights established four Crusader states along the Syrian and Palestinian coasts.

Almost 50 years later, one of these states fell to the Muslims, an event that precipitated the disastrous Second Crusade, which ended in a complete rout of the West. The Third Crusade was inspired by the reconquest of Jerusalem in 1187 by a brilliant Islamic commander named Saladin (SAL-uh-din). In contrast to the bloody Christian takeover, Saladin allowed no slaughter of Jerusalem's civilian population. This distinguished Muslim was soon confronted by equally distinguished European warriors: King Richard the Lion-Hearted of England, King Philip of France, and Emperor Frederick Barbarossa of Germany. In spite of their efforts, Jerusalem remained in Saladin's hands.

In the Fourth Crusade, noble purpose fell victim to mismanagement and greed. The pope had organized a new band of crusaders, but had not given them the money to carry out their plans. Arriving penniless in Venice, they were persuaded to attack the Byzantine empire's capital of Constantinople. The crusaders captured the city, looted it of its riches and holy relics, and massacred thousands of Orthodox Christians in the process.

After this disgraceful episode, the Crusades lost their momentum. The Crusader states declined and eventually fell to the Muslims. Jerusalem would remain under Islamic control until the 1900s.

Effects of the Crusades. Historians argue over the effects of the Crusades. Most surely they accomplished few of the purposes for which they were launched.

Spiritually, the Crusades seem to have introduced a mood of distrust about the role of the church in world affairs. Politically, they helped to speed up the decline of feudalism by killing many of the nobility. Economically, the Crusades brought both losses and gains. For years, the church and the nobility of Europe suffered from the enormous cost of financing these expeditions. On the other hand, the Crusaders brought back to Europe an appetite for many of the products they encountered in their travels. Merchants, bankers, and shipowners grew rich taking advantage of these new opportunities for trade. In so doing, they stimulated the rapid growth of an economy based on money rather than on land. The immediate beneficiaries of this trade were Italian city-states like Venice, Florence, and Genoa. The Italian cities, in turn, came to serve as bankers for the European monarchs, offering them loans to finance various large-scale enterprises.

The cultural effects of the Crusades are questionable. Most European contact with Islamic science, philosophy, and medicine had taken place centuries before in Spain, not in Asia Minor or the Holy

Land. Still, the experience of traveling and living in foreign lands must have generated a curiosity and openness in Europeans, so that they were prepared for the cultural awakening that began as early as the 1100s and 1200s.

THE DECLINE OF THE MIDDLE AGES

The Late Middle Ages, or 1300s and early 1400s, was an age of anxiety and adversity, brought on by a burdensome number of natural and human catastrophes. The result was unparalleled physical suffering, economic hardship, social strife, and spiritual crisis.

Economic Decline.   The weather in Europe over many years inflicted alternating bouts of unnaturally heavy rain and frost, causing frequent crop failures. With scanty harvests, famine spread throughout the continent, causing starvation, illness, and ultimately a decrease in population.

The Black Death.   More devastating than crop failure was the **Black Death,** an epidemic of bubonic plague that swept through the world in the 1300s. The disease, which caused a quick, painful death, was called the "Black Death" because of the characteristic black blotches that appeared on the skin. It was carried by fleas on rats, but no one at the time had any understanding of infectious disease. Indeed, the total inability to understand, prevent, or control the epidemic made it "the most terrible of all the terrors," as a priest of the time described it. Many thought it the judgment of God against a sinful people and feared that it might be the means by which the world would come to an end.

The epidemic probably originated in Central Asia and spread to Europe via rats on merchant ships. It first reached Sicily in 1347, from where it was carried by ships along coasts and up rivers to most of the major cities in Europe. In heavily populated areas, it killed for about four to six months, let up during the winter months, and then reappeared in the spring to rage for another six months. The total death toll was perhaps 20 million people—about one quarter to one third of the European population.

The Hundred Years' War.   The Black Death was to recur six times in the next six decades. During periods of abatement, a long, destructive war between French and English troops claimed additional lives and created more social and economic hardship.

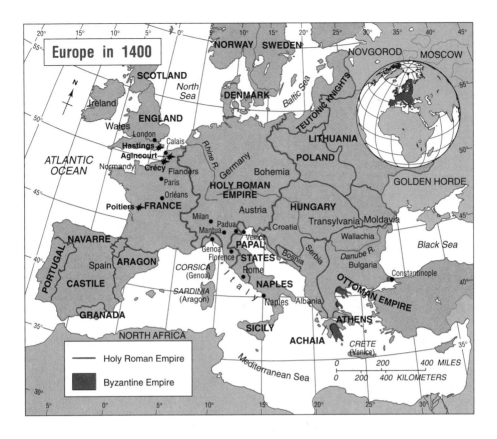

Europe in 1400

Holy Roman Empire

Byzantine Empire

The causes of this conflict, known as the **Hundred Years' War** (1337–1453), are a tangled tale of dynastic marriage, disputed land claims, shifting feudal loyalties, and trade rivalries. As descendants of French nobility, the kings of England were also French feudal lords who resented the loss of their land to the French monarchy. In retaliation, they laid claim to the French crown themselves and were supported by some of the French nobility, as well as by merchants in Flanders (in present-day Belgium and northern France) who needed British wool to produce cloth, their major export.

During the first period of the war, a spectacular advancement in military technology gave the advantage to the British. At the battles of Crécy (kray-SEE) in 1346 and Poitiers (pwah-tee-YAY) in 1356, French knights on horseback were no match for English **archers**—men on foot wielding a new weapon called a longbow, which fired up to 10 or 12 arrows a minute.

In a later phase of the war, the English seemed close to total victory after Henry V's display of strength at the Battle of Agincourt (AJ-in-kort) in 1415 and the conquest of Normandy soon after. Then, with French morale at its lowest ebb, a new and completely unexpected leader emerged. An illiterate peasant girl named Joan of Arc claimed that God had commanded her to rescue the country from foreign tyrants. In three short years, she was able to rally the French troops and lead them in battle to liberate the besieged city of Orléans (or-lay-AWN) in 1429. When she was captured and sold to the English, whose French allies burned her at the stake as a witch, she became a martyr whose example inspired the French. By 1453 the English had been driven out of all parts of France except the port city of Calais. As a result of Joan's patriotic vision, the old feudal loyalties weakened further. A new spirit of national loyalty began to redefine the way people thought about themselves and their country.

Peasant Rebellions.   During the course of Hundred Years' War, a terrible new scourge was visited on the French peasantry. Bands of English soldiers roamed the countryside, robbing farms, villages, castles, monasteries—whatever potential source of loot lay in their path. Gangs of French knights, impoverished by the war, joined in the pillage.

Eventually the resentment of the peasants, who were known as *Jacques* (ZHAHKS), boiled over into active rebellion. After seeing their crops, animals, and tools stolen, and still being taxed by the nobility to help pay for the war, they banded together for revenge. In 1358, wielding clubs, pitchforks, scythes, and hatchets, the peasant army attacked castles and manors, killing, burning, and looting as it went. The French nobility finally put down this revolt, known as the **Jacquerie** (zhahk-REE), killing some 20,000 peasants in the process.

The Jacquerie, the most dramatic of many peasant uprisings that occurred in the Late Middle Ages, indicated a new consciousness of the injustices of the medieval class system. An English contemporary expressed the resentment of the peasantry: "Ill have they used us! And for what reason do they hold us in bondage? Are we not descended from the same parents, Adam and Eve? And what can they show, or what reasons give, why they should be more the masters than ourselves?"

THE RENAISSANCE IN ITALY

In the latter part of the Middle Ages, a new world-outlook began to evolve in the city-states of northern Italy. These well-developed urban centers had the wealth and the freedom to cultivate the arts and to find inspiration in the classical works of art and literature that could still be found there. It was in this environment that the **Renaissance** was born.

The term *Renaissance* comes from the French word for *rebirth*. Originally it referred to a revival, at the end of the Middle Ages, of interest in the ideas, values, and styles of classical Greek and Roman culture. Later historians have applied it to other periods of rebirth, such as the Carolingian Renaissance (see page 48).

The Renaissance is both an historical period and an intellectual movement. As a period, it lasted from about 1350 to 1600. As a movement, it began in Italy and gradually spread to the rest of Europe.

The Environmental Influence.   Northern Italian city-states were nominally part of the Holy Roman Empire during the Middle Ages. However, because the German emperors were continually embroiled in political struggles with the papacy, the Italian city-states were able to develop as independent political units.

These city-states were not only politically independent, but economically secure as well. Because of their location near the Mediterranean Sea, cities like Venice and Genoa had been able to establish a flourishing sea trade with Asia, which had increased during and after the Crusades. Because this trade required a commercial and banking system to support it, a rich merchant class soon arose in these cities and also in such cities as Florence, Milan, Mantua, and Padua.

In this commerce-oriented environment, money, not land, became the major value. A wealthy business class, rather than a feudal nobility, formed the upper levels of society. Without benefit of noble titles, the rich merchant-bankers sought other means of self-glorification. Without vast estates, they sought to beautify their cities. They found their status symbols in the works of literature, art, and architecture that they began to sponsor. Members of the upper classes became patrons of the arts, paying talented individuals to design their villas and the public buildings of their city, to paint pictures for their galleries, to sculpt statues for their gardens, and to write books to fill their libraries.

Most influential of all the Renaissance patrons of the arts was a rich family called the Medici (MED-uh-chee). The Medici built a banking empire in the city of Florence, a city-state that became the fountainhead of the Italian Renaissance.

The Renaissance World-View.   The artists and writers of the Renaissance soon developed a world-view inspired by classical literature and art. This outlook, which made human beings rather than God the central focus of all study and artistic expression, became known as **humanism** (HYOO-muh-niz-uhm).

Although humanism was not un-Christian, its emphasis was on the secular, or worldly, aspects of life. Whereas the medieval world view looked to life after death, humanism shifted attention to the here and now. It tried to discover the best ways to live in this life, not the next.

Another hallmark of humanism was its emphasis on the importance and dignity of the individual. Inspired by the ancient Greek ideal of excellence, the humanists believed that a major goal in life should be the individual's pursuit of honor and glory.

Writers of the Italian Renaissance. The earliest humanist was Petrarch (PEE-trahrk) (1304–1374), who is sometimes called the "father of humanism." He collected the works of ancient Greek and Roman writers and studied the languages in which these works were written. At a time when most writing was in the Latin of the church, Petrarch also became interested in the **vernacular**, the everyday spoken language of the people. In his own work, especially his love poems, he introduced the use of vernacular Italian in place of Latin.

Following in Petrarch's wake were writers concerned with history and political science. Political writing of the time often took the form of advice books to rulers of the various city-states. Typically, these books measured a ruler's success by how polite he was and how many different things he knew how to do. A more realistic, and more cynical, guide book was written by Niccolo Machiavelli (mak-ee-uh-VEL-ee). In *The Prince*, published about 1513, Machiavelli told rulers how to succeed in the real world, not the world as it ought to be. His primer for the practice of the politics of realism has led scholars to call its author "the world's first modern political thinker."

Renaissance Art. Under the patronage of the merchant-bankers, Renaissance artists applied the classical ideals of balance, proportion, and harmony to their works. At the same time, they gave their creations a striking realism, the hallmark of all Renaissance art.

Classical themes took their place alongside Christian subjects. Even when artists used Christian topics, they depicted the characters as thinking, feeling human beings, not as the stiff and formal figures of medieval art.

The most illustrious trio of the Italian Renaissance were Leonardo da Vinci, Michelangelo, and Raphael. All were closely associated with Florence. Leonardo da Vinci (lay-uh-NAHR-doh dah VIN-chee) (1452–

1519) is best remembered for his paintings, such as *The Last Supper* (1498) and the *Mona Lisa* (1505). Michelangelo (meye-kuhl-AN-juh-loh) (1475–1564) was an architect, sculptor, and painter. His mastery of human anatomy helped him to create a sense of reality in such statues as *David, Moses,* and *The Dying Slave*. The painter Raphael (RAH-fah-el) (1483–1520) was a master of color, harmony, and design. While his sweet-faced Madonnas represent one aspect of his art, his masterpiece, *The School of Athens* (1510), is the perfect embodiment of the classical spirit of the times.

THE NORTHERN RENAISSANCE

Many of the ideas and attitudes of the Renaissance spread to Germany, France, England, and Spain during the late 1400s and 1500s. They were brought to these countries by the merchants, bankers, diplomats, and scholars who travelled to and from Italy. In these northern countries, however, Renaissance writers and artists expressed themselves different-ly, due to a different set of social, political, and economic circumstances.

The Diffusion of New Ideas.   The speed with which the ideas of the Renaissance spread was enhanced by two developments. First, a new era of peace and prosperity had finally dawned in Europe, after decades

Moses, a sculpture by Michelangelo, was intended to decorate the tomb of a pope. However, the tomb was never completed, and the stat-ue is now in a church in Rome.

of war and distress. With newly found money and leisure time, people were able to turn their efforts to refining the quality of their lives. Most notable in this respect was the founding of schools and colleges where humanistic studies began to replace the study of church texts. The goal of these new studies, known as the **humanities**, was to educate the whole person—intellectually, spiritually, physically, and artistically.

A second factor encouraging the diffusion of the Renaissance was the invention of printing by Johannes Gutenberg (GOOT-uhn-burg) about 1445. Up to this time, all texts had been painstakingly copied by hand. Gutenberg's use of movable metal type made it possible to produce books much more quickly and inexpensively than before. As a result, books could now reach a much larger audience. This "communications revolution" also stimulated a dramatic increase in literacy.

Christian Humanism.   The books and works of art that began to circulate freely among northern Europeans were different in form and substance from Italian ones. Writers and artists applied the ideas of humanism to the institution they knew best, the church. **Christian humanism,** as this combination of ideas came to be known, focused on the human potential for goodness and knowledge, in contrast to the medieval emphasis on sinfulness. Christian humanists applied themselves to studying and carefully editing the texts on which Christianity was based. They believed these works should be available to all and not interpreted solely by the church hierarchy.

The greatest of the Christian humanists was Erasmus (ih-RAZ-muhs). Born in the Netherlands in 1466, he traveled extensively throughout Europe as a teacher and biblical scholar. He attacked abuses of the church in a famous satiric work called *In Praise of Folly* (1511). However, he refused to enter the religious disagreements of his contemporaries, pleading instead for tolerance, peace, and unity.

The seeds planted by the Christian humanists took root in many parts of Europe. In France, Michel de Montaigne (mahn-TAYN) (1533–1592), used the Socratic method in his Essays to question his own innermost thoughts and beliefs. In Spain, Miquel de Cervantes (suhr-VAN-teez) introduced satire in his adventure novel *Don Quixote* (dahn kee-HOHT-ee), written between 1605 and 1615.

Humanism in England found its greatest expression in William Shakespeare (1564–1616), who gave voice to the Renaissance belief in the human capacity for achievement on a grand scale. It was Shakespeare's ability to be a child of the Renaissance and yet to transcend his age that lifts him into the realm of true genius.

Chapter 3:
CHECKUP

REVIEWING THE CHAPTER

I. Building Your Vocabulary

In your notebook write the correct term that matches the definition.

fealty	hierarchy	Islam
fief	humanism	secularism

1. attention to worldly rather than religious concerns

2. land making up a feudal estate

3. the obligation of loyalty assumed by a vassal

4. the organization of a church government

5. the religious faith of Muslims

6. the revival of classical learning and ideas during the Renaissance

II. Understanding the Facts

In your notebook write the numbers 1 to 5. Write the letter of the correct answer next to its number.

1. From which group of people did the Normans descend?
   a. Magyars   b. Seljuks   c. Vikings

2. What was the basis of the economy under manorialism?
   a. land   b. money   c. trade

3. Who was an early spokesperson for Christian humanism?
   a. Erasmus   b. Petrarch   c. Pope Urban II

4. The reconquest of which city inspired the Third Crusade?
   a. Antioch   b. Constantinople   c. Jerusalem

5. In which country was political unity achieved earliest?
   a. France   b. England   c. Germany

III. Thinking It Through

In your notebook write the numbers 1 to 6. Write the letter of the correct answer next to its number.

1. Under feudalism, a vassal was obliged to:
   a. give his lord military service.
   b. give his lord a portion of his harvest.
   c. pay rent to his lord.
   d. work on his lord's manor.

2. Medieval anti-Semitism was partly caused by:
   a. the ideals of chivalry.
   b. the growth of secularism.
   c. reactions against the tithe.
   d. Jews not being allowed to own land or to enter most professions.

3. The German nobility remained powerful throughout the Middle Ages because of:
   a. alliances with the Holy Roman Empire.
   b. financial loans from Italian city-states.
   c. riches won during the Jacquerie.
   d. support from the papacy.

4. As a result of the Crusades:
   a. Europeans adopted Islamic cultural values.
   b. Latin Christendom regained Muslim-held lands.
   c. trade between East and West was stimulated.
   d. the population of Europe increased.

5. Florence became the center of the Italian Renaissance due largely to:
   a. the influence of the Italian nobility.
   b. the patronage of the Medici family.
   c. the presence of many artists and architects.
   d. its wealth as a seafaring city-state.

6. Writers and artists of the northern Renaissance were less likely to use classical themes because:
   a. they disapproved of secular models.
   b. they had little exposure to Greco-Roman models.
   c. they wanted to focus on church reforms.
   d. they were unable to use the Latin vernacular.

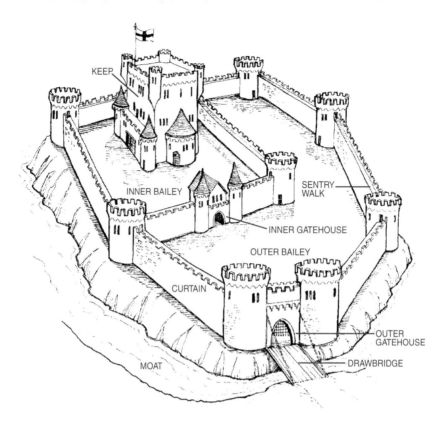

KEEP

SENTRY WALK

INNER BAILEY

INNER GATEHOUSE

OUTER BAILEY

CURTAIN

OUTER GATEHOUSE

MOAT

DRAWBRIDGE

MAKING HYPOTHESES ABOUT A DIAGRAM

The diagram shows the different components of a typical stone castle of the Middle Ages. A castle's primary purpose was to provide protection to everyone on a lord's manor during times of attack. With that fact in mind, it is possible to form reasonable hypotheses about the functions of the various architectural details.

1. What was the purpose of the moat and drawbridge?

2. The "toothed" gaps in the wall, or curtain, are called *crennels*. What purpose might crennelated walls have served?

3. Which part of the castle might have "kept" the lord and his family?

4. Into which part of the castle might peasants and animals have been herded during an attack?

5. What was the purpose of putting long, narrow windows in the curtain towers?

6. Remains of castles like this one can still be found throughout Europe and in Turkey, Syria, and Jordan. How can you explain their presence in Middle Eastern countries?

DEVELOPING CRITICAL THINKING SKILLS

1. Explain the statement that feudalism established "a great web of give-and-take" insofar as the duties and privileges of medieval life were concerned.
2. Show how the actions and policies of William the Conqueror helped to create political unity in England.
3. Discuss the immediate and more far-reaching reasons for the Crusades.
4. Describe the basic differences between the world-view of the Early and High Middle-Ages and that of the Renaissance.
5. Describe how Florence became a cultural as well as a commercial center.

ENRICHMENT AND EXPLORATION

1. As a class project, collect examples of medieval and Renaissance art and architecture. Present and explain each in class, showing how it exemplifies the values of the period in which it was created.
2. By consulting travel agents or tourism councils, draw up an itinerary for a tour of medieval sites and buildings in England, France, or Germany. Be prepared to explain why you chose the sites listed on your itinerary.
3. Working in small groups and using library resources, plan a television documentary on the Hundred Years' War. Different groups should gather information about causes of the war, the various parties involved, specific battles, military technology, and the personalities that influenced the outcome. Prepare a script for a 30-minute program and stage the presentation in class.
4. Consult the text or an encyclopedia to learn names of medieval and Renaissance authors. Read a tale, poem, or play by one of these authors and write a review. Explain what light the work sheds on the spirit of the times.
5. Using library resources, make costume designs for a play set in medieval times. Include clothing for a knight, a lady, a Crusader, a page, and a peasant. Display these designs on the class bulletin board. Carefully label the different parts of the clothing.

EXPANDING EUROPE
1440–1815

1440–1460	Henry the Navigator encourages expansion into Africa.
1453	*Ottoman conquest of Constantinople*
1492	Columbus reaches San Salvador, Hispaniola, and Cuba.
1498	Vasco da Gama reaches India.
1517	Martin Luther posts his Ninety-Five Theses.
1519–1522	First circumnavigation of the globe
1521	Cortés conquers the Aztecs.
1533	Pizarro conquers the Incas.
1534	Henry VIII is declared head of the Church of England.
1545–1563	The Council of Trent
1556	*Akbar the Great becomes Mogul emperor of India.*
1572	Saint Bartholomew's Day Massacre
1598	Edict of Nantes
1641	*Japan ends trade with Europeans and isolates itself.*
1642–1645	Cromwell's Roundheads defeat the Cavaliers.
1643–1715	Reign of Louis XIV
1649	Charles I is executed.
1685	Louis XIV revokes Edict of Nantes.
1687	Publication of Newton's *Principia Mathematica*
1688–1689	The Glorious Revolution
1762	Rousseau publishes *The Social Contract.*
1775–1783	*The American Revolution*
1776	Adam Smith publishes *The Wealth of Nations.*
1789–1799	The French Revolution
1799	Napoleon seizes power in France.
1815	Napoleon is defeated at Waterloo and banished.

4 Expanding Europe

From the time of the Italian Renaissance, the outlook and institutions of the Middle Ages began to disappear from Europe, and Europeans laid the groundwork for modern society. With newly felt self-confidence and optimism, they expanded in many directions at once—not only geographically, but also in the areas of culture, economics, science, and politics.

THE AGE OF EXPLORATION

In the Middle Ages, Europe had been largely isolated from the rest of the world. In the late 1400s and throughout the 1500s, this trend was reversed. Now Europeans burst the geographic bonds of their continent and traveled to the farthest corners of the world.

Riches of the East.   The force driving these discoveries was largely economic. Europeans wanted to take part in the trade with Asia for jewels, silks, porcelain, and spices. Spices were used to preserve meats in the days before refrigeration.

Europeans had long known about the lands that produced these precious goods. The tales of Marco Polo's incredible adventures in China and Southeast Asia in the 1200s were avidly read by increasing numbers of people. Moreover, the travels of the Crusaders had whetted an appetite for exotic goods. But as demand increased, so did price. In 1453 the Ottoman Turks had conquered Constantinople, destroying the last vestiges of Byzantine power. This gave Muslims a virtual monopoly on all trade coming from Asia. The only others profiting from this trade were Venetian and Genoese merchants who acted as agents for the trade, skimming a handsome profit. Trade through the Mediterranean was closed to the rest of Europe. New routes were needed "to the Indies where the spices grow."

Seafaring Technology.   This period also saw important advances in seafaring. Most fleets had already abandoned their slow, oar-powered galleys in favor of ships with sails. Mounted on these ships were guns, which the recent development of firearms had made possible. Equally important were improvements in navigational aids, such as the **compass**, which indicates direction, and the **astrolabe**, which helped identify location. These instruments made it possible to cross open seas rather than hugging the coastline.

Early Portuguese Expeditions.   The first countries to actively apply these new technologies were Portugal and Spain. Portugal, a small country on the west coast of the Iberian peninsula, was in a good location for exploring the Atlantic Ocean. In the mid-1400s, Prince Henry of Portugal, known as Henry "the Navigator," became interested in launching a new crusade in North Africa. Although not a sailor himself, he hired experienced Italian seafarers to teach the Portuguese seamanship, geography, and navigation. Henry also sponsored a number of expeditions. Before his death in 1460, these crews had ventured down the west coast of Africa as far as modern-day Sierra Leone, establishing trading posts as they went.

Henry's early successes convinced the Portuguese that they could reach Asia by sailing around the African continent. In 1487, Bartolomeu Dias (BAHR-too-loo-MEE-oo DEE-uhsh) rounded the cape at Africa's southern tip. Anticipating that Dias had found the way to India, the king of Portugal named it the Cape of Good Hope.

The Race to the Indies.   In the meantime, an Italian sailor from Genoa named Christopher Columbus persuaded Queen Isabella and King Ferdinand of Spain to sponsor a daring expedition westward across the Atlantic Ocean. Columbus was sure this route would prove to be the shortest way to Asia. Earlier, he had tried to sell his plan to the Portuguese. With their superior geographical knowledge, the Portuguese had rejected it, not because they thought the earth was flat, but because they felt Columbus had seriously miscalculated the distance between Europe and Asia. The Portuguese were right about the distance, which was much greater than Columbus had imagined. How were they to know that another continent lay to the west between Europe and Asia?

80

In October 1492, Columbus's three ships, the *Niña*, the *Pinta*, and the *Santa María*, made landfall at one of the islands of the Bahamas, which Columbus named San Salvador. Soon after, he arrived at Hispaniola (his-puhn-YOH-luh) (now Haiti and the Dominican Republic) and Cuba. He returned home triumphant, convinced that he had indeed reached Asia.

The Portuguese were skeptical that Columbus had found Asia. Where, they wondered, were the spices and other riches? Sticking with their original plan, King Manuel sent Portuguese navigator Vasco da Gama to follow in Dias's path. After many difficulties, the expedition rounded the Cape of Good Hope, sailed up the east coast of Africa, and crossed the Indian Ocean. In May 1498, da Gama arrived in Calicut, India. The Islamic trade monopoly on Asian goods had finally been broken. Portugal soon was established as an economic power.

Around the World. Columbus remained convinced all his life that he had reached Asia. However, later Spanish voyages made clear that he had found what to Europeans was a "New World," soon to be called "America." In 1513, Vasco Núñez de Balboa (bal-BOH-uh) led an expedition across the isthmus of Panama and became the first European since Marco Polo to gaze upon the Pacific Ocean.

This map of the 1500s shows the world as it was then known to Europeans. A line on the map traces the route around the world of Magellan's voyage.

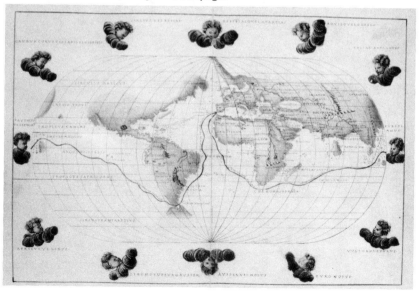

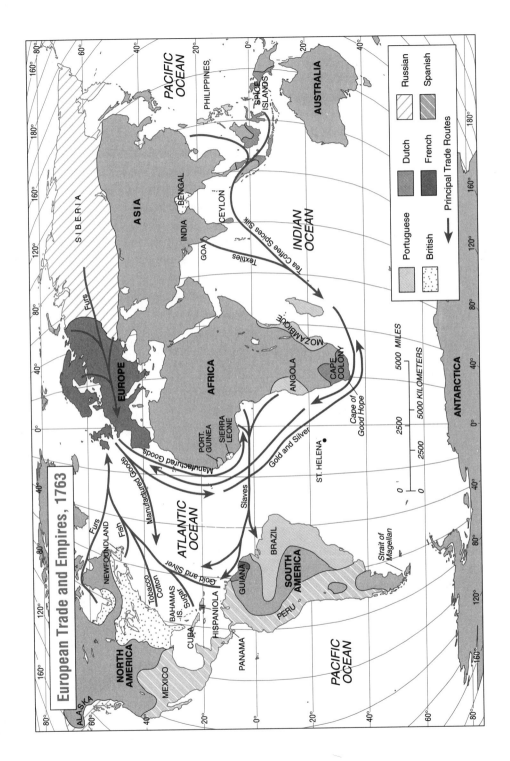

European Trade and Empires, 1763

PACIFIC OCEAN

PHILIPPINES

SPICE ISLANDS

AUSTRALIA

ASIA

BENGAL

INDIA

CEYLON

GOA

Textiles

Tea Coffee Spices Silk

INDIAN OCEAN

SIBERIA

Furs

EUROPE

AFRICA

MOZAMBIQUE

ANGOLA

CAPE COLONY

Cape of Good Hope

5000 MILES

5000 KILOMETERS

2500

2500

0

0

ANTARCTICA

Manufactured Goods

PORT. GUINEA

SIERRA LEONE

Manufactured Goods

Gold and Silver

ST. HELENA

Slaves

ATLANTIC OCEAN

Gold and Silver

ALASKA

NORTH AMERICA

Furs

Fish

NEWFOUNDLAND

Tobacco

Cotton

BAHAMAS IS.

Sugar

CUBA

HISPANIOLA

MEXICO

PANAMA

GUIANA

BRAZIL

SOUTH AMERICA

PERU

Strait of Magellan

PACIFIC OCEAN

Gold and Silver

Legend:

Portuguese

British

Dutch

French

Russian

Spanish

→ Principal Trade Routes

82

Six years later, in 1519, the skilled Portuguese navigator Ferdinand Magellan (muh-JEL-uhn) was engaged by King Charles I of Spain to lead an expedition that would attempt to reach Asia by sailing around South America. Magellan sailed with five ships and 240 sailors and soldiers. Near the tip of South America, he found the passage to the Pacific now known as the Strait of Magellan. Magellan then crossed the Pacific to the present-day Philippine Islands, where he was killed in battle. Two of his ships reached the Spice Islands, now part of Indonesia, in September 1522. Only one of these ships, carrying 18 exhausted survivors, finally made it across the Indian Ocean, around the Cape of Good Hope, and home to Spain. In three long years (1519–1522), Magellan's surviving crew had traveled more than 50,000 miles. They were the first to **circumnavigate** (suhr-kuhm-NAV-uh-gayt) (sail around) the globe. The single cargo of spices they carried back was valuable enough to pay for the entire expedition.

The New World. The Spanish found no spices in America, but they were richly rewarded with land and precious metals. In 1519 Hernán Cortés (kor-TEZ) landed on the Mexican coast with 600 soldiers. Within two years, he had subdued the Aztec empire, acquired a vast hoard of Aztec gold, and claimed the Aztecs' land for Spain. A decade later (1531–1533), Francisco Pizarro (pih-ZAHR-oh) conquered the Incan empire in the mountains of present-day Peru. Here, too, rich stores of gold and silver were the reward. Although later "treasure hunts" by such adventurers as Francisco de Coronado and Hernando de Soto failed to match the Aztec and Incan prizes, they made lands available to Spanish settlers and made possible Europe's first real colonial empire. Soon slaves were brought from Africa to work the newly-established plantations.

A Global Network. More explorations and conquests followed, many of them similarly inspired by the lust for gold and silver. These foreign ventures had profound results. Within a century, the entire world became a vast interconnected trading system. Geographic horizons stretched far beyond the world the Romans had known, to include the Americas, East Asia, Southeast Asia, and India.

As gold and silver bullion from the Americas made European monarchs rich, there was a great redistribution of wealth. Even more significantly, there was a redistribution of the world's population, as settlers came to the new lands voluntarily and slaves were transported against their will. The Americas, in particular, became the most racially mixed region in the world.

Plants and animals were also redistributed. From Europe to the Americas came various domestic animals, such as horses, cattle, and sheep. From the Americas to Europe came plants such as corn, potatoes, tomatoes, sweet potatoes, and squash. Today these Native American foods account for about half of the world's food supply.

The lives of ordinary people in Europe, however, changed slowly. Most people continued to toil endlessly in the fields. Productivity of crops had been improved by such breakthroughs as the use of horses to pull plows and the cultivation of new vegetables. Gradually the diets of people improved and began to include more meat and cheese.

Future patterns of global economic activity were also set in motion. The Americas, eastern Europe, Africa, and Asia began to furnish the majority of the world's raw materials. Africa and Asia provided much of the labor. Europe began to produce manufactured goods.

Worldwide trade created new jobs in towns and cities of Europe. More and more people moved to the towns, and competition for the new jobs was fierce. European cities became filled with homeless people begging and looking for work. Some of them resorted to stealing. Since poor people in the towns could not farm, they were the first to starve in times of famine. Extended families, which had been the basis of social life in the Middle Ages, gave way to smaller nuclear families in the towns, so that townspeople had less family to rely on in hard times.

THE REFORMATION

While Europeans were forging a worldwide economic order, the spiritual unity that had once characterized Latin Christendom was rapidly coming undone. Seeds of discontent planted centuries earlier now blossomed into a full-blown religious movement called the **Reformation**. The result was the establishment of a number of Protestant churches and religious groups.

Background of the Reformation. Protest against the church had been developing throughout the latter part of the Middle Ages. Power struggles within the church hierarchy, displays of church wealth, and the sometimes worldly and corrupt lifestyles of high-ranking clergy had all helped to erode public confidence.

During the Renaissance, cultural, political, and economic conditions made the mood of discontent more intense. The spirit of inquiry championed by Renaissance thinkers led many to question church authority. Moreover, the Renaissance ideal of individualism clashed with the church's insistence on its role in the salvation of individual human beings (see pages 57–58). As literacy rose and the printing press made available the works of the Christian humanists, these radical new ideas became widespread.

Politically, conflicts between European monarchies and the papacy grew more intense as monarchs continued to gain power. More and more people moved to the cities, abandoning their feudal loyalties and tying their interests to those of the king or queen. Thus, not only the monarchs, but also large numbers of the middle class, began to regard the pope as a foreigner with no right to meddle in their nation's affairs.

Economically, public resentment grew over the heavy taxes imposed by the church. To this was added the perception that church life was driven by greed. The church was criticized for selling religious offices. Its reputation was even worse for selling **indulgences**, or pardons from some of the punishments a sinner would suffer after death. When a monk named Martin Luther publicly criticized the sale of indulgences, a momentous revolution was set in motion.

The Reformation in Germany.   Martin Luther was a monk and professor of theology in Wittenberg, Germany. In 1517 he posted a document called the **Ninety-Five Theses** on the door of the castle church. Each thesis was a statement, or "proposition," that he offered to defend in a debate. The theses condemned the entire notion of selling indulgences. Luther's attack gained widespread attention. The church soon branded him a **heretic**, or person whose beliefs defied church authority. He was excommunicated, and he might have been executed if he had not been protected by a powerful German noble.

Luther had set the Reformation in motion. While in hiding from church authorities, he translated the New Testament into German and began to teach that every individual could discover its meaning without the help of the clergy. Also central to Luther's teachings was the notion that personal salvation depended on faith alone. This viewpoint challenged church doctrine that salvation rested not only on faith, but also on "good works," sometimes interpreted as giving money to the church.

The Spread of Protestantism.   Luther's ideas spread like wildfire, due partly to the new printing technology. In Germany and Scandinavia, these ideas formed the basis of the Lutheran church. At almost the same time, other Protestant reform movements developed in other countries. In Switzerland, John Calvin proposed a religious community

Martin Luther as he appeared in 1546, shortly before his death

organized around a council of elders, or *presbyters* (PREZ-bih-tuhrz). The Presbyterian Church of Scotland developed from Calvin's ideas, as did other Calvinist communities in Hungary, Germany, the Netherlands, and France. Calvin's followers in France were called **Huguenots** (HYOO-guh-nahts). Under France's Catholic kings, they endured a series of brutal religious wars (1562–1598) and a devastating massacre on Saint Bartholomew's Day in 1572. This slaughter stopped only after the French king issued the Edict of Nantes in 1598, the first document ever to order a degree of religious toleration.

In England, Henry VIII broke away from Rome, not so much for religious reasons as because he wished to have his marriage annulled, a request the pope had denied. In 1534 the English Parliament declared Henry the head of the church in England. English Protestantism, known as Anglicanism, retained many rituals and doctrines of the Roman Catholic Church, although modifications during the reign of Queen Elizabeth I (1558–1603) made it more like other Protestant churches in some ways.

The Counter-Reformation. The Roman Catholic Church responded to the Protestant reform movements in several ways. Many loyal Catholics worked to revive the spiritual leadership of the Catholic Church. This movement became known as the **Counter-Reformation.**

Catholic institutions and individuals reacted to the Protestant challenge by actively reforming themselves. In 1534 Ignatius Loyola founded the Society of Jesus, commonly known as the **Jesuits** (JEH-zoo-ihts). This religious order dedicated itself to teaching and preaching a reformed Catholicism on a worldwide basis. By the 1600s, the Jesuits

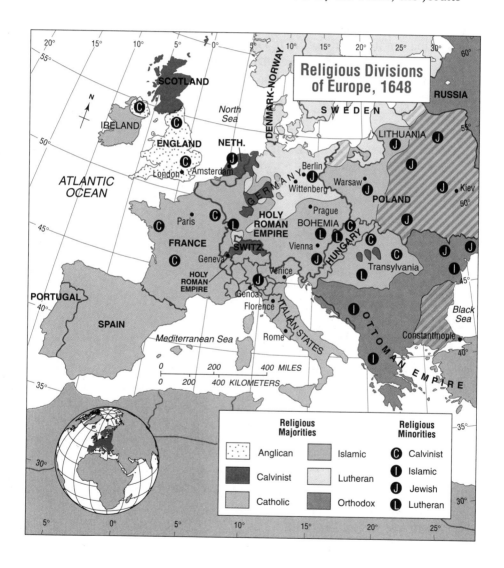

Religious Divisions of Europe, 1648

had become the greatest religious teachers in Europe. Jesuits traveled to new lands and won many converts to Catholicism.

Under the leadership of Paul III, pope from 1534 to 1549, many able scholars and reformers were appointed to high office. In 1545, the pope convened a group of leaders at the Council of Trent in order to reform abuses and to clarify doctrine. The council continued until 1563. During the course of these meetings, many corrupt practices, including the selling of indulgences, were abolished. Catholic rulers in Italy, Spain, and France enthusiastically supported the reforms.

Effects of the Reformation.   In spite of the efforts of the Counter-Reformation, the unity of Latin Christendom was permanently shattered. To this day, Europe remains a checkerboard of Protestant and Catholic areas. The northern part of Europe is predominantly Protestant, and the southern part predominantly Catholic. Although in time a spirit of toleration became the rule, isolated instances of deep-seated antagonism remain, as in northern Ireland.

The Reformation had other significant effects. Politically, it marked the increasing transfer of power from the church to the state. Moreover, with its emphasis on individualism, it paved the way for ideas about political liberty.

Economically, many Protestants—especially Calvinists—emphasized thrift and hard work in everyday life. This attitude, known as the "Protestant Ethic," has been seen by some as a great impetus to the growth of industry and the spirit of capitalism.

THE AGE OF ABSOLUTISM

During the 1500s and 1600s, a unique political unit, the national state, came of age in Europe. The creation of strongly centralized governments was almost invariably the work of powerful monarchs. Their power was so much greater than that of earlier monarchs that the period came to be known as the Age of Absolutism. **Absolutism** is a political system that concentrates power in the hands of one person.

To justify their policies, absolute monarchs invoked the theory known as the **divine right of kings**. They justified their iron-fisted control over all aspects of government by claiming that God had selected them to rule over others.

A Case Study of Absolutism.   The long reign of France's Louis (LOO-ee) XIV (the fourteenth), from 1643 to 1715, presented a near-perfect example of absolutism in action. The "Grand Monarch" gave voice to the concept in his famous statement *"L'état c'est moi"* ("I am the state").

When Louis inherited the throne in 1643, France was already on its way to becoming an absolute monarchy. From 1624 to 1642, his father's chief minister, Cardinal Richelieu (RISH-loo), had crafted a policy based on humbling the nobles and turning France into a military power.

After Richelieu's death, however, his policies caused a revolt called the *Fronde* (1648–1653). Having witnessed the *Fronde* as a child, Louis vowed that he would become so absolute in power that no such dissent would ever be possible again.

Domestic Control.   Louis worked long and hard to create an administrative staff of 1,000 officials who loyally carried out his every command. To stimulate industry and trade and to improve tax methods, he used the services of a brilliant official named Jean Colbert (ZHAHN kohl-BEHR). As was the case throughout Europe at this time, the largest share of the tax burden fell on the peasants. However, their resentment did not develop into active rebellion during Louis's lifetime, probably because they feared Louis's huge military machine—over 300,000 soldiers and armed police.

Part of the palace of Versailles, now a museum open to the public. The palace took more than 40 years to build and, when completed, had more than 1,300 rooms.

The middle class, another possible source of rebellion, was also kept in check. Many of these city dwellers were Huguenots who suffered harsh persecutions from the staunchly Catholic government. In 1685, Louis revoked (canceled) the Edict of Nantes. As a result, most of the remaining Huguenots fled the country, costing France some of its most productive citizens.

Louis used a completely different tactic to gain control over the French aristocracy. Although he had dispensed entirely with their services as government decision-makers, he kept them amused and occupied by lavish entertainments held at his sumptuous new palace at Versailles (vuhr-SEYE), just outside Paris. Here a level of extravagance and style was attained that would never be equaled again. The king himself led the court revels with such dazzling splendor that he became known as the "Sun King."

A Flawed Foreign Policy. Louis's fatal flaw lay in his overly ambitious foreign policy. In 1689 he mounted a military campaign to conquer part of the Holy Roman Empire, and in 1701 he tried to bring Spain under his control. The conflict that resulted, the War of the Spanish Succession (1702–1713), drained the royal treasury and brought no significant gain to France. On the contrary, Great Britain emerged as a force strong enough to balance the military might of France in Europe.

In 1715, at the end of his reign—the longest in modern European history—Louis left behind a highly organized and powerful nation. But he also left behind a bankrupt economy and social resentments that would one day erupt as a full-scale revolution.

LIMITED MONARCHY IN ENGLAND

The pattern established by Louis XIV was followed and imitated by monarchs throughout Europe. In England, however, the development of government took a different course. By the end of the 1600s, absolutism had given way to a limited, constitutional monarchy.

The Medieval Foundation. During the Middle Ages, the Norman kings had been able to unify England quickly and with little resistance from the nobility. During the following centuries, institutions arose that eventually led to a monarchy limited by the law: Magna Carta, the Common Law, and a consultative body called Parliament, composed of two houses. Unlike councils on the continent, one of these English houses, the House of Commons, was elected. Its members represented people whose right to vote was based on property ownership rather than on noble birth. This characteristic gave the emerging middle class a voice in governmental affairs.

Tudors and Stuarts. After the Hundred Years' War, England underwent a civil war, called the Wars of the Roses because the symbols of the opposing sides were a red rose and a white rose. In 1485, the Tudor family emerged victorious. The Tudor dynasty (1485–1603) included Henry VII, Henry VIII, and Elizabeth I.

The Tudors were generally popular with the people, especially the middle classes. These monarchs were, at heart, almost as absolutist as the French kings. However, they allowed Parliament to meet and even used it to legalize the break with the Catholic Church. In late Tudor times, many of the middle class became **Puritans**, members of a Calvinist sect that wanted to "purify" the Church of England by eliminating its ritual and reforming its doctrine. The Puritans held many of the Protestant ideas about individualism and freedom from oppression.

In 1603, the Tudor dynasty was succeeded by the Stuart dynasty, who were also kings of Scotland. The first Stuart kings, James I and Charles I, did little to maintain the good will that had existed between the Tudors and Parliament. As staunch believers in divine right, they dismissed Parliament and tried to raise money without its consent.

Cavaliers and Roundheads. A crisis came in 1640, when Charles was forced to convene Parliament to ask for taxes in order to put down a Scottish invasion. The Parliament ignored his request and instead insisted on a number of far-reaching demands, including reform of the Church of England. Charles refused, and war broke out in 1642 between his supporters, called **Cavaliers,** and supporters of Parliament, called **Roundheads** because of their short haircuts.

These developments began a political revolution that ultimately changed the character of the English monarchy. During the first stage of the English Revolution, from 1642 to 1645, an army led by a Puritan member of Parliament named Oliver Cromwell defeated the Cavaliers. Charles was publicly executed by order of Parliament in 1649. Cromwell became the head of an English republic called the **Commonwealth.** In 1658, Cromwell died and was replaced by his son, Richard, who proved to be a weak leader. In 1660, dissatisfied with Richard Cromwell and tired of the strict Puritanism of the Commonwealth, the English people reinstated the Stuart dynasty.

From 1660 to 1688, a period called the **Restoration**, England was ruled first by Charles II, then by James II. These kings once more tried to downplay the role of Parliament and angered middle class and nobility alike with their support of the Catholic Church.

The Glorious Revolution.   The final stage in the English Revolution took place in 1688 and 1689. In 1688, a group of Anglicans, aristocrats, and parliamentarians overthrew James II in a bloodless *coup d'état* (KOO day-TAH), or sudden overthrow of the government, known as the **Glorious Revolution**. The monarch was replaced by his daughter Mary and her husband, a Dutch prince named William of Orange. (*Orange* is the family name of the rulers of the Netherlands.) William and Mary were named king and queen, ruling jointly, by an act of Parliament.

In 1689 William and Mary accepted the Bill of Rights, which expressed Parliament's right to convene regularly, raise taxes, and maintain an army. It established the basic civil rights of the people, including trial by jury. The new monarchs also agreed to a **Toleration Act**, which allowed all Protestants the right to worship as they saw fit.

The Glorious Revolution was England's last great political upheaval. By establishing a **constitutional monarchy**—a monarchy lim-

A member of Parliament offers the crown to William and Mary. Although he is kneeling before them, it was Parliament that now had the upper hand in England.

ited by law—a flexible political system had been put into place. Over the next centuries, it would evolve into a full democracy. It also would serve as a model for systems later developed by the United States and France.

In 1707, England and Scotland united to form the kingdom of Great Britain. After this time, the government is referred to as "British" and the united country as "Great Britain" or simply "Britain." English and Scottish law remained separate, however, as did the churches of England and Scotland.

WINDS OF CHANGE

The English Revolution was but one in a host of profound changes sweeping like shifting winds over Europe between 1500 and 1800. The economic, scientific, and philosophical transformations of this period were among the most momentous in history.

The Commercial Revolution. Ways of doing business underwent a radical change. There were several reasons for the change. Explorations and discoveries increased trade and brought large amounts of gold and silver into Europe. A population explosion led to the demand for more food and goods and caused prices to rise. **Subsistence farming,** in which almost everything is raised locally, gave way to **commercial agriculture,** in which one or two crops are grown and sold for cash.

Guilds gave way to **cottage industries,** in which people were paid to do work in their homes. Although most of the home-based industries were run by men, some women became successful business owners. Other women learned trades and worked outside the home. Women were employed in such diverse occupations as brewing, tailoring, and manufacturing silk. They also were employed as spinners and weavers of wool cloth, one of the major items of trade in Europe.

Banks and insurance companies were formed to support the new commercial ventures. The net result of all this activity was a new class of individuals called **entrepreneurs** who were prepared to risk their capital in enterprises that might bring profit in the future. In this way, the modern economic system of **capitalism** began to emerge. In capitalism, private investors make the main economic decisions of what, when, where, how much, and at what price to produce, buy, and sell goods.

European states encouraged early capitalism through a group of policies called **mercantilism.** One of mercantilism's chief aims was a "favorable balance of trade," which was achieved by exporting more goods abroad than were imported into the country. A favorable balance of trade, it was argued, caused gold and silver to accumulate. These could then be used for yet more capitalistic ventures. The theory failed to consider that if foreign countries or colonies were unable to sell their own products, eventually they would lack the purchasing power to buy anyone else's.

Initially, mercantilism did much to subsidize new businesses, stimulate colonization, and charter trading companies. In the long run, however, these policies led to intense national rivalries in the colonies and produced resentment and rebellion on the part of the colonized people.

The Scientific Revolution. During the years from 1500 to 1800, scholars began to look at the natural world in a completely new way. Thinkers from earliest times had tried to unravel the mysteries of nature. Only now, however, were they able to begin transforming their speculations into scientific facts.

The changes were so great they are called the **Scientific Revolution**. Europeans came to see the universe as an complicated machine that is governed by certain unchanging laws. They also evolved a new way of gaining knowledge, called the **scientific method**. Scientists and philosophers such as Copernicus (koh-PUHR-nih-kuhs), Galileo (gal-uh-LAY-oh), Newton, and Harvey, established the fundamentals of the scientific method in the course of their work. These fundamentals are still in use today: observation, experimentation, and rational deduction.

The outstanding figure of the Scientific Revolution was the English physicist Isaac Newton, who did pioneering work in physics and mathematics. His major contribution was the discovery of the law of universal gravitation, which states that every body in the universe exercises a force on every other body—a force that can be explained by a mathematical formula. From the time Newton's law was published, in a book called *Principia Mathematica* (1687), it transformed the way human beings thought about nature and the universe. Newton also made important discoveries about the nature of light, explaining why objects appear to have colors. The esteem in which the great scientist was held during his own lifetime was expressed in Newton's epitaph, which was written by the poet Alexander Pope:

> Nature and Nature's Laws lay hid in Night.
> God said, "Let Newton be!" and All was Light.

The new scientific outlook gave Europeans the self-confidence not only to understand the world but to master it. The knowing *why* of science inspired the knowing *how* of technology, the practical use of knowledge. The Scientific Revolution laid the groundwork for the Industrial Revolution that was to follow. It also became the one aspect of European civilization most respected and adopted by other countries and cultures.

The Enlightenment. The 1700s are called the *Age of Reason*, the *Age of Enlightenment*, or simply the **Enlightenment**. Directly inspired by the Scientific Revolution, writers of the Enlightenment used the scientific method to try to discover natural laws governing society. Once they had developed theories about such laws, these early social scientists set about examining human institutions to determine how they could be managed and changed for the better. Everything from government and economics to religion, education, slavery, crime and punishment, and the status of women was examined under the microscope of the human ability to reason.

Most Enlightenment writers, because they were members of the middle class, rejected the ideas and institutions of the Middle Ages, especially the medieval class structure, which favored the nobility and the clergy. Instead, the ***philosophes*** (fee-luh-SAHFS), as these writers were known, insisted on the right of the individual to operate freely— free from the authority of church, state, or school. The French writer Voltaire (vawl-TEHR), in his letters and in books like *Candide* (1759), probably did more than any other *philosophe* to popularize these ideas and to criticize established authority.

Using the printing press to spread their message, the *philosophes* shaped new outlooks on many subjects. Although most of the *philosophes* were men, women also contributed to the creation and spread of Enlightenment ideas. Wealthy women held **salons**, or informal gatherings, attended by the key figures of the Enlightenment—writers, artists, and thinkers. These gatherings provided a place for people to present their work, share their ideas, debate, and create new concepts. The interaction that took place at these gatherings fueled the development of Enlightenment ideas. Wealthy women also became patrons for *philosophes*, providing guidance and financial assistance.

The greatest influence of the *philosophes* was in the areas of politics and economics. Three major political thinkers and numerous minor ones rejected the concept of the divine right of kings. In its place, they put the idea of democratic government based on a "social contract"

CASE STUDY:

The Rights of Women

The thinkers of the Enlightenment were often silent about the rights of women. Only late in the 1700s were women's voices heard, the most passionate being that of the English feminist Mary Wollstonecraft (1759–1797). In her most famous book, A *Vindication of the Rights of Woman* (1792), she attacks the wrongs inflicted on women by a culture that believes in women's inferiority.

> To account for, and excuse the tyranny of man, many ingenious arguments have been brought forward to prove, that the two sexes, in the acquirement of virtue [excellence], ought to aim at attaining a very different character: or, to speak explicitly [clearly], women are not allowed [acknowledged] to have sufficient strength of mind to acquire what really deserves the name of virtue. . . .
>
> Men complain . . . of the follies and caprices of our sex. . . . Behold, I should answer, the natural effect of ignorance! The mind will ever be unstable that has only prejudices to rest on. . . . Women are told from their infancy, and taught by the example of their mothers, that a little knowledge of human weakness, justly termed cunning, softness of temper, *outward* obedience, and a scrupulous [careful] attention to a puerile [childish] kind of propriety, will obtain for them the protection of man; and should they be beautiful, every thing else is needless, for, at least, twenty years of their lives. . . .
>
> The most perfect education, in my opinion, is . . . calculated to . . . enable the individual to attain such habits of virtue as will render it independent. . . .

A *Vindication of the Rights of Woman* by Mary Wollstonecraft. From *The Norton Anthology of Literature by Women*, edited by Sandra M. Gilbert and Susan Grebar. New York: Norton, 1985

1. How does Wollstonecraft explain the "follies and caprices of our sex"?

2. What does Wollstonecraft think the goal of education should be?

3. How do you think Wollstonecraft would view the status and behavior of modern U.S. women?

between rulers and ruled. The English philosopher John Locke stated in *Two Treatises of Government* (1690) that the right to govern was based on the consent of those governed. If a state governed unjustly by refusing to recognize and protect the rights of the individual, then it forfeited the loyalty of its subjects, who could legitimately overthrow it.

The French *philosophe* Charles de Montesquieu (mahn-tuhs-KYOO) had little sympathy with revolution. However, in such works as *The Spirit of the Laws* (1748) he argued for a constitutional monarchy in place of absolutism. Montesquieu proposed an ideal state in which the executive and legislative branches keep each other from getting too powerful through a system of checks and balances.

Democracy found its most impassioned champion in the French writer Jean Jacques Rousseau (roo-SOH), who began his book *The Social Contract* (1762) with the stirring words, "Man was born free, and everywhere he is in chains." Rousseau's political ideal was the small Greek city-state, in which every citizen played a role. He felt that if people put aside their selfish interests, they would be capable of making their own laws serve the common good.

Most Enlightenment political thinkers were more interested in the rights of property owners than in the rights of all individuals. In attempting to discover universal laws governing property and other forms of wealth, the science of economics was born. Enlightenment economics tended to favor capitalism and the entrepreneur. It rejected mercantilism in favor of a new kind of capitalism. In *The Wealth of Nations* (1776), the great Scottish economic thinker of the Enlightenment, Adam Smith, lashed out against government regulation. He proposed instead that business people should be allowed to make whatever economic decisions they chose, an idea usually expressed by the French term *laissez-faire* (leh-say-FEHR). Left to its own devices, Smith said, the market would be governed by "the invisible hand" of the law of supply and demand.

TWO REVOLUTIONS

At first, the ideas of the Enlightenment had little practical effect on the political life of Europe. It was overseas, in Great Britain's 13 North American colonies, that change first took place. In Europe, the American Revolution came to be seen as a sort of laboratory where the ideas of the *philosophes* were proved to be practical and workable.

The American Revolution (1775–1783). To protect its American colonies, Britain had fought the French and Indian War (1754–1763) with France. Britain had won, and France was driven from North America. Now, in 1763, Britain found its treasury depleted. Rather than impose new taxes on its subjects at home, the government found it only natural to tax the colonists for the protection it had given them. The colonists thought otherwise, regarding the taxes as a form of tyranny.

Adding fuel to the flames of resentment was English-born Thomas Paine, whose pamphlet *Common Sense* (1776) echoed the well-known Enlightenment views on natural rights, political equality, tolerance, civil liberties, and the dignity of all human beings.

When the quarrel turned to bloodshed, delegates from the colonies met and in 1776 adopted the Declaration of Independence, written mainly by Thomas Jefferson. In it, Jefferson borrowed heavily from Locke's theory of natural rights, declaring that government receives its powers from the people, and that people have a right to change or overthrow a government that deprives them of their "unalienable rights."

As the war progressed, France entered on the side of the colonists. Britain, frustrated by long supply lines, distracted by fighting the French in the West Indies, and lacking commitment to a long, sustained struggle, gave up fighting in 1781. The North Americans were then free to create a new and different kind of government, a republic in which the ultimate power rested with the people. In Europe and Latin America, the American Revolution was seen as a great victory over tyranny and a powerful justification of the ideas of the Enlightenment.

A European Revolution. The French were the first Europeans to follow the example of the American Revolution. Here, in the home of the Enlightenment, the people enjoyed none of the privileges of a free society. Under the Old Regime, as the existing government came to be called, gross inequalities existed. King Louis XVI (the sixteenth) ruled as an absolute monarch. Society was divided along strict class lines into three "estates," a system dating back to the Middle Ages. The First Estate, the clergy, and the Second Estate, the nobility, comprised only about 2 percent of the population. Yet they owned 35 percent of the land and were exempt from most taxation. The Third Estate, which included both peasants and the middle class, comprised the vast majority of people. They bore the lion's share of the taxes, in addition to the tithe, another holdover from feudal days. The peasants, especially, felt the economic burden, while the complaints of the middle class focused more on their lack of political power.

Such conditions made France ripe for revolution. All that was needed was an event to set it off. That event occurred when Louis found his
treasury depleted after aiding the colonists during the American
Revolution. To raise money, he proposed a property tax, which angered
the landed nobility and the clergy. In 1787 they forced the king to convene a national parliament, called the **Estates-General**, for the first time
in 173 years. The aristocracy hoped to regain some of the power it had
lost. Instead, the meeting unleashed a revolutionary fervor that swept
through all levels of society, causing power shifts from one group to
another. The revolution grew steadily in intensity, finally reaching a
crescendo of violence known as the Reign of Terror.

Power Struggles.   The first shifts of power were from the king and the
aristocracy to the middle class. In the Estates-General, the Third Estate
had more numbers than the other two estates combined. Even so, it had
only one third of the vote, since the three estates voted as separate
units. In June 1789, the Third Estate broke away from the other two

*The storming of the Bastille was a turning point in
French history. Each year the French celebrate July 14,
its anniversary, as their national holiday.*

estates and declared itself an independent body. Ten days later it changed its name, declaring itself to be the **National Assembly.**

Yet another shift of power came when the rumor spread that aristocrats were plotting to attack the National Assembly. This led the people of Paris to arm themselves. On July 14, 1789, a large number of Parisians attacked and captured the Bastille (bas-TEEL), an ancient castle and prison that had become a symbol of royal oppression. Mass revolution also occurred in the countryside, with peasants taking arms, seizing land, and burning down manors.

Faced with these threats, nobles and clergy in the National Assembly agreed to reforms that abolished their exemption from taxes and their exclusive right to hold office. The assembly then confiscated church lands, reorganized the government and the courts, and in August 1789 adopted the *Declaration of the Rights of Man and of the Citizen.* This document, modeled after the English Bill of Rights and the U.S. Declaration of Independence, was an expression of most of the political ideas of the Enlightenment. It contained the slogan "Liberty, Equality, Fraternity [Brotherhood]," which became the battle cry of the revolution.

Mounting Terror.   In 1791, the assembly drafted a new constitution. Although this constitution described the government as a limited monarchy, Louis by now was virtually powerless, as were most aristocrats. Many nobles fled the country and tried enlist the help of foreign powers against the revolutionary government in France. They found allies in Austria and in the German kingdom of Prussia. Later Britain, Holland, and Spain joined the aristocrats' coalition.

As a result, the assembly, now composed mainly of the middle class, had to deal with the threat of war. A group of radicals called the **Girondists** (jih-RAHN-duhsts) favored the war because they hoped it would bring about the removal of the king and the creation a true republic. They also wanted to spread the revolution to other countries.

At first the conflict went badly for the revolutionaries. When it looked as if Louis might soon be welcoming royalist invaders, the people of Paris took him prisoner. The National Assembly called a National Convention at which Louis was tried and convicted of treason. On January 21, 1793 he was executed. By September of that year, the French people had rallied to defend their country against the royalist invaders. By 1795 the coalition was completely smashed.

Meanwhile, the National Assembly had grown increasingly radical and divided as a new, far-left group called the **Jacobins** (JAK-uh-bihnz) entered a deadly power struggle with the Girondists. In time, the Jacobins triumphed and set up a group called the *Committee of Public Safety* as the main arm of government. With extremist zeal and a complete disregard for civil and human rights, the committee ruled the country during what is now called the **Reign of Terror**. During this period, in 1793 and 1794, more than 17,000 people were convicted of treason and executed, including Marie Antoinette, widow of Louis XVI.

The End of Revolution. Eventually the people were sickened by a terrorist revolution that was "devouring its own children." In the National Assembly, power shifted once more, this time to a group of conservatives, who in 1795 scrapped the constitution and replaced the government with a five-man *Directory*, which tried and executed many of the Jacobin leaders. The Directory ended, as did the ten-year-old revolution, on November 9, 1799, when a general named Napoleon Bonaparte [nuh-POH-lee-uhn BOH-nuh-pahrt] staged a *coup d'état*.

Although the French Revolution failed to establish a lasting democracy, it destroyed the Old Regime, inspired a spirit of **nationalism**, or devotion to one's country, and laid the groundwork for a free society dominated by the middle class. The removal of the last traces of mercantilism and feudalism was achieved after the revolution by a dictator.

THE AGE OF NAPOLEON

Napoleon Bonaparte, as a young man, had been a member of the Jacobin party. But after seizing power, he showed no interest in the republican ideas of the Jacobins. Rather, he was a military dictator with a genius not only for battle, but for administration. In 1804 he took the title *Emperor of the French* and thereafter was known, like all royalty, by only his first name.

Domestic Reforms. Napoleon immediately set about designing an efficient and highly centralized government. He reorganized the administration of the various departments (political divisions) of France and established a national system of education. He stabilized the economy through setting up a new tax structure and founding a national bank.

His greatest domestic achievement was in collecting and revising the entire body of French laws into seven codes. These codes incorporated some of the goals of the Revolution, such as religious toleration and the abolition of serfdom. One of them, called the Napoleonic Code,

As the pope looks on, Napoleon crowns his wife, Josephine, Empress of the French. Earlier, Napoleon had seized his own crown and put it on his head himself.

still forms the basis for modern French civil law, and also for the law of other countries in Europe and Latin America. In the United States, the law of the state of Louisiana is based on the Napoleonic Code.

A Military Rise and Fall.   Napoleon's domestic policies made him extremely popular with the people. However, his military ambitions eroded that good will and ultimately brought about his downfall.

At first, Napoleon's brilliant military strategies enabled France to defeat one European power after another. By 1810 he ruled a large empire that covered much of western and central Europe. Ultimately, however, the people in the conquered areas came to believe that their own national development was being held back by the French. Many also suffered economic hardships because of Napoleon's policy of blocking the import of British goods.

In 1805, the British admiral Lord Horatio Nelson destroyed a combined French and Spanish fleet in the battle of Trafalgar (truh-FAL-guhr), named for a nearby cape on the southern coast of Spain. This victory gave Britain mastery of the seas and guaranteed that Napoleon would not be able to invade Great Britain.

Even more disastrous to Napoleon was his invasion of Russia in 1812. With his "Grand Army" of 600,000 men, he hoped to engage the

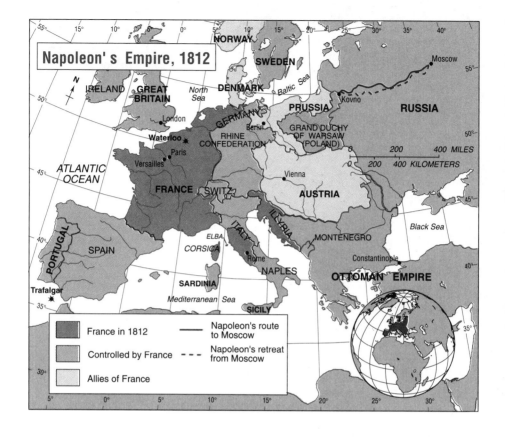

Napoleon's Empire, 1812

France in 1812	Napoleon's route to Moscow
Controlled by France	Napoleon's retreat from Moscow
Allies of France	

czar's troops in battle. Instead, the Russians retreated, drawing Napoleon's troops ever deeper into the vast country. When the Grand Army finally arrived in Moscow, they found the city nearly deserted, and soon much of it was on fire. Napoleon waited for the czar's surrender, but none came. In the face of bitter Russian resistance, the oncoming Russian winter, and the long supply lines that made it impossible to feed the troops, Napoleon decided to retreat. In the end, only 100,000 of his soldiers made it home. The rest starved, froze, or were shot or captured by the Russians.

In disgrace, Napoleon was forced in 1814 to abdicate and go into exile on the small island of Elba, off the northwest coast of Italy. A year later, he attempted a comeback. Within months, he suffered another humiliating defeat at the hands of Britain's duke of Wellington and Prussia's Marshal von Blücher (BLOO-kuhr) at the battle of Waterloo (1815) in Belgium. This time Napoleon was exiled to the barren island of St. Helena in the South Atlantic Ocean, where he died six years later.

REVIEWING THE CHAPTER

I. **Building Your Vocabulary**

In your notebook write the correct term that matches the definition.

absolutism   *coup d'état*   heretic

laissez-faire   entrepreneur   mercantilism

1. an economic system in which a nation seeks to increase wealth through strict government regulations

2. government in which all the power rests with one person

3. allowing business people to do as they choose

4. someone who dissents from established church doctrine

5. the sudden overthrow of an existing government by a small group

II. **Understanding the Facts**

In your notebook write the numbers 1 to 5. After each number, write the term that best completes the sentence.

Edict of Nantes   Social Contract   Toleration Act

Ninety-Five Theses   Theory of Gravitation

1. The Huguenots were given a degree of toleration by means of the _____.

2. One result of the Glorious Revolution was adoption of the

   _____.

3. In his book called *The* _____ Rousseau stated that "Man was born free."

4. The way people thought about nature and the universe was changed by the _____.

5. When Luther posted the _____, he began the Reformation.

III. Thinking It Through

In your notebook, write the numbers from 1 to 5. After each number, write the letter of the correct answer to the question.

1. How were Louis XIV and Henry VIII alike?
   a. Both believed in limited monarchy.
   b. Both believed in the divine right of kings.
   c. Both were executed.

2. A major factor influencing the emergence of capitalism was:
   a. the presence of a new class of wealthy individuals.
   b. the Counter-Reformation.
   c. the ideas of Jean-Jacques Rousseau.

3. Enlightenment thinking had a profound effect on
   a. the delegates to the Council of Trent.
   b. court life at Versailles.
   c. the leaders of the American Revolution.

4. Which statement best describes the reasons for Napoleon's downfall?
   a. His acquisition of a foreign empire bankrupted the treasury.
   b. His domestic policies caused a breakdown in central control.
   c. His military campaigns eventually angered the people.

5. Which of the following did *not* occur as an aftereffect of the Reformation?
   a. The Protestant Ethic encouraged the rise of capitalism.
   b. Protestants were able to unite in a single religious community.
   c. The Protestants' emphasis on individualism influenced political thinking.

DEVELOPING CRITICAL THINKING SKILLS

1. Explain how overseas exploration and discovery stimulated the commercial revolution.

2. Show the shifts in power that took place from the beginning of the French Revolution to its conclusion.

3. Explore the reasons why England moved toward a limited monarchy more quickly than France did.

4. Discuss the main characteristics of the scientific world view that developed between 1500 and 1800.

INTERPRETING A MAP

The map on page 82 shows the global trading network that had developed by 1763. Study the map, and then answer the questions that follow.

1. What three European countries controlled most of North and South America?

2. From which area did most of the gold and silver come? For what products was it spent?

3. Why did most of the slaves come from the west coast rather than the east coast of Africa?

4. Compare the raw materials of North America with those of Southeast Asia.

ENRICHMENT AND EXPLORATION

1. Using library sources, research the life of one of the individuals mentioned in this chapter. Then consult a book with models of professional résumés for job applications. Create a résumé for the individual you have selected, briefly describing "professional goals," "work experience," "skills," and "background." Conclude the résumé with "a personal statement of belief."

2. As a class project, collect information on court life during the reign of Louis XIV, including art and architecture, Gobelin tapestries, furniture, formal gardens, costumes, and the literature of Molière, Racine, La Fontaine, Madame de Sévigne, and La Rochefoucauld. Combine a bulletin board display with oral reports. Include posters that use the sayings of La Rochefoucauld.

3. Using library resources, including if possible record, tape, or compact disc collections, obtain information about one of the composers of eighteenth century classical music, such as Handel, Bach, Rameau, Gluck, Haydn, or Mozart. Make an oral report, explaining how the composer was influenced by the ideas of the age. If possible, play a musical excerpt to illustrate the composer's style.

4. Imagine that you are a print or television journalist covering the French Revolution. Use library resources to find out about a particular event. Then either write or deliver orally your "first-hand" account.

5 The Rise of Modern Europe

During the 1800s, two powerful forces came together that deeply influence our world today. One of these, the growth of the nation-state, was political. The other, the Industrial Revolution, was at first economic, but had important social and political effects as well. Together, these forces generated new loyalties, new wealth, and a new spirit of optimism and self-confidence.

These strengths became weaknesses, however, when they were carried to extremes. The development of industry came to depend on exploiting workers and, sometimes, other countries. Patriotism deteriorated into intense national rivalry that finally exploded in a bloody conflict of global proportions, World War I.

NATIONALISM IN THE 1800s

The nation-state was an entirely European invention. A **nation** is a community of people with a distinctive culture and, usually, its own territory and language. A **nation-state** is a government that takes in one nation and one nation only.

In other parts of the world and in earlier times, there had been narrower allegiances—to the tribe, to the city, to the feudal lord. There also had been some wider allegiances—to the Greek gods, to the Roman Empire, to Latin Christendom. But only in Europe of the 1700s and 1800s had loyalty to a nation taken shape. In some places it came slowly, by evolution, as in Britain. In others it developed rapidly, by revolution, as in France.

Once unleashed, the forces of nationalism seemed to take on a life of their own. They survived the Napoleonic era, and they survived the conservative forces that tried to bring back the Europe that had existed before the French Revolution.

THE RISE OF MODERN EUROPE
1815–1920

1815	Congress of Vienna
1821–1829	Greek War of Independence
1830	Revolution in France forces king to abdicate.
	Polish and Belgian revolts
1848–1849	Revolts in Paris, Vienna, Venice, Berlin, Milan, Rome, and Warsaw
1848	Publication of the *Communist Manifesto*
1854	*Perry opens Japan.*
1861	Independent kingdom of Italy proclaimed.
1861–1865	*U.S. Civil War*
1864	Prussia and Austria fight Denmark.
1866	Seven Weeks' War (Austria vs. Prussia)
1867	Austro-Hungarian Dual Monarchy established.
1870–1871	Franco–Prussian War
1871	German Reich proclaimed
1880–1914	Era of High Imperialism
1901	The Triple Alliance
1904	Triple Entente
	Russo–Japanese War
1908	Austria-Hungary annexes Bosnia-Herzegovina.
1911	*Revolution in China*
1914–1918	World War I
1917	Russian Revolution
	United States joins Allies.
1918	Wilson's Fourteen Points speech
1919	Treaty of Versailles
1920	League of Nations holds first meeting at Geneva.
1921	Irish Free State established.

Conservative Backlash in Vienna. In 1815, a group of monarchs, aristocrats, and diplomats met in Vienna. For ten months, delegates to the **Congress of Vienna**, as this meeting was called, attended glittering balls, theater productions, the opera, fox hunts, and gala banquets. When not busy at social events, they worked at restoring the old order as it had existed before the French Revolution. The chief architect of this plan was the foreign minister of Austria, Prince Klemens von Metternich (MET-uhr-nihk). He arranged for the return to their former sovereigns of lands conquered by Napoleon. He put monarchs like the brother of Louis XVI in France back on their thrones. Most important, he established a finely tuned **balance of power** among the nations of Europe. A balance of power is a distribution of power that keeps any one nation from becoming dangerous to the others.

These arrangements helped to keep peace in Europe for most of the next hundred years. But it was an uneasy peace. The return of the old order led to new upheavals and revolutions. In 1830, an armed revolt in Paris brought France a new king and inspired revolutions in Belgium and Poland. In 1848 another upheaval in France brought down the monarchy and replaced it with a republic. This revolution ignited other revolutions in many parts of Europe. These included Italy and Germany, which until this time had remained divided into numerous small states.

The Unification of Italy. Italy, as the birthplace of the Renaissance, had long been exposed to ideas challenging traditional values and institutions. It was not until Napoleon conquered the peninsula, however, that Italians began to dream of a united country, free of foreign control.

At the Congress of Vienna, most of Italy was carved up into several small kingdoms, and the remainder of it was given to Austria. Metternich asserted that Italy was nothing more than "a geographic expression"—a place on the map without a political core.

In defiance, Italian nationalists began a drive toward unification that became known as the **Risorgimento** (ree-sawr-jee-MEN-toh), meaning "resurrection." Inspiring others to action was Giuseppe Mazzini (maht-TSEE-nee), who wrote, "A country is not a mere territory . . . it is the sentiment of love, the sense of fellowship which binds together all the sons of that territory."

If Mazzini was the soul of *Risorgimento*, Count Camillo Cavour (kah-VOOR) was its brain. As premier of the kingdom of Sardinia-Piedmont, Cavour attempted to make that region a model state from which to stage his unification drive. He allied his small kingdom with

France, working out an arrangement by which Sardinia would cede two provinces to France, if France would join Sardinia in a war against Austria. As a result of this war, the Austrians were expelled from Lombardy in northern Italy. Lombardy joined Sardinia as the nucleus of a new kingdom of Italy, a victory that inspired other uprisings throughout northern Italy.

Parts of southern Italy were won by the dashing Giuseppe Garibaldi (gar-uh-BAWL-dee). With a volunteer force of 1,000 "Red Shirts," he successfully invaded Sicily and convinced the Sicilians to join Sardinia. By 1860, all Italy had been united except for Rome and Austrian-controlled Venetia (vi-NEE-shee-uh) in the north.

Cavour, who died in 1861, did not live to see Italy completely united. But in 1866, his successors allied with Prussia in a war against Austria, which gained them Venetia. Four years later, when French troops in Rome returned to France, Italian troops took possession of the city and made it the capital of a fully united Italy.

Bismarck Unites Germany.   The Germans were also late in achieving unity. Like the Italians, German nationalists had rankled under French occupation during the Napoleonic era. They then saw their hopes for nationhood dashed by the peacemakers at the Congress of Vienna. The Congress restored a loose confederation of princely states dominated by the Habsburg dynasty, who now called themselves the emperors of Austria. (Napoleon had abolished the Holy Roman Empire in 1806.)

In 1848, a series of revolutions erupted in the German states, but efforts to create a democratic, united Germany were unsuccessful. Instead, the drive toward unification was taken up by conservative, militaristic Prussia. Prussia was a kingdom in northeastern Germany, with its capital in Berlin. For more than a century, it had been increasing its territory and power. Now, under the leadership of Otto von Bismarck, it was ready to challenge the Habsburgs of Austria for leadership in Germany. Bismarck was dedicated to *Realpolitik* (ray-AHL poh-lee-TEEK), or policies based on practical considerations rather than on theory or morality. He made this obvious in his first speech to the Prussian parliament, when he said, "The great questions of the time are not decided by speeches and majority decisions . . . but by iron and blood."

Following his own advice, the "Iron Chancellor," as Bismarck came to be known, led Prussia into three wars designed to strengthen it and weaken other European powers. First, he joined forces with Austria in a war against Denmark (1864), which resulted in Prussia and Austria taking over two Danish provinces. Next, a quarrel with Austria over the

Otto von Bismarck, chancellor first of Prussia and then of Germany, was Europe's strongest and most effective statesman from the 1860s to 1890.

administration of these provinces gave him the excuse he needed to turn on his former ally. Austria was soon defeated in the so-called "Seven Weeks' War" of 1866. With Austria's influence in Germany now weakened, Bismarck formed the **North German Confederation**, which united 22 states under a federal government. Finally, in 1870, he master-minded an argument with France over who should inherit the Spanish throne. By leaking a carefully edited telegram to the press, he inflamed the passions of both the French and German public to such a degree that war became inevitable.

Emerging victorious from this war, called the **Franco–Prussian War**, Prussia added all the southern German states except Austria to the fed-eration. On January 18, 1871, the Prussian king, William I, was crowned **Kaiser** [KEYE-zuhr], or emperor, of a new German **Reich** (RIKE), or empire. With his "blood and iron" tactics, Bismarck had achieved the unification of Germany, but at the cost of a free and democratic system.

Multinational Empires. Not all of Europe was formed into nation-states. Three large empires continued to hold sway over large areas containing many different nationalities. In these empires, too, the stirring of discontent was evident.

In the Balkan peninsula was the Ottoman Empire, so corrupt and inefficient that it had been contemptuously dubbed "the sick man of Europe" by the czar of Russia. Once a military power that had threatened Europe as far north as Vienna, the Ottoman Empire had been steadily losing territory to Austria and Russia since the 1700s. During the 1800s it also lost Greece, Serbia, and Romania, all of which became independent. As its hold weakened on the remainder of the Balkan Peninsula, other nationalities there began to seek their independence as well.

Austria-Hungary had its own minority problems. This "Dual Monarchy" was created in 1867 in response to Hungarian demands for autonomy within the Habsburg empire. As a compromise, Austrians and Hungarians now shared a monarch and ministers of foreign affairs, defense, and finance. In other respects, they were separate countries. Their emperor (of Austria) and king (of Hungary), Francis Joseph, ruled over a large area that included many other restless nationalities, most of them Slavic.

The Russian Empire appeared to hold a tighter rein on its minorities, which included Poles, Jews, Ukrainians, Finns, Turkic Moslems, and others. Seemingly the strongest of the three empires, it shocked the world when it suffered a humiliating defeat in a war with Japan in 1905.

THE INDUSTRIAL REVOLUTION

Occurring at the same time as the rise of the European nation-state was a phenomenon of even greater global significance: the **Industrial Revolution**. By the latter part of the 1700s, the British economy experienced what is called a "takeoff" in economic development. A new system of producing goods in factories was established. The factory system allowed large quantities of goods to be produced at much lower costs than previously. Britain's economic takeoff seemed sudden and dramatic. In fact, it required many years to develop and just the right combination of factors.

Why Britain Was First. Large investments of capital were essential in order to build factories, hire workers, and buy raw materials. Thanks to Britain's well-developed trading system, profits had poured in from around the world—from the fur trade in Siberia and North America, the

112

gold and silver mines of South America, the slave trade in Africa, and the many trading companies in India, the West Indies, and Africa. This money became the basis for funding new factory ventures.

A factory system also required people to work in the factories. High prices for wool had encouraged British landowners to *enclose*, or fence in, their farmlands so that sheep could be grazed there. The **enclosures**, put into effect between 1714 and 1820, forced poor peasants off the land to seek work elsewhere. It was an appalling situation, for many thousands of people died of hunger and exposure. It did, however, assure that new industries would have a plentiful supply of labor.

Well-established markets were another condition that Britain had already achieved. General trade within Great Britain and Ireland was made easy by an open market, free of tariffs. Overseas, a brisk trade with the colonies had created a demand for such goods as textiles, weapons, hardware, and ships.

Britain also had a plentiful supply of the resources that were the basis of its early metal and textile industries. It had large deposits of coal, found in central and northern England. Methods were developed to turn the coal into coke, the fuel with which iron could be smelted. In addition, Britain had the water resources necessary to power the early machinery used in the textile industry.

Lastly, Britain's geography helped it to become a major seafaring power. Most important were its many ports and thousands of merchant

An iron and steel mill belches smoke over northwestern England in the middle 1800s. At the time, scenes like this were seen as signs of progress and prosperity.

ships. In addition, as factories multiplied, Britain built a connecting network of roads and canals. Such a system was essential for moving raw materials to factories and goods to markets.

The Technology Explosion.   **Technology,** applying scientific principles in practical ways, is also a requirement for industrialization. The invention of new ways of doing things followed the rule that "necessity is the mother of invention." Initially, there was a demand for cotton cloth. Therefore, Britons saw a need for machines that would quickly and efficiently produce cotton thread. Soon several newly invented devices achieved that goal. With the abundance of thread that resulted, there was now a need for a loom that could weave the thread faster than by the old hand method. Thus, in 1785 came Edmund Cartwright's loom, which at first was powered by horses.

Now came a need for a more plentiful and reliable power source than horses. The response was the application of an earlier invention, James Watt's steam engine (1769), to Cartwright's machine. It was but one of the many uses found for this wonderful invention, which ended forever humanity's complete dependence on animal, wind, and water power.

Industrialization on the Continent.   The spread of industrialization from Great Britain to other parts of Europe took place at different rates, depending on the presence of the necessary conditions. Belgium, with its rich deposits of coal and long manufacturing tradition, became the first nation on the continent to industrialize. France was next, achieving takeoff during and immediately after the French Revolution. Germany lagged somewhat behind. However, the establishment of a common economic market (*Zollverein*) among the states in 1818 and Bismarck's unification in 1871 remedied the situation. By 1900, Germany was well on its way to overtaking Britain as Europe's most industrialized nation.

Other parts of Europe were slower to develop. Southern Europe, for example, lacked capital and such essential resources as coal and iron. Russia under the autocratic czars remained an underdeveloped country, without the necessary middle class and commercial wealth to establish an early factory system. It was not until the 1890s that this slumbering giant began to exploit the tremendous quantity and variety of its natural resources.

A Brave New World?   The world created by the Industrial Revolution was a far different place from what had been before. In economic terms, it began a system in which goods were produced not by hand but by machine, not in cottages but in factories, not singly but by highly efficient mass-production methods. But there were other results that went wider and deeper into the social, economic, and political fabric of people's lives.

Populations increased throughout Europe. The major reason for larger populations was advances in medicine and hygiene. Improved sewage systems and clean water supplies dramatically decreased death rates. So, too, did the discovery of vaccines and the realization that persons with infectious diseases should be quarantined.

As populations increased, so did the sizes of cities. With improved transportation bringing food supplies from afar, cities sprang up around factories. The "dark satanic mills," as the poet William Blake called them, had smokestacks that blackened the sky above the tenements where workers lived. In spite of these negative aspects, European cities in the 1800s were exciting, vibrant places, full of the latest mechanical wonders and buzzing with new ideas, new products, and a rich cross-section of humanity. By 1914, a majority of the populations of many European nations lived in cities.

Class Distinctions.   Another major effect of industrialization was an increase in the size and vitality of the middle class of merchants, bankers, and industrialists. Supporting their efforts were a host of engineers, lawyers, shopkeepers, civil servants, and journalists. With new wealth filling the bank accounts of a burgeoning middle class, a large-scale, consumer-oriented society was born. Businesses soon found ways to tap consumer wealth by developing techniques of advertising, mail-order merchandising, and credit and discount plans.

For people outside the middle class, however, life often was not so pleasant. Workers toiled at jobs for 12, 14, even 16 hours a day. Working conditions also were bad. Most people worked in factories filled with noxious fumes, ear-splitting noise, and dangerous machinery. When workers were hurt in accidents, which were frequent, they were fired with no compensation.

Wages were so low that one person's wage could not support a family. Women and children often worked along with men to try to earn enough money to feed their families. Many factory owners preferred to hire women and children, because they could pay them lower wages, using the excuse that their incomes were only supplementing those of men. In reality, many families had only women or children working, because men often could not find jobs.

In the early industrial cities, children often had to fend for themselves. These boys were photographed in a London street in the 1890s.

The Industrial Revolution radically changed the way most people lived their lives. Before, most Europeans had been farmers. As the Industrial Revolution gained momentum, more and more people were drawn into the new industrial system. Cities around factories and mines seemed to spring up almost overnight.

Workers in the cities also had little social support. Families from different parts of the country were packed together in the tenements, and often they remained strangers to one another. In rural communities, people could rely on support from their neighbors. In the cities, thousands of people milled together without any ties and with little personal contact. Competition for jobs was fierce, and city dwellers found themselves pitted against other workers in a fight for survival.

Living conditions in these cities often were horrendous. Housing, sanitation, and water systems had not been designed for so many people. Workers were packed into tenement houses, sometimes with as many as 15 people living in one room, and with no plumbing systems. Disease spread quickly in these conditions, and many workers and their family members died. Yet in spite of these harsh conditions, laborers from the countryside continued to flood into the new industrial cities.

Women in the Industrial Revolution.   The roles of women were profoundly changed by the Industrial Revolution. Many women were hired to work in the new factories and mines, and this added to their existing responsibilities. Like male workers, women worked 12 to 16 hours a day. Then they had to do domestic chores as well. Cleaning and cooking at the end of an exhausting working day was difficult enough, but these women also had to do these chores under the crowding, poor sanitation, and lack of clean water that characterized life in the new industrial cities.

As the middle class grew, working-class women were employed in increasing numbers as domestic servants. These women, who were usually single, served as cooks, maids, and nannies for middle-class households. In contrast, middle-class women usually did not work outside the home, believing that a woman's role was to raise children and manage the household so that it ran smoothly.

RESPONSES TO INDUSTRIALISM

The changes brought by the Industrial Revolution stimulated new thinking about how economic matters related to the social and political environment. A new group of thinkers calling themselves **economists** developed theories that were applied with varying degrees of success in the real world.

Classical Liberalism.   The prevailing economic and political theory during the early days of industrialism in Great Britain was **classical liberalism**. Its economic tenets were most clearly expressed in Adam Smith's argument for *laissez-faire* capitalism (see page 97). Liberalism was closely associated with middle-class beliefs and interests. These included freedom of the individual, the importance of "natural law," and the protection of property rights. In the world of industry, these principles meant unrestricted competition, free trade, and a factory system ruled by the law of supply and demand rather than by government regulations. Such principles gave industrialists a moral justification for the system under which they prospered, but the principles did little to better the lot of the workers.

The Shift to Democratic Liberalism.   By the late 1800s, the working class could no longer be ignored. As workers became better educated and more assertive, and as revolutions swept through Europe, the masses began to acquire the same political rights as those the property owners had won before them. Workers and those sympathetic to them used their voting power to strengthen the government's role in looking after the welfare of all its citizens. This new approach, known as **democratic liberalism**, resulted in social reform programs that remedied many of the terrible working conditions. Led by Germany, most European countries passed legislation that allowed their governments to set minimum wages, limit working hours and child labor, and monitor factory conditions. Governments also began to take responsibility for unemployment compensation, health insurance, and old-age benefits. In this way, conditions for laborers gradually improved. The elements of Europe's modern **welfare states**, which provide generous benefits to citizens, were put into place.

Socialism. While classical liberalism was softening to meet the new realities, an entirely different economic theory was being developed. Where liberalism extolled the freedom of the individual, **socialism** emphasized the welfare of the community. Socialists believed that people could design the best political and economic systems for the greatest number of people. In the same way, socialist economists rejected the idea of a free market in favor of a planned economy.

Some of the earliest socialists were social reformers who envisioned ideal communities in which the means of production—money, land, factories, machinery, and so on—would be owned **collectively**, that is, by everyone. The Welsh industrialist Robert Owen, for example, tried to establish a cooperative community in Indiana. But the **Utopian Socialists**, as they were called, seldom put their ideas into action. One of these dreamers, a Frenchman named Charles Fourier, sat in his room at noon for 12 years waiting for a response to his newspaper advertisement seeking supporters for his commune. No one ever came.

Marxism. Karl Marx, known as the father of modern socialism, was different from the Utopian Socialists. Living in an era of vast economic change, he came to believe that economic forces—and economic forces alone—shaped history. He contended that throughout the course of human events, a struggle had taken place between two classes of people, the "haves" and the "have-nots." The "haves" were all-powerful because they controlled the means of production. The "have-nots," in contrast, were forced to work for the "haves" merely in order to survive.

Putting the class struggle into present-day terms, Marx identified the "haves" of the middle 1800s as the capitalists—the middle class—

and the "have-nots" as the working classes, which he called the **proletariat** (proh-luh-TEHR-ee-uht). He was convinced, however, that the situation was only temporary, that capitalism would soon be destroyed. The wages that capitalists paid to the masses would destroy the masses' purchasing power. Without the ability to sell their goods, the capitalists would then be forced to close factories, causing widespread unemployment and a deep economic depression. In desperation, the proletariat would revolt and overthrow the system. In its place, they would establish a state-controlled society. In the new system, the government, as the owner of the means of production, would take no profits. Thus it would always be able to pay workers a living wage. Eventually, the state would "wither away," and control would pass to the people of the new, classless society. Marx and a colleague, Friedrich Engels, attempted to hasten the process by publishing a short propaganda tract called *The Communist Manifesto* (1848), in which they wrote, "The proletarians have nothing to lose but their chains. They have a world to win. Working men of all countries, unite!"

Marx's predictions about the course of socialism were badly off the mark. In most of Europe, the reforms of democratic liberalism improved the general standard of living. Most workers accepted a capitalist system tempered by the "security net" of the welfare state. In addition, moderate socialists chose to work within the system rather than to overthrow it. They formed their own political parties, which in time became part of the legislatures of most European nations.

However, **Marxism**—systems of thought derived from Marx's ideas—was not yet dead. During World War I, the czarist government of Russia was overthrown. A few months later, a radical Marxist party called the **Bolsheviks** took control of the Russian government, establishing a political and economic system that came to be called **communism**.

THE ERA OF HIGH IMPERIALISM

By the early 1800s, the European powers had all given up the old mercantilist notions of government regulation of trade. As a result, they paid little attention to the expansion of their colonial empires. But in the latter half of the century, as nationalism and industrialism became powerful forces in European society, there was renewed interest in overseas possessions. Many nations, especially Britain, Germany, and France, became gripped with "imperialist fever." **Imperialism** is the policy of building empires by taking control of other countries.

Reasons for the New Imperialism. The new era of imperialism, from about 1880 to 1914, was the result of a complex mixture of economic, political, and social causes. First and foremost were certain economic conditions brought on by the Industrial Revolution. Many industries that had prospered in the early years of industrialization now discovered that their European markets had become saturated. Sales were down, in part because of the recent introduction of high protective tariffs. More important, a prolonged and widespread depression had reduced general purchasing power. Trading arrangements with colonies seemed to promise a whole new market for European goods. Selling to one's own colonies removed any possibility of trade barriers.

With ocean transportation improving, industrialists also saw colonies as attractive sources for foods, such as tea and coffee; raw materials, such as cotton, wool, and minerals; and new tropical products, such as bananas, palm oil, and rubber. Moreover, a capitalist who invested his surplus profits in a colonial plantation could expect a high return, because of the plentiful supply of cheap labor.

Politically the main reason for the new imperialism was the nationalist rivalry among the European nations. One author has suggested that in their race for power and prestige, the European nations used the entire world like a giant Monopoly board, on which the player with the

In spite of his turban, this Englishman in India looks out of place on a camel. Efforts by Europeans to adopt the customs of their colonies did not always succeed.

best collection of possessions won the game. Moreover, they coveted certain areas for national strategic and military advantages. The Suez Canal in Egypt, for example, was a strategic link between Great Britain and its most valued colony, India. The Indian Ocean islands of Réunion, Madagascar, and Ceylon were important as coaling stations and naval bases.

Social and cultural factors also figured in empire-building. As opportunities narrowed at home, adventurous young people often sought their fortunes overseas. In addition, many Europeans believed that they had a moral obligation to spread their "superior" civilization and religion to the rest of the world. Today this attitude is seen as unacceptably **ethnocentric** (believing that one's own nation or group is superior). In the late 1800s, however, it was in keeping with the spirit of the age. English writer Rudyard Kipling could publish a patriotic poem about "The White Man's Burden" without a tinge of irony or shame. English empire-builder Cecil Rhodes could say smugly, "I would annex the planets if I could; I often think of that. It makes me sad to see them so clear and yet so far."

The Scramble for Colonial Domination. In a single generation, Europeans achieved domination over much of the rest of the world. The entire continent of Africa was colonized, with the exception of Ethiopia and Liberia. First there were the Belgians in the Congo, the British in the south and east, and the French in the north and west, including the vast Sahara. The Germans and the Italians joined the scramble late in the game, so received a smaller share of the spoils.

In Asia, Britain moved eastward from its Indian colony and took over Burma and the Malay States. France added Annam and Tonkin to Cochin-China and Cambodia, creating the extensive colony of Indochina. The Russians, intent on extending their own land-based empire, colonized large parts of Central Asia. By 1914, of the 16,819,000 square miles (43,561,000 square km.) in Asia, no fewer than 9,443,000 square miles (24,457,000 square km.) were under European rule.

Even in areas that were not directly colonized, the imperial powers carved out "spheres of influence" by putting indirect, diplomatic pressure on other governments. In this way, France and Britain came to dominate the politics and economy of Egypt, although officially it remained part of the Ottoman Empire. In the decaying empire of China, the western powers were joined by a new, Asian imperialist force, Japan. Together they divided the country into spheres of influence and obtained special trading rights at "treaty ports."

Imperialism's Balance Sheet. By 1914, Europe, the western tip of the Eurasian peninsula, had gained domination over the entire globe. Within a half century, however, all was lost. Imperialism's balance sheet contained both debits and credits. Certainly on the negative side was the ease with which the imperialists either destroyed or ignored the local cultures with which they came into contact. By carving out political boundaries without respect for existing nations, they planted the seeds for future strife among minorities. Moreover, they exploited the conquered territories without bringing them lasting economic development, and they profited from the labor of workers who received little in return.

There also were credits, though it often appeared that the blessings of European civilization carried with them a hidden curse. For example, the imperialists improved the quality of agriculture, but often they did so by introducing single-crop economies that destroyed a region's ability to feed its own people. They introduced western educational ideas, yet they were unwilling to give people the freedom to use their educations. They introduced modern sanitation and medical knowledge, but the decrease in death rates helped to create the population explosions that occurred in such countries as India.

It is ironic that perhaps Europe's finest gift to its colonies was completely unintentional. Exposure to European ideas about democracy and nationalism finally inspired the colonized peoples to rise against their conquerors in order to gain those same benefits for themselves.

MOVING TOWARDS WAR

By the early 1900s, intense rivalry among European nations festered into an ugly sort of patriotism called **jingoism**, in which hatred and suspicion of another nation overshadowed the love of one's own country. This tension was particularly strong between Britain and Germany, probably because Germany was beginning to overtake Britain as an economic power. But negative feelings also characterized relations between France and Germany and between Austria-Hungary and Russia. Taken singly, these economic and political rivalries were probably not enough to plunge the continent into an all-out war. But they combined with other factors to fuel a seemingly unstoppable drive toward death and destruction.

Militarism.   One such factor was a growing spirit of militarism. All nations, but especially Germany and Britain, engaged in a race to build up armies, navies, and weaponry. Military advisers occupied key positions in government and were quick to propose military solutions to international problems in place of more peaceful approaches. By 1914, Europe had become a field of armed camps, all ready to do battle.

Entangling Alliances.   The European powers also sought safety in numbers through alliance systems. Germany, feeling threatened by its geographic position between France and Russia, allied itself in 1901 with Austria-Hungary and Italy in a mutual-defense agreement called the **Triple Alliance**. Britain, increasingly suspicious of Germany, sought to restore the balance of power by secretly allying itself with France and Russia to form a "cordial understanding" known as the **Triple Entente** (ahn-TAHNT) in 1904.

Nationalism in the Balkans.   Added to this explosive mix were the hopes and expectations of the national minorities in the Balkan Peninsula. As you have read, the Ottoman Empire, Austria-Hungary, and Russia struggled to maintain control as the many ethnic groups within their borders sought ways to gain their freedom. With pockets of ethnic Serbs, Croats (KROH-ats), Macedonians, Bulgarians, Albanians, Hungarians, Greeks, Romanians, and others all demanding the right of self-determination, the Balkans became known as the "Tinder Box of Europe," with only a spark needed to ignite the fires of war.

Showdown at Sarajevo.   Serbia had won its freedom from the Ottoman Empire in 1878. However, a sizable number of ethnic Serbs still lived in neighboring Bosnia-Herzegovina (BAHZ-nee-uh hehrt-suh-goh-VEE-nuh), which Austria-Hungary had taken from the Ottomans in 1908. This move infuriated the Serbs. Now, in 1914, Serbia had designs on Bosnia-Herzegovina and hoped to act as a magnet that would attract Serbs everywhere to the nationalist cause.

In June 1914, the Archduke Francis Ferdinand, heir to the Austro-Hungarian throne, was assassinated while visiting Sarajevo (sar-uh-YEH-voh) in Bosnia. His murderer was later identified as a member of a local ethnic Serbian terrorist group. Austria-Hungary, however, decided to blame the Serbian government for the assassination. This gave Austria-Hungary a pretext for crushing Serbian nationalism before it was too

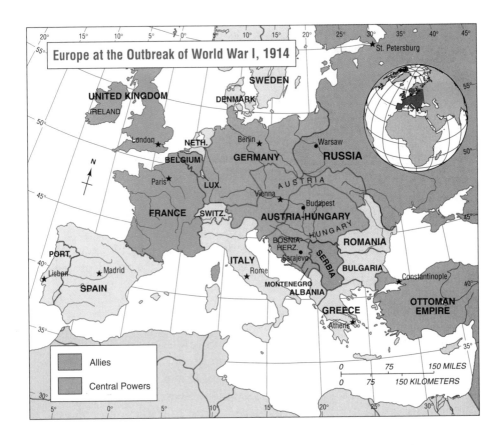

Europe at the Outbreak of World War I, 1914

late. Germany urged Austria-Hungary on, assuming that the conflict could remain a local affair, as it had so often in the past.

After Austria-Hungary declared war on Serbia on July 28, the entangling alliances came into play, ensnaring all the great powers and their allies. Russia decided to support the Serbs and ordered mobilization on July 30. To **mobilize** is to prepare an army for war. This move caused Germany to declare war on Russia on August 1. On August 3, it declared war on France, which was Russia's ally. On the same day, Germany put into effect a plan to attack France by sweeping around French fortifications and attacking from the north through Belgium. Germany hoped that by quickly defeating France before Russia had a chance to fully mobilize, a war on two fronts could be avoided.

After Germany invaded Belgium, Britain declared war on Germany on August 4. To gain public support, the British government claimed that it was defending Belgian neutrality. The real reason that Britain entered the war was its secret alliance with France.

The two conflicting groups became known as the **Allies** and the **Central Powers**. Initially, the Allies included Great Britain, the British Empire, France, Russia, Serbia, and Belgium. The Central Powers were originally Germany and Austria-Hungary, later joined by the Ottoman Empire and Bulgaria. Eventually the war involved 35 nations and 65 million troops.

WORLD WAR I

When the war began, both sides expected it to be short. Instead, it became long, deadly, and costly. It was the world's first **total war**, in which an all-out commitment of human and material resources was demanded.

Weapon Technology. In World War I, new weapons changed the ways in which battles were fought. On the western front, for example, it soon became obvious that the traditional massed infantry charge was suicidal against the frightful new artillery and machine-gun fire. Hence, both sides dug deep, elaborate trenches, above which was strung yard after

The first World War I trenches were simple ditches, but as the war dragged on, they became ever more elaborate and fortified. This trench is in northeastern France.

CASE STUDY:
The Human Cost of War

Flanders, a region of western Belgium and northern France, was the scene of the British Army's first major battle in World War I. Each side lost nearly 100,000 soldiers. The next year, at a second battle in the same location, the Germans introduced a new horror of war: poison gas. Soon afterward, the following poem by a Canadian soldier appeared in the British magazine *Punch*.

In Flanders Fields

In Flanders fields the poppies blow
Between the crosses, row on row,
   That mark our place; and in the sky
   The larks, still bravely singing, fly
Scarce heard amid the guns below.

We are the Dead. Short days ago
We lived, felt Dawn, saw sunset glow,
   Loved and were loved, and now we lie
      In Flanders fields.

Take up our quarrel with the foe:
To you from failing hands we throw
   The torch; be yours to hold it high.
   If ye break faith with us who die
We shall not sleep, though poppies grow
   In Flanders fields.

—John McCrae

1. In the first stanza, what visual detail is used as a contrast with the rows of graves?

2. What auditory (sound) detail is used as a contrast to the guns?

3. How does the mood of the poem shift in the third stanza?

4. As a result of this poem, poppies became part of remembrance ceremonies on Memorial Day and Veterans Day. What do you think they symbolize?

yard of spiraling barbed wire. Between these trenches lay a desolate combat zone, which the soldiers called "no-man's land."

Throughout most of the war, each side attempted to flush out the other with new instruments of death. The Germans introduced poison gas. The British introduced tanks. Both sides developed ways to turn the newly invented airplane into fighter planes and bombers. But the battle line, established in the early days of the war and stretching across France from the English Channel in the west to the Swiss border in the east, did not shift more than ten miles in either direction from 1914 through 1917. Thus, the conflict became a war in which each side tried to wear down the other.

Another front was opened when Italy came into the war on the Allied side in 1915. Originally a signer of the Triple Alliance, Italy experienced a change of heart after the Allies promised that Italian-speaking areas of Austria and Hungary would be a reward for participation. Italian attempts to invade Austria were unsuccessful until late in the war. Here, as in France and Belgium, the war bogged down into a marathon of endurance.

On the eastern front, the vast distances and poor transportation lines led to a more traditional war of movement. An initial Russian advance into Germany was stopped by a stunning German victory in late August 1914. Thereafter, Russia was gradually pushed out of Poland. Russian morale sagged, and confidence in the czarist government eroded.

Naval Blockades. At sea, Germany and Great Britain resorted mainly to blockades of each other. Britain's superior fleet of warships roamed the globe, stopping merchant ships and preventing them from transporting foods and raw materials to Germany. The Germans, in retaliation, used submarines, or **U-boats**, to attack ships bound for Great Britain. Until late in the war, when special listening devices were invented, U-boats could attack without being detected.

These blockades had a profound effect on the **home front**, as the people at home were called. As the war dragged on and resources became scarcer, governments introduced harsh economic planning and strict controls, such as fuel and food rationing. Working people, too, were in short supply. With all available manpower dispatched to the battlefront, women filled many of the jobs formerly reserved for men. Although most such positions reverted to men after the war, the war experience gave women a taste of the economic and social freedom they were to achieve more fully later in the century.

The Tide Turns. After three years of virtual stalemate, several events in 1917 dramatically changed the war. The first of these was the overthrow of the Russian czar in March. The monarchy was replaced by a moderate government, but it too failed to respond to public demands for immediate peace and redistribution of land. In the fall of that same year, a second revolution took place, this one staged by Bolsheviks. After taking control, they ordered a cease-fire, which led to a treaty with Germany and Russia's departure from the war in March 1918.

With Russia out of the war, Germany moved the bulk of its forces to France. At the same time, it redoubled its efforts to break the British blockade by following a policy of unrestricted submarine warfare. This decision proved to be a fatal mistake, for it brought the United States into the war. Although most Americans had been vaguely pro-British, they had remained neutral throughout most of the war, content to supply the Allies with financial and military aid. However, with U.S. freedom of the seas violated and its trade in jeopardy, President Woodrow Wilson asked Congress for a formal declaration of war in April 1917.

The "Yanks" were immediately shipped to Europe, their ears ringing with Wilson's promise that they were "making the world safe for democracy" by participating in "the war to end all wars." Their presence on the battlefield swelled the ranks of Allied troops and rekindled the resolve to press on to victory. The U.S. Navy joined with the British fleet to create a convoy system in which warships accompanying supply ships were able to break through the German submarine blockade.

Reeling from millions of casualties and faced with perilously low supplies of food and raw materials, the demoralized Germans retreated toward their own border. Finally, at 11 a.m. on November 11, 1918—the eleventh hour of the eleventh day of the eleventh month—an armistice was signed. The war had ended. It left in its wake 10 million people dead, 20 million wounded, and four autocratic monarchies swept away. Henceforth, a shattered Europe faced "the beginning of the end" of its era of global dominance.

THE AFTERMATH OF WAR

Seven months after the cease-fire, the Allies began a series of conferences to draw up four peace treaties, one for each of the Central Powers. The first of these conferences, the one dealing with Germany, took place at Versailles in 1919. Attending were the leaders of the "Big

The "Big Four" of the Versailles conference: left to right, Lloyd George of Great Britain, Orlando of Italy, Clemenceau of France, and Wilson of the United States.

Four" powers: President Woodrow Wilson of the United States and Prime Ministers Georges Clemenceau (KLEH-muhn-soh) of France, David Lloyd George of Great Britain, and Vittorio Orlando of Italy. Of these men, only Wilson had a clear vision of a postwar world dedicated to the principles of peace. The others were driven more by a desire for revenge against Germany.

The American president had expressed his postwar policy in a speech before Congress the year before. In it, he outlined **Fourteen Points** that he believed were necessary to ensure a just and lasting peace. These principles included freedom of the seas, self-determination for all peoples, arms reduction, and a "general association of nations" to guarantee peace and freedom "to great and small states alike." The latter provided the framework for the world's first international political forum, the League of Nations.

When Wilson arrived at Versailles, he was greeted by ecstatic crowds, who hailed him as "King of Humanity" and "Prince of Peace." However, when he sat down at the conference table with his European colleagues, he was unable to sell them on his complete program. In the end, he was forced to compromise on a number of crucial issues.

The Treaty of Versailles.   The European leaders at the peace table were more interested in revenge. Clemenceau, nicknamed "the Tiger," was openly scornful of Wilson's idealism. "Mr. Wilson bores me with his Fourteen Points," he sneered. "Why, God Almighty has only ten."

With Clemenceau's goading, the other European powers drew up terms designed to bring Germany to its knees. Germany was to lose one tenth of its territory in Europe and all its colonies abroad. Britain and the United States resisted France's demands that the Rhineland, an important military and industrial zone, be permanently severed from Germany, but they did agree on a 15-year Allied occupation and complete **demilitarization** (removal of all military force). All participants agreed that the German military would be reduced to 100,000 men, with a prohibition on heavy artillery, tanks, airplanes, and submarines.

Most galling of all to Germany was a "war-guilt" clause, which laid the entire blame for the war on the defeated nation. As retribution, Germany was required to provide **reparations**, or payment for damages, of $5 billion in gold and goods immediately, with the promise of another $28 billion at a future time. Germany's humiliation and resentment over these aspects of the treaty were later to help bring about the rise of Nazi dictatorship under Adolf Hitler.

The Versailles treaty, as well as the treaties with other defeated countries, did include a covenant (charter) setting up the League of Nations. Ironically, the success of the League was compromised from the very beginning by the refusal of the U.S. Congress to ratify the treaty. However, even if its membership had included all the major powers, it is doubtful that the league would have been entirely successful. It lacked the authority to form an armed peace-keeping force, and thus was unable to control aggression.

Remaking the Map.   The respective peace treaties also followed— albeit only partially—Wilson's policy of national self-determination. As a result, the postwar map of Europe was far different from its prewar counterpart. Alsace and Lorraine, two provinces that Germany had taken from France in 1871, were returned to France. A new Poland was carved out of former Russian, German, and Austrian provinces. Czechoslovakia emerged from the wreckage of Austria-Hungary as a new nation. Italy also gained territory from Austria-Hungary. Russia lost territory along the Baltic Sea, with the creation of Finland, Estonia, Latvia, and Lithuania. Yugoslavia was created out of prewar Serbia, Montenegro, and various former Austrian territories containing Slavic

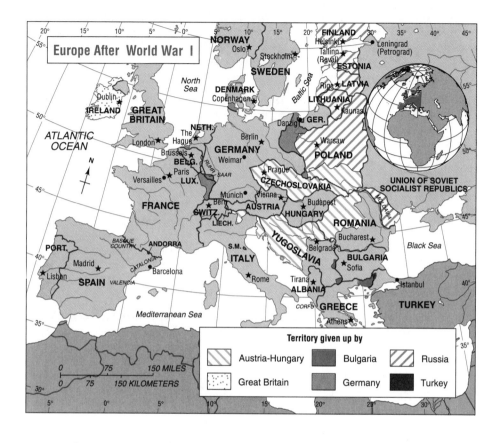

Territory given up by

| | Austria-Hungary | | Bulgaria | | Russia |
| | Great Britain | | Germany | | Turkey |

peoples. Austria and Hungary became two separate nations. In a development unrelated to the war but occurring at about the same time, Britain granted independence to the greater part of the island of Ireland.

Although the principle of self-determination was not respected in every case, in general the new map of Europe was a better reflection of national interests than the old one had been. Abroad, however, the Allied powers clung tenaciously to their colonial possessions. Germany's and Ottoman Turkey's former colonies were made League of Nations **mandates**, territories administered but not owned by member nations. Middle Eastern peoples were particularly outraged at the way their lands, once part of the Ottoman Empire, were divided into French and British mandates. So grave and so persistent did problems in that area become that one historian has ironically called the treaty that established the arbitrary boundaries "the peace to end all peace."

REVIEWING THE CHAPTER

I. Building Your Vocabulary

In your notebook, write the correct term that matches the definition.

enclosure   proletariat   reparations
mandate   *Realpolitik*   *Risorgimento*

1. land taken from farmers between 1714 and 1820
2. the movement for Italian political unity
3. payment for damages as a result of hostilities
4. policies grounded in practical considerations rather than theoretical or ethical ideals
5. former German territory ruled but not owned by member nations of the League of Nations
6. the working class in industrial societies

II. Understanding the Facts

In your notebook, write the numbers 1 to 5. Write the letter of the correct answer to each question next to its number.

1. Italian unity was masterminded by:
   a. Cavour   b. Garibaldi   c. Metternich
2. Which of the following was not a nation-state in 1815?
   a. France   b. Germany   c. Great Britain
3. Marx believed that capitalism would be replaced by:
   a. liberalism   b. nationalism   c. socialism
4. World War I was triggered by the nationalistic ambitions of:
   a. the Balkans   b. Bosnia   c. Serbia
5. Which of the following nations was created after World War I?
   a. Bulgaria   b. Serbia   c. Yugoslavia

III. Thinking It Through

In your notebook, write the numbers from 1 to 4. After each number, write the number of the correct answer to the question.

1. "The questions of the time are . . . decided . . . by iron and blood." These words of Bismarck reflect:
   a. a growing spirit of militarism.
   b. a trend toward freedom and democracy.
   c. a plea for rapid industrialization.

2. Which of the following was not a result of the enclosures?
   a. An increased labor supply was available.
   b. Agricultural land was left unused.
   c. Many people were put off the land.

3. Which of the following was true about the new imperialism?
   a. It brought industrialism to the rest of the world.
   b. It reflected mercantilist policies.
   c. It satisfied capitalism's need for new markets.

4. Because of Wilson's leadership, the Versailles Treaty:
   a. contained a "war-guilt" clause.
   b. demanded reparations from Germany.
   c. included a covenant creating the League of Nations.

INTERPRETING A STATISTICAL TABLE

Using the table below and information in this chapter, answer the questions on the next page.

European Army Sizes, 1870–1944				
DATE	GERMANY	FRANCE	GREAT BRITAIN	RUSSIA
1870	1,200,000	454,000	345,000	716,000
1900	524,000	715,000	624,000	1,162,000
1914	3,400,000	1,000,000	650,000	2,000,000
1929	115,000	666,000	443,000	570,000
1937	766,000	825,000	645,000	1,324,000
1944	9,125,000	—	4,500,000	5,500,000

Source: P. Q. Wright, *A Study of War*, II (Chicago, 1942), pp. 670–1;
M. Howard, *War in European History* (Oxford, 1976)

1. By comparing troop sizes for Germany in 1870 with the major event listed for that year in the Time Box, what conclusion can you draw about the reason for such a large army?

2. In 1914, how many more soldiers did Germany have than France and Britain combined? What might these figures have led Germany to believe about the duration of the war on the western front?

3. In 1929, which European country had the smallest army? What historical event accounted for this reduction in troops?

DEVELOPING CRITICAL THINKING SKILLS

1. Explain why Italian and German nationalistic movements did not spark a world war, while a generation later Serbian nationalism did.

2. Show how most European countries were able to solve many of the social problems created by industrialism without becoming Communistic states.

3. Explain why Germans might have felt that the "war-guilt" clause of the Versailles Treaty was unjust.

ENRICHMENT AND EXPLORATION

1. Choose one aspect of industrial technology, such as a particular energy source, a form of transportation, a type of communication, a branch of medicine, photography, or cinematography. By consulting encyclopedias and other library resources, create a time line of significant inventions, developments, and events within the subject area you have chosen. Make a display of these time lines on the bulletin board.

2. Organize a classroom exhibit of European art of the late 1800s and early 1900s. By researching various artists and artistic movements, attach captions to the pictures that explain how the styles and subject matter reflect the historical era. Include Romantics such as Géricault and Delacroix; Impressionists such as Manet, Monet, Renoir, and Degas; post-Impressionists such as Cézanne, Van Gogh, and Gauguin; and Modernists such as Picasso, Matisse, Léger, and Duchamp.

6 World War II and the Cold War

As the 1920s opened, Europeans were trying to return to a normal existence. However, the economic, social, and political effects of World War I continued to trouble the continent through the 1920s and 1930s, until war once again engulfed the world. Only in the nervous stability of the Cold War that followed World War II would Europe regain a semblance of normality.

The early 1920s were years of hardship for most Europeans. Business had boomed for a few brief months after the armistice, but then it went bust. Many factories closed. People went hungry. Not until the mid-1920s would economic life in Europe begin to stabilize. Economic hardships added to other problems, such as the mass movements of refugees across newly redrawn borders and the seething hatreds that divided many ethnic groups. The bleakness of everyday life fed the tendency of people to try to find scapegoats for their unhappy condition. In the defeated nations, in particular, a sense of injustice fed a desire for revenge.

FASCISM IN ITALY

Although Italy had been on the winning side in World War I, many of its people felt cheated by the peace settlement. The Allies had kept some of their secret promises—for example, to let Italy take over two sections of Austria where many Italians lived. But the peace treaties had denied Italy other territory that it had expected. In the chaos that followed the war, many Italians were ready to follow any leader who seemed likely to restore stability, strengthen the state, and make people proud of being Italians.

EUROPE AND THE WORLD

1919–1970s

1919	Weimar Republic founded in Germany.
1922	Mussolini's "March on Rome"
1923	German money plummets in value.
1931	Republic established in Spain.
1933	Hitler comes to power in Germany.
1935	Italy attacks Ethiopia.
1936–1939	Spanish Civil War
1937	Rome–Berlin–Tokyo Axis formed.
1938	Germany takes over Austria.
	Munich Agreements allow Hitler to annex Sudetenland.
1939	Germany invades Poland; World War II begins.
1940	Battle of Britain
1941	Germany attacks Soviet Union.
	U.S. enters World War II.
1941–1942	Holocaust begins.
1943	Soviets win Battle of Stalingrad.
1944	D-Day landings by Eisenhower in Normandy
1945	Germany and Japan surrender.
1945–1946	Nuremberg war crimes trials
1947	Cold War begins.
1948–1949	Berlin Blockade
1948	Yugoslavia breaks with Soviet Union.
1949	West Germany and East Germany created.
1956	Soviets suppress Hungarian revolution.
1968	Soviets suppress "Prague Spring" in Czechoslovakia.
1970s	Solidarity movement begins in Poland.

Benito Mussolini.   A former elementary school teacher named Benito Mussolini wanted to do just that. Mussolini had once been a leader of Italy's Socialist party, but he had broken with his party by supporting Italy's entry into World War I. Mussolini then soon swerved to the political right. In 1919, he began to organize "combat groups" of black-shirted toughs to break up strikes and to fight street battles against Communists and Socialists. His "combat groups" became the basis of the **Fascist** (FASH-ist) party. Mussolini and the Fascists had no clear political program, but they spoke of a need for order, for discipline.

The "March on Rome" of 1922.   In the parliamentary election of 1921, the Fascists won a mere 35 seats out of more than 500. However, none of Italy's other quarreling parties was able to provide firm leadership. Mussolini and his supporters soon resolved to seize power. They organized a "march on Rome" of tens of thousands of Fascists in October 1922. Government leaders wanted to arrest Mussolini and have troops block the marchers. However, King Victor Emmanuel III refused to permit this. Instead, he asked Mussolini to form a new government.

Duly voted into office by parliament, Mussolini set out to "establish order" and end the country's chaos. Seemingly, he succeeded. Within

Benito Mussolini liked to strike dramatic poses, eyes closed and chin forward. His goal was to return Italy to the glory it had known under the Roman empire.

two years, Mussolini had become **dictator** of Italy, that is, a ruler with absolute power. He dissolved all political parties but the Fascists, established strict censorship, and established a Fascist military organization. Mussolini came to be called by his party title, *Il Duce* (eel DOO-chay)— the Leader.

Italian Fascism in Action. Under fascism, Italy took on the trappings of a **totalitarian** state. In a totalitarian state, the government monopolizes power and demands strict obediance from the people, who have few if any political rights. Totalitarian governments seek to control almost every aspect of people's lives.

Both communism and fascism were totalitarian systems. They shared such features as a dependence on one-party rule, a reliance on secret police to enforce conformity, a denial of political rights, and a refusal to allow labor unions to operate freely. But communism and fascism were different in two basic ways. First, in theory at least, communism was **internationalist**, claiming to speak for the working-class people of all nations against the wealthier classes of all nations. On the other hand, fascism was **nationalist**. It glorified one nation to the exclusion of others. Second, communism stressed public ownership of industry. Under fascism, private owners remained in charge of industry.

Mussolini and the Catholic Church. Mussolini worked to heal a long-standing quarrel between the Italian state and the Catholic Church. Bad feelings dated back to 1870, when Italian soldiers had completed the unification of Italy by marching into Rome and claiming it for the king. Up to that time, the pope had ruled over the city and the area around it. After 1870, hostility grew between the church and the state.

In signing a series of accords with church leaders, Mussolini pleased Italian Catholics and boosted his own popularity. Under the Lateran Agreements of 1929, Italy recognized the pope as a sovereign ruler over a 109-acre portion of Rome known as Vatican City. The agreements also recognized Catholicism as Italy's state religion. Henceforth, classes in Catholic doctrine would be required courses in all public schools. This provision remained in effect until the 1980s.

NAZISM IN GERMANY

The early 1920s brought turmoil to Germany as well as to Italy. At first, Germany's young democracy weathered a series of crises. But it could not stand the shock of the worldwide Great Depression that began in the United States in 1929. Eventually, Germany too succumbed to its own form of fascism.

Democratic Interlude: 1919–1933.   As World War I drew to a close in 1918, Germany's emperor was overthrown and a republic proclaimed. The following year, a group of leaders meeting at Weimar (WEYE-mahr) wrote a constitution for the new republic. The democracy that they established, known as the **Weimar Republic**, lasted until 1933.

Its government faced constant challenges. The greatest came in 1923, when inflation, which already was severe, went completely out of control. Before World War I, the German mark had been worth about 25 cents. In the fall of 1922, 4,500 marks bought one U.S. dollar. Thirteen months later, it took 4.2 trillion marks to buy a dollar.

Germany's economy was devastated. People now needed a wheelbarrow full of money just to buy a few groceries. Even worse, the money that people had been keeping in banks was now worthless. Most working-class people had had little savings to begin with. But many middle-class people who had scrimped and saved lost their whole life's savings. They lost all sense of economic security, and they lost confidence in the ability of the government to protect their interests. This was a blow to German democracy, for without public support a democratic system cannot survive.

The Weimar Republic managed to scrape through the crisis of 1923, but only after great political turmoil. One incident in particular deserves mention—an uprising in Munich led by a 34-year-old war veteran named Adolf Hitler. The Austrian-born Hitler had become leader of a small political party called the National Socialist German Workers' Party. From the German pronunciation of the word *National*, it was called the **Nazi** (NAHT-see) party. Hitler's 1923 "beer hall *Putsch* [coup]," so called because it began with a rowdy meeting in a Munich beer hall, failed utterly. Police fire broke up a Nazi mob, and the authorities threw Hitler into jail.

By 1924, Germany seemed to have settled down again. But Germany and the world had not heard the last of Adolf Hitler.

Hitler Comes to Power.   During the nine months he spent in jail, Hitler wrote a book setting forth his political ideas. He titled the book *Mein Kampf*—"My Battle." Out of the jumble of Hitler's thoughts, two ideas leaped forth. One was the racist notion that "pure" Germans were a master race and that other groups, especially Jews, were inferior. The other was a crude belief in the need for force to bring "order" to Germany and to avenge its defeat in World War I. Upon his release from jail, Hitler set out to expand his Nazi party and win control over the German government.

Hitler got his big chance at the start of the 1930s, when the world economy collapsed. American bankers demanded immediate repayment of their loans to German industry. World trade shriveled. German factories closed down. Unemployment soared. The one bright spot for Germans was an international decision in 1932 to put an end to Germany's reparations payments.

But economic misery kept spreading, and Germans increasingly turned to extremist parties. As had happened in Italy, young toughs joined political "armies" that battled in the streets. The Nazis' brown-shirted Storm Troopers enlisted tens of thousands of young men.

In two parliamentary elections during 1932, Hitler's Nazis won more seats than any other party, although still less than a majority. In January 1933, a rival right-wing party, the Nationalists, agreed to join the Nazis in forming a coalition government. Although Hitler would become chancellor (the German equivalent of prime minister), Nationalist leaders thought such a coalition would be "safe." After all, only a minority of the cabinet positions would go to Nazis.

Thus, Hitler came to power by following the forms of democracy. However, he did not follow those forms for long. Within six months, he persuaded parliament to grant him sweeping powers, dumped the Nationalists, seized firm control of the army, created a secret police called the **Gestapo**, dissolved all political parties except the Nazis, and abolished the Weimar Republic. In its place, he erected what he called the **Third Reich** (Third Empire). (The first two empires were the Holy Roman Empire and the German Empire of 1871–1918.)

The _Führer_. Many Germans adored their new leader, or _Führer_ (FYOO-ruhr). After the chaos and insecurity of the 1920s and early 1930s, much of the middle class saw Hitler as a savior who would restore German traditions and values. So did many business people who were fed up with the instability of the Weimar Republic. Millions of Germans shared Hitler's conviction that Germany needed a strong leader who could arouse the pride of his people.

In 1934 the aged German president, Paul von Hindenburg, died, and Hitler merged the office of president into his own position of _Führer_. He submitted his decision to a **plebiscite**, or yes–no vote of the people. Nearly nine voters in ten voted yes.

Adolf Hitler reviews a group of Hitler Youth at a Nazi party rally. Children over ten were required to join the Hitler Youth or a similar organization for girls.

Race Laws and Concentration Camps.   In many ways, Hitler's dictatorship in Germany resembled Mussolini's in Italy. The Nazis adopted many of the features of Italian fascism, but they also added features of their own. The biggest difference was the Nazis' brutal policy of anti-Semitism. Fearing what might lie ahead, many of Germany's 500,000 Jews left in the first years after the Nazis gained power. Those who remained suffered under a series of harsh laws. One law forbade marriages between Jews and "Aryans" (as the Nazis called Germans they considered "pure"). Another barred Jews from government jobs. Still another required Jews to carry special identity papers. Moreover, racist mobs attacked Jews on the streets and sacked Jewish businesses. In 1938, the government began rounding up Jews and sending them to prisons called **concentration camps.**

German Rearmament.   Hitler had a solution to Germany's economic distress. He began massive programs of public works—and a rapid buildup of the German armed forces. Such programs put the unemployed back to work and boosted Hitler's popularity. The German economy quickly revived. However, rearmament alarmed the victor nations of World War I and boosted the risk of war.

141

THE SPANISH CIVIL WAR

Meanwhile, dictators were coming to power elsewhere in Europe. Most of the new states that emerged from World War I had tried to create democratic governments. However, during the 1920s and 1930s, one after another succumbed to dictatorship. Among the new countries, only Czechoslovakia, with a well-balanced industrial economy, seemed to be making democracy work.

Democracy also stumbled in older nations like Portugal and Spain. Following a military coup in 1926, Portugal drifted into a right-wing dictatorship. The dictator was Antonio Salazar, an admirer of Mussolini. In the late 1930s, the world focused its attention on Portugal's neighbor, Spain, as forces clashed in the Spanish Civil War of 1936–1939.

The Background.   After the glory days of its empire in the Americas, Spain had declined into genteel poverty. During the early 1900s, it had a parliamentary form of government, but true power was in the hands of a few wealthy people and the king. Then, in 1931, the monarchy was overthrown and a republic established. An election early in 1936 resulted in victory for a **Popular Front**—a combination of parties that ranged from moderates to Socialists to Communists. The Popular Front victory stirred expectations of major change. When it became obvious that the Popular Front government planned only moderate reforms, some turned to revolutionary actions. Peasants seized land from large landowners. Extremists burned Catholic churches and attacked members of the clergy. Extremists on the other side retaliated with more violence. Anarchy (total absence of government) threatened as political parties formed their own private armies.

Outbreak of War.   Civil war broke out in July 1936 when military officers in Spanish Morocco revolted against the Popular Front government. The rebellion spread quickly to Spain itself. The military insurgents, led by General Francisco Franco, were known as the **Nationalists**. They drew support from rural landowners, monarchists, the Catholic clergy, and many devout Catholics. Pro-government forces were called the **Republicans** or **Loyalists**. Their backers included urban moderates, factory workers, Communists, and supporters of democracy.

Within weeks,the war split Spain's territory into two unequal halves. Nationalists held the greater part of the country. Republicans controlled only the capital Madrid, the Basque country in the north, and the eastern regions known as Catalonia (KAT-uh-LOH-nee-uh) and Valencia.

The Spanish Civil War quickly took on international dimensions. Outside forces poured in to help one side or the other. The Fascist powers, Italy and Germany, supported Franco's Nationalists. Anti-Fascists organized "international brigades" of volunteers to fight alongside the Republicans.

After three years of bitter fighting, in which as many as a million people died, the Nationalists won the war. The Republicans surrendered the Catalonian capital of Barcelona (bahr-suh-LOH-nuh) in January 1939. Two months later, Madrid also fell to the Nationalists. General Franco became dictator. Spain was now a one-party state with Fascist leanings.

PLUNGING TOWARD A NEW WORLD WAR

Even before the Spanish Civil War began, international tensions had started to build. Through the 1930s, Italy and Germany made increasingly aggressive moves. Yet democratic nations like Britain, France, and the United States did little more than protest weakly.

The Rome–Berlin Axis. Germany withdrew from the League of Nations in 1933. Soon after, Hitler began shaking off the Versailles Treaty. In 1935, he announced he would ignore the treaty's limits on German armaments. In 1936 he sent soldiers into the Rhineland area of Germany, which had been demilitarized.

Italy, bent on expanding its small empire in Africa, invaded Ethiopia in 1935. The League of Nations imposed **sanctions**, or penalties, on Italy, but they had little effect. The failure of sanctions showed how toothless the League really was.

Italy and Germany moved closer and closer together, forming an alliance that came to be called the **Rome–Berlin Axis**, or just the **Axis**. (The idea was that Europe would now revolve around a new axis, the line from Rome to Berlin.) Japan, an ally of Hitler's, was also a member of the Axis.

Making *Lebensraum*. Hitler had declared in *Mein Kampf* that one of his goals was to give Germany more *Lebensraum* ("living room," or space for expansion). He began to expand German territory in March 1938 by marching German soldiers into Austria and taking over the country. Many Austrians welcomed the *Anschluss*, or union, of the two German-speaking nations.

Next Hitler turned his attention to Czechoslovakia, where 3 million Germans lived in border areas called the **Sudetenland** (soo-DAY-tun-land). Hitler's demands for this territory became more and more strident. France and the Soviet Union had military alliances with Czechoslovakia, and the Soviet Union had offered military aid. But neither France nor Britain was willing to risk war, and both distrusted the Soviet Union. In September 1938 British Prime Minister Neville Chamberlain and French Premier Édouard Daladier flew to Munich to meet Hitler. The resulting Munich Agreement let Germany take over the Sudetenland. Upon returning to London, Chamberlain claimed that the agreement had insured "peace in our time." However, the agreement did no such thing. The policy of seeking to meet Hitler's demands was called **appeasement**.

The Failure of Appeasement.   The policy of appeasement followed by Britain and France in seeking to meet Hitler's demands was aimed at avoiding war at almost any cost. At the time, the policy had broad public support. British and French leaders wanted to believe that Hitler's goals were limited ones—that he would be satisfied when German-speaking peoples were united within Germany. But Hitler had far more ambitious goals, and he pursued them ruthlessly. Within 12 months Europe was plunged into a new war, and **Munich** became a code word for "spinelessly caving in to an aggressor."

Without its border fortifications in the Sudetenland, Czechoslovakia was unable to defend itself when, in March 1939, Hitler took over the rest of the country. This time he could not argue that he was only "rescuing Germans from foreign rule." It appeared that his next target would be Poland. Britain and France braced for war, declaring that they would defend Poland if Germany attacked. The Soviet Union, snubbed by the democracies because of its efforts to spread communism, took a different tack. Dropping its stance of bitter hostility to Hitler and the Nazis, it stunned the world by signing a nonaggression pact with Germany on August 22, 1939. Secret **protocols** (supplemental agreements) provided for dividing Poland into German and Soviet "spheres" and paved the way for a Soviet takeover of the Baltic states.

Ten days later, keeping to a schedule he had drawn up months before, Hitler sent the German armed forces storming into Poland. Germany's **Blitzkrieg** (BLITS-kreeg)(lightning war) quickly overcame Polish defenses. Britain and France, having abandoned the policy of appeasement, responded with declarations of war on Germany. World War II had begun.

WORLD WAR II IN EUROPE

Like World War I, this new war spread to far corners of the earth and involved many non-European nations. The United States entered in December 1941, when Japan attacked Pearl Harbor in Hawaii. From then on, the war raged on two fronts, Pacific and European. But until 1945 the United States and its allies devoted their major resources to the European front, seeing Hitler's Germany as the most dangerous of the three Axis powers.

German Victories. Germany's attack on Poland in September 1939 triggered a matching Soviet invasion of Poland from the east. As they had agreed, the two invaders divided the country between them. That wiped Poland once again from the map. Shoring up its defensive position along the Baltic, the Soviet Union established naval bases in Estonia, Latvia, and Lithuania. Soon after, in 1940, the Soviet Union annexed those nations outright. When Finland resisted Soviet demands for territory, Soviet troops attacked and defeated the Finns in the Winter War of 1939–1940. The Soviets got the land they wanted, but Finland kept its independence.

In the west, the winter of 1939–1940 was a time of "phony war." French troops dug in behind their fortified Maginot (MAZH-uh-noh) Line and waited warily for a German attack.

The Nazis resumed their *Blitzkrieg* in April 1940. German forces quickly occupied Denmark and Norway. Soon they were smashing through the Netherlands, Belgium, and Luxembourg. Trapped in the French port of Dunkirk, 215,000 British and 120,000 French soldiers barely escaped to England in a motley assortment of vessels.

The German victories in the north allowed them to make an end run around the Maginot Line. Meanwhile, Italy attacked France from the southeast. Outgunned, outmaneuvered, and divided, the French government surrendered in June 1940. German forces occupied three fifths of France, including Paris. The French government moved south to the small town of Vichy (VEE-shee). There Marshal Henri-Philippe Pétain (pay-TAN), a hero of World War I, established a government patterned after Mussolini's fascism. The rule of the Vichy régime was limited to unoccupied portions of France and to French colonies overseas.

The Battle of Britain. The German *Luftwaffe* (LOOFT-vah-fuh), or air force, launched air attacks on British targets in the summer of 1940. That September the Nazis began nightly bombing raids on London and other cities. This was the **Battle of Britain,** by which Hitler aimed to terrorize the people and soften up British defenses in preparation for a German invasion.

A new prime minister, Winston Churchill, rallied the British people with somber appeals. "Blood, toil, tears, and sweat," he said, were all he could offer. Churchill had been an outspoken critic of appeasement through the 1930s, and his moral authority and well-chosen words helped the British to make it through "the Blitz." Armed with radar, then a new and highly secret invention, and with high-performance Spitfire and Hurricane fighter planes, the heroic pilots of the Royal Air Force forced the Germans to drop their invasion plans. "Never in the field of human conflict was so much owed by so many to so few," Churchill exclaimed.

The Nazi Attack on the Soviet Union. By the middle of 1941, Hitler had conquered much of continental Europe. Then, on June 22, 1941, he launched an attack on the Soviet Union. Finland attacked the Soviet Union soon after, hoping to take back territory lost in the Winter War.

Catching Soviet defenders by surprise, German armies drove deep inside Soviet borders. They quickly reached the outskirts of Leningrad (present-day St. Petersburg) and Moscow. The Soviets moved entire industries east to the Ural Mountains and kept churning out war goods. Soviet losses were staggering, but the Red Army kept on fighting.

Turning Points. With the Japanese attack on Pearl Harbor in December 1941, the United States entered the war against the Axis. The United States, Britain, and the Soviet Union became partners in the fight against fascism. They were called the **Allies.** The balance of power began to shift against the Axis.

Prior to Pearl Harbor, the wish to avoid foreign "entanglements" had kept the United States from a formal alliance with Britain. However, President Franklin D. Roosevelt had persuaded Congress to supply the British with arms and other assistance under a program called **lend-lease.** In November 1941, Roosevelt's "lend-lease" aid was extended to the Soviet Union. After Pearl Harbor, the flow of aid increased.

What the Soviets wanted most, however, was a second front in western Europe. Most of the fighting in the European war was now on the eastern front, in the forests of Russia and the wheat fields of Ukraine. The Soviet Union started pushing back the Germans with a decisive victory at Stalingrad (present-day Volgograd) in February 1943.

Soviet soldiers edge toward a ruined building during the battle of Stalingrad. The battle lasted five months and ended with the capture of 90,000 German soldiers.

The German siege of Leningrad dragged on some 28 months until January 1944, costing the lives of a million Soviet citizens.

Postponing an attack on German forces in France, for which Stalin pleaded, the western Allies invaded North Africa. They aimed to block an Axis threat to the Suez Canal, a vital lifeline between Britain and its colonies in Africa and Asia. Led by the dashing Sir Bernard Montgomery, British troops drove west from Egypt. American troops under General Dwight Eisenhower struck east from Morocco and Algeria. By May 1943, the Allies had defeated the forces of German General Erwin Rommel, known as the "Desert Fox."

Next the western Allies crossed the Mediterranean to attack what Churchill called "the soft underbelly of Europe." First they struck Sicily, then mainland Italy. The attack caused a change of heart among a number of Italian leaders. They deposed Mussolini, declared an end to fascism, and sought to pull Italy out of the war. But German troops poured into Italy to hold the line against advancing Allied armies. Italy became one of the bloodiest battlegrounds of the war.

The D-Day Landings. With Allied armies making slow but steady progress, the **Big Three** leaders—Roosevelt, Churchill, and Stalin—met in Iran's capital city of Teheran late in 1943. Roosevelt joined Stalin in pushing for an invasion of northern France. They did not share Churchill's fears of becoming bogged down in murderous trench warfare, as in World War I. The leaders decided that General Eisenhower would lead a cross-Channel invasion in the spring of 1944.

D-Day, the day for the big attack, fell on June 6, two days after Allied armies entered the Italian capital of Rome. Under a deadly hail of German artillery fire, Allied soldiers splashed ashore in wave after wave along the coast of Normandy. They suffered heavy casualties as they advanced through barbed wire and mine fields. But they managed to established a beachhead and fan out into the countryside. By August, General George Patton, a flamboyant tank commander, was leading a mad dash across northern France.

French fighters helped to liberate their country. General Charles de Gaulle had refused to accept the French surrender in 1940. He escaped to London and organized an army of "Free French" soldiers that cooperated with the Allies. Meanwhile, anti-Fascists in occupied France had fashioned an underground movement known as the **Resistance.** Its agents engaged in sabotage and other operations against the Germans. In August 1944 they launched street battles against the occupiers of Paris, paving the way for De Gaulle's triumphal entry on August 25.

Victory for the Allies.   In the face of stubborn German resistance, Allied armies closed in from both east and west. In the east, the Red Army was battling 2 million German soldiers, twice as many as were fighting in France and Italy. Soviet troops moved forward on a broad front from Poland to the Balkans. On the western front, a German counteroffensive stymied the Allied advance in the Ardennes Mountains of Belgium. German soldiers lunged westward through the wooded mountains in December 1944, creating a bulge in the Allied ranks and threatening havoc. After a nerve-wracking few weeks, this "Battle of the Bulge" ended in an Allied victory.

As winter turned to spring in 1945, German positions crumbled one by one. American, British, and French troops crossed the Rhine River into Germany. German troops surrendered in Italy, Hungary, and Austria. Allied bombers devastated one German city after another, destroying Dresden in a hail of firebombs that turned the city into a deadly inferno. At the end of April, Soviet forces smashed into Berlin. There, holed up in an underground bunker, Hitler committed suicide to avoid being captured. On May 7, the German high command signed an unconditional surrender.

The calculated murder of millions of Jews was an official policy of the Nazi state, carried out with ruthless efficiency by thousands of faceless bureaucrats. The policy is a horrifying example of genocide, the deliberate murder of an entire nation or religious group. Top Nazis referred to their plan, adopted in 1941 or early 1942, as "the final solution" to "the Jewish problem." Today, the murder of an estimated 6 million European Jews is known as the Holocaust.

There were millions of other victims of Nazi brutality. In addition to the Jews, the Nazis attempted to eliminate all the Gypsies in Europe. In every occupied country, many civilians lost their lives. The Slavic countries were especially hard hit. More than 6 million non-Jewish civilians died in the Soviet Union, more than 2.5 million in Poland, and more than 1.3 million in Yugoslavia. Some were killed in air raids or other acts of war, but many others were deliberately murdered.

After the war, the Allied nations put high officials of the Axis states on trial. The charges included not only "crimes against humanity" (such as genocide) but also violations of the laws of war. The most notorious defendants were tried before a special court at Nuremberg, Germany, in 1945–1946. Most were either sentenced to prison or hanged. Many Nazis escaped trial, however, in some cases by fleeing to South or North America. "Nazi hunters" have continued to track down people who worked in death camps, and trials for war crimes were still being held in the 1990s.

A Weaker Europe. The Europe that emerged from World War II was greatly changed from the Europe of 1939. Germany's formidable military and economic power had been smashed. Its cities were in ruins, and its people were now governed by occupying powers. Moreover, despite the Allied victory, Britain and France were scarcely in better shape. Both had been greatly weakened and faced uncertain futures. Before long, both would find themselves forced to give up their colonial empires in Africa and Asia.

Finally, the world power balance had shifted. Before the war, Britain, France, Germany, and Italy had all been considered major military powers. That was true no longer. The United States had developed an immensely powerful new weapon, the atomic bomb, and used it against Japan. Another nation, the Soviet Union, had suffered more than any other in the war. Yet at war's end, it had the world's largest army and would soon have nuclear weapons as well. The military might of those two nations so dwarfed the capabilities of all other nations that they were called **superpowers**.

World War II had taken an awesome human toll in Europe. In death camps, on the battlefield, and in bombing raids, more than 30 million people had died, 20 million in the Soviet Union alone. Millions more had been wounded.

At war's end, many of Europe's cities lay in ruins. Millions of people were living in dank cellars or refugee camps. Bombs and artillery had destroyed much of the continent's railroad trackage and cratered many of its roads. Many factories had only walls—no roofs, no windows, no machinery that worked. Heroic measures would be needed to put Europe back on its feet again.

The newly created United Nations began pouring aid into Europe almost at once. Allied nations had met in 1944 to lay plans for the United Nations as a successor to the now-defunct League of Nations. Even before the war ended, the United Nations Relief and Rehabilitation Agency (UNRRA) began funneling help into devastated areas. Such outside aid helped Europe to avoid epidemics and famine in the months after the war ended.

Emergence of the Cold War. Political quarrels erupted among the Allies almost as soon as they had clinched victory. Such wrangling complicated the recovery process and gave it a political spin.

In meetings in 1945 at Yalta (in the southern Soviet Union) and Potsdam (in Germany), the Allied leaders laid plans for the postwar era. At Yalta, in February, surface feelings remained smooth. By the time of the Potsdam conference in July, disputes were erupting into the open. On one side were the democratic powers, the United States and Britain. On the other side was the citadel of world communism, the Soviet Union. Two key issues were paramount: what to do about Poland, and how to treat Germany.

At Yalta, Roosevelt and Churchill agreed to Stalin's proposals on Poland, where the Red Army was in control. Poland would have to give up land in the east to the Soviets. In return, it would gain land in the west from the Germans. A Polish government dominated by Communists would continue to exercise power. However, the Allies agreed that "free elections" would be organized in Poland and all the other liberated nations of central and eastern Europe. Stalin later refused to hold truly free elections in any of the countries. Poland would be the first of many European nations where the Soviet Union installed Communist governments.

152

The Allies decided to split Germany into four zones of occupation. The Soviet Union occupied the east, Britain the northwest, the United States the south, and France the southwest. Although the German capital, Berlin, lay deep within the Soviet zone, it too was divided into four zones of occupation. But plans for a joint council to make decisions for Germany as a whole quickly collapsed.

Other issues also divided the Allies, and by 1947 the two sides were engaged in bitter quarrels that stopped just short of a shooting war. The **Cold War**—a long period of hostility between Communist nations, led by the Soviet Union, and western nations, led by the United States—had begun.

The Marshall Plan. American leaders worried that the slow recovery of Europe's economy was causing suffering and discontent that might push Europeans to try extremist solutions. The main worry was Communists. In June 1947, the United States proposed a sweeping program of economic aid. That program was called the **Marshall Plan**, after U.S. Secretary of State George Marshall.

Originally, the Marshall Plan offered to assist any European nation that needed help. But the Soviets ordered the leaders of eight Soviet-influenced countries in eastern Europe not to participate. Seventeen other nations, from Ireland to Turkey and including the western part of Germany, accepted gratefully.

Over the next several years, the Marshall Plan gave more than $12 billion to Europe. As western European economies recovered, the appeal of communism faded. By the early 1950s industrial production had leaped past prewar levels. Expressing thanks for American generosity, Winston Churchill lauded the Marshall Plan as "the most unsordid act in history."

EASTERN EUROPE IN THE SOVIET ORBIT

As the Soviet Union tightened its grip on eastern Europe, an "Iron Curtain" clanged down across the continent. To the west, democratic nations with capitalist or moderately socialist economies prevailed. To the east, behind the Iron Curtain, Communist systems followed the Soviet pattern of totalitarianism. They featured command economies, one-party rule, secret-police terror, and rigid ideological control.

The Communist-run nations went through wrenching social change, aimed at destroying the power of the old ruling classes and establishing "people's democracy." In theory, the new system aimed to put ordinary people—workers and peasants—in the driver's seat. In reality, "people's democracy" meant rule by the Communist few.

Two Germanys.   A series of developments hardened the division of Europe. With the former Allies unable to agree on a common occupation policy, Germany became a focus of Cold War tensions. In 1948, the western powers announced the merger of their three zones into one and took the first steps toward reviving the German economy. The Soviets responded with the Berlin Blockade. Soviet soldiers blocked traffic on all land routes to West Berlin (the U.S., British, and French sectors of Berlin). Rather than risk war by sending armed convoys through the Soviet-occupied zone, the western nations began an airlift. Cargo planes flew day and night, supplying West Berlin with food, coal, and other supplies. After 321 days, the Soviets gave in and lifted the blockade.

In 1949, both western and eastern sections of Germany formed their own governments. West Germany, a parliamentary democracy, was known officially as the Federal Republic of Germany. East Germany became a Communist dictatorship, calling itself the German Democratic Republic. The four wartime Allies retained their occupation rights, and periodic crises erupted over the two Germanys.

In 1961, a dangerous crisis flared up in Berlin. For many years, people had been able to pass freely between East and West Berlin. Tens of thousands of East Germans had used this gateway as an escape to West Germany. To plug this hole in the Iron Curtain, East German police in August 1961 began construction of a wall that completely surrounded West Berlin. Henceforth, the Berlin Wall became a symbol for Communist oppression. Worldwide sympathy for the people of Berlin was voiced by President John F. Kennedy in 1963, when he visited the city and told an excited crowd, "All free men, wherever they may live, are citizens of Berlin. And therefore . . . I take pride in the words, 'Ich bin ein Berliner [I am a Berliner].'"

Two Alliances.   Cold War rivalries in Europe led to the creation of two rival military blocs. The west set up **NATO**—the **North Atlantic Treaty Organization**—in 1949. Six years later, the Soviet Union spearheaded the formation of a group called the Warsaw Pact. Each bloc created a joint military command that could call on the forces of many countries. NATO members eventually included the United States, Canada, and 14 European nations. Warsaw Pact members included the Soviet Union and most of the Communist nations of eastern Europe.

The Berlin Wall winds through the center of Berlin. The Brandenburg Gate, in the background, became a symbol of the Cold War division of Europe.

Communist Nations: Satellites and Mavericks. Soviet influence over eastern Europe varied from country to country. Yugoslavia's Communists had come to power without Soviet help and did not rely on the Soviet army to stay in power. Breaking openly with Stalin in 1948, Yugoslav leaders followed independent policies and even got aid from the United States. In 1961, Albania, too, broke with the Soviets.

Other nations of eastern Europe were so completely dominated by the Soviet Union that they were called **satellite** nations. Like the moon orbiting the earth, they seemed unable to escape the Soviet Union's strong gravitational pull. The satellite nations were East Germany, Poland, Czechoslovakia, Hungary, Romania, and Bulgaria.

Popular uprisings sometimes tried to shake off Soviet domination of the satellite nations. Soviet troops crushed strikes and demonstrations that shook East Germany in 1953. In October 1956, Polish unrest brought to power an independent-minded Communist, Wladyslaw Gomulka (VLAH-dih-slahv goh-MOOL-kah), who managed to reduce Soviet influence over Poland. Later that month, revolution broke out in

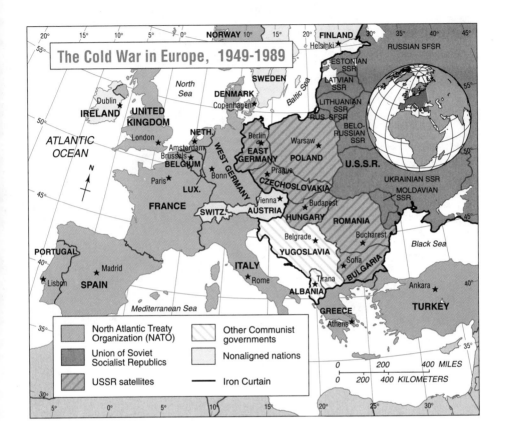

The Cold War in Europe, 1949-1989

NORWAY · FINLAND · Helsinki · RUSSIAN SFSR
SWEDEN · ESTONIAN SSR · LATVIAN SSR · LITHUANIAN SSR · RUS. SFSR
North Sea · DENMARK · Copenhagen · BELO-RUSSIAN SSR
IRELAND · UNITED KINGDOM · Dublin
ATLANTIC OCEAN · London · NETH. · Berlin · Warsaw
Amsterdam · EAST GERMANY · POLAND · U.S.S.R.
Brussels · BELGIUM · WEST GERMANY · Prague · UKRAINIAN SSR
Paris · LUX. · Bonn · CZECHOSLOVAKIA · MOLDAVIAN SSR
FRANCE · SWITZ. · Vienna · AUSTRIA · Budapest
HUNGARY · ROMANIA
Belgrade · Bucharest · Black Sea
PORTUGAL · YUGOSLAVIA · Sofia · BULGARIA
Madrid · ITALY · Rome · Tirana · Ankara
Lisbon · SPAIN · ALBANIA · TURKEY
Mediterranean Sea · GREECE · Athens

North Atlantic Treaty Organization (NATO)
Union of Soviet Socialist Republics
USSR satellites
Other Communist governments
Nonaligned nations
Iron Curtain

0   200   400 MILES
0   200   400 KILOMETERS

Hungary. A local Communist leader, Imre Nagy (IM-ruh NAHJ), announced reforms and tried to pull Hungary out of the Warsaw Pact. But Soviet troops ousted Nagy's government and brutally repressed the revolution. Later, Nagy was put on trial and executed.

Czechoslovakia was the next satellite nation to challenge the Soviet rulers. In what was called the **Prague Spring** of 1968, Communist reformers led by Alexander Dubcek (DOOB-chek) tried to nudge their country onto a more independent course. Soviet-led Warsaw Pact troops invaded Czechoslovakia and ousted the reform government.

In the 1970s and early 1980s, workers in Poland organized the most tenacious challenge of all to Communist control. They formed a labor union called **Solidarity**, mobilizing broad support among workers and intellectuals. As you will read in later chapters, Solidarity became a powerful movement that eventually toppled Communist rule in Poland.

Chapter 6:
CHECKUP

REVIEWING THE CHAPTER

I. Building Your Vocabulary

In your notebook, write the term from the list below that best completes each sentence. (The list contains one extra term.)

sanctions   appeasement   genocide
Solidarity   satellite

1. The British and French followed a policy of _____ in giving in to Hitler's demands at Munich.

2. Dominated by the Soviet Union's immense power, Poland became a(n) _____ in the postwar years.

3. Hitler's "final solution" to "the Jewish problem" was _____.

4. The League of Nations policy of using _____ against Italy did not keep Italy from taking over Ethiopia.

II. Understanding the Facts

In your notebook, write the letter of the word or phrase that best completes each of the following sentences.

1. Mussolini's Fascist party came to power:
   a. through a military coup.
   b. by peaceful parliamentary procedures alone.
   c. through a combination of bullying street tactics and parliamentary procedures.

2. A key difference between communism and fascism was that:
   a. communism was totalitarian but fascism was not.
   b. fascism was nationalist but communism was internationalist.
   c. Only fascism depended on state ownership of industry

3. The term "Weimar Republic" refers to:
   a. an independent nation between Germany and Austria.
   b. the German government that emerged after 1945.
   c. the democratic system created in Germany after World War I.

4. Which of the following did *not* influence the outcome of the Battle of Britain?

   a. Winston Churchill's speeches bolstered British morale.

   b. The British used radar to detect approaching enemy aircraft.

   c. The United States Air Force was fighting alongside the British.

III. Thinking It Through

In your notebook, write the letter of the word or phrase that best completes each of the following sentences.

1. All of the following contributed to the rise of Fascism except:

   a. weaknesses of democratic systems.

   b. economic hardships, especially among the middle classes.

   c. secret financial support to Fascist parties from the Soviet Union.

   d. a desire for revenge over the outcome of World War I.

2. The most devastating effect of the collapse of Germany's currency in 1923 was that it:

   a. robbed middle-class people of their savings and undermined their faith in democracy.

   b. forced Germany to stop paying war reparations.

   c. caused French troops to occupy the Ruhr industrial area, provoking German rearmament.

   d. destroyed people's morale and contributed to a Nazi victory in the 1924 parliamentary elections.

3. The Spanish Civil War grew out of a situation in which:

   a. the Spanish people were so sharply divided that no government could satisfy their wishes.

   b. an elected government was creating a police state.

   c. an absolute monarch refused to permit democratic elections.

   d. the Spanish Catholic Church was demanding sweeping social changes to end inequality.

4. The importance of the German–Soviet agreements of August 1939 was that they:

   a. forced Britain and France to support Poland.

   b. freed Germany to attack Poland without having to fight the Soviet Union too.

   c. allowed Germany to take over the Sudetenland.

   d. secretly provided for the Soviet Union to create satellite nations in eastern Europe.

DEVELOPING CRITICAL THINKING SKILLS

1. What circumstances made it possible for Mussolini and Hitler to come to power? Were the circumstances unique, or might they happen again? Explain your reasoning.

2. Evaluate actions taken by democratic nations like the United States, Britain, and France in response to the crises of the 1920s and 1930s.

3. What was the Marshall Plan? How did its origins and execution reflect the Cold War tensions of the time?

INTERPRETING MAPS

Study the maps on pages 131 and 156. Use the maps and information contained in the chapter to answer the questions below.

1. What countries had more territory after World War II than they had after World War I?

2. From which country or countries did Poland gain territory after World War II? To which country or countries did it give up territory?

3. How did the borders of Romania change between the two maps?

4. What countries were independent at the end of World War I but not after World War II? What happened to them?

ENRICHMENT AND EXPLORATION

1. Divide the class into groups and have each group find out more about one of the following subjects: (a) life in Mussolini's Italy; (b) life in Hitler's Germany; (c) the Resistance movement in France; (d) life in a Soviet satellite nation. Have each group present its findings to the entire class.

2. Read a book that deals with the Holocaust—one that either gives an overview or describes someone's personal experiences. Write a report summarizing the contents of the book.

3. Use library resources to learn more about life in the satellite nations under Soviet domination. Make a classroom display of pictures and articles that describe conditions and events in those nations between the late 1940s and the late 1980s. Include such events as the Hungarian Revolution of 1956 and the Prague Spring of 1968.

EUROPE IN TRANSITION
1949–Today

1949	Comecon created.
	Communist government established in China.
1950	Schuman proposes a coal and steel authority.
1953	European Coal and Steel Community created.
1957	European Community and Euratom created.
1960	European Free Trade Association created.
1964	*Jawaharlal Nehru dies.*
1967	European Commission takes authority over Euratom and ECSC.
1968	Hungary introduces "goulash communism."
	Martin Luther King, Jr., is assassinated.
1973	Britain, Ireland, and Denmark join European Community.
1981	Greece joins European Community.
1985	*Mikhail Gorbachev begins reforms in Soviet Union.*
1986	Spain and Portugal join European Community.
1989	Communism collapses in former Soviet satellites.
	Berlin Wall torn down.
1990	European Bank for Reconstruction and Development created.
1991	Comecon dissolves.
1991	Yugoslavia breaks into several pieces.
	EC, EFTA nations agree to form European Economic Area.
	Soviet Union dissolves; 11 republics form Commonwealth of Independent States.
1993	Scheduled start of European Community's "single internal market"
1999	Projected date for European currency

7 *Europe in Transition*

How long should it take to travel 270 miles by train? Four hours? Three hours? Guess again. On the high-speed line from Paris to Lyon (lee-AWN), in France, special high-speed trains zip along at speeds that reach 186 miles per hour. The Paris–Lyon trip takes just two hours. Such speeds are becoming more common as the European Community puts into effect its plan for a high-speed rail network linking many of Europe's major cities. Additional high-speed trains run from Paris to Bordeaux in France, from Hanover to Würzburg (WURTS-buhrg) in Germany, and from Madrid to Seville (suh-VIL) in Spain. Year by year, the network is expanding.

Train travel is but one example of the major changes that have been taking place in Europe since the 1940s. Europeans have been tearing down barriers and building new institutions to unite people from different countries. Having passports checked and luggage examined at borders is becoming a thing of the past. The European Community is the most far-reaching of the new institutions, but it is far from the only one.

THE MOVEMENT TOWARD EUROPEAN UNITY

The idea of a "united Europe" has bubbled to the surface many times in the course of history. In the past, it was often part of a plan for military conquest or religious unity. But since the 1940s, Europeans have been exploring other ways of realizing the ancient dream. The Marshall Plan of 1947 (see page 153) showed what could be accomplished when many nations cooperated in reaching a common goal. In 1948, the **Benelux** nations (*Belgium, Netherlands,* and *Luxembourg*) formed a **customs union,** eliminating tariffs and other restrictions on trade among their

161

countries. Steps toward further cooperation began in the early 1950s, and picked up speed as time went on.

The European Coal and Steel Community.   In 1950, French Foreign Minister Robert Schuman proposed creating an international authority to oversee the coal and steel industries of France, West Germany, and neighboring countries. Coal and steel products would circulate among the countries without regard to borders or tariffs. This would have two important consequences. First, it would unite key elements of the countries' economies, making it harder for them to go to war against one another. Second, it would give the coal and steel industries of the European countries a larger market for their products. This would make them more competitive with companies in the United States, which produced in large volume for the vast American market.

The **European Coal and Steel Community**, or ECSC, went into operation in 1953. Besides France and West Germany, its members were Italy, Belgium, the Netherlands, and Luxembourg.

The European Community.   The ECSC nations, known as **"the Six,"** carried their experiment further by founding the European Atomic Energy Agency (**Euratom**) and the **Common Market** in 1957. Euratom promoted the joint development of peaceful atomic energy. The Common Market had a more sweeping goal. It extended the idea of the

The headquarters building of the European Community in Brussels, Belgium

ECSC to products other than coal and steel. That is, it removed tariffs and other trade barriers on a wide variety of products. It also created common tariffs for goods imported from outside the Six. The Common Market was an economic union, but it aimed ultimately to forge also a political union of European states.

The official title of the Common Market was the European Economic Community. As it expanded its scope and inched closer to its goal, people began to call it simply the **European Community**, or EC.

The European Community has created a number of groups to carry on its work. The top policy-making body is a Council of Ministers, to which each member government sends one representative. Day-to-day operations are the responsibility of a 17-person executive body called the European Commission, with headquarters in Brussels, Belgium. Since 1967, this Commission has also run both the ECSC and Euratom. Finally, a European Parliament meets once a month in Strasbourg, France. Its 518 members are directly elected by the voters of the member nations. However, the parliament has only limited powers. Government ministers—not elected representatives—are the most powerful decision-makers in the EC.

The European Free Trade Association. As the Six moved forward with their plans for economic unity, seven other European nations started a rival trade group in 1960. Its name: the **European Free Trade Association**, or EFTA.

Leaders of the EFTA nations saw the economic advantages of lower trade barriers. But they did not want strong institutions like the European Commission and Parliament. They were not ready to consider steps toward political union. They thought the voters in their nations would be unwilling to give up part of their national sovereignty. **Sovereignty** is the power of a nation to make all decisions for itself.

EFTA's original members were Austria, Britain, Denmark, Norway, Portugal, Sweden, and Switzerland. Later, Finland, Iceland, and Liechtenstein also joined.

Expansion of the European Community. During the 1960s, some EFTA nations decided they had more to gain by joining the European Community than by staying out. They decided to leave EFTA for the EC, believing that their economies would do better in the larger, stronger organization. But admission to the EC was not automatic. President Charles de Gaulle of France twice vetoed a British application for membership.

CASE STUDY:

How to Sell to Europe

The unification of Europe means that industries will one day be able to market an item for sale throughout Europe. However, there also are major problems along the way to a single market, as an advertising executive notes.

> There seems to be a general view that markets for packaged consumer goods will become very much more competitive, and that the winners of the battle will be those who . . . [extend] their national brands into giant "Euro-brands" distributed in enormous quantities all over Europe. . . .
>
> But there will be no Euro-consumers in the foreseeable future! Life-styles and consumption patterns differ greatly across Europe. The reasons for this are varied: history, climate, religion, work habits, language. No legislation will be able to try, let alone succeed, in changing these inherent differences. . . .
>
> A [package] printed in English would be understood by at most 2 out of 5 consumers in the EC, and in other languages by even fewer. It would need to have at least five languages printed on it to be of use to as many as 9 out of 10 Europeans. . . .
>
> Much has been written about potential savings in production costs by (for example) shooting one commercial and running it all over Europe. . . . [But] one advertisement may not *work* all over Europe. A model or background perfectly appropriate and suitable for a product in one country may not be suitable in another. . . . A blonde model will seem glamourous and exotic in Italy, but look like "the girl next door" in Sweden!

Alan Wolfe. "The Single European Market: National or Euro-Brands?" *International Journal of Advertising*, 1991, Vol. 10, pp. 49-58.

1. Why would advertisers and people who package products be happy to sell to "Euro-consumers"?

2. List two reasons why the author does not think "Euro-consumers" will appear in the near future.

3. Does the author accept the idea that almost every European speaks English?

After de Gaulle retired, the EC expanded to nine members by admitting Britain, Ireland, and Denmark in 1973. Later, three relatively poor nations of southern Europe joined: Greece in 1981, and Portugal and Spain in 1986. Having doubled its size to 12 members, the EC began to plan further steps toward economic and political unity.

The EC as a Single Market. Even after trade barriers had come down, trade wasn't totally "free." For example, truck drivers carrying goods from Belgium to Italy had to stop at numerous border crossings as they passed through EC countries. Each time, customs officials would check them over before waving them on. Manufacturers, too, had problems in meeting the standards of 12 separate EC countries. For example, there was the question of what kind of plug to put on electrical appliances. Philips, the Dutch electronics giant, found itself making 36 different plugs because the wall sockets in the 12 EC countries came in so many shapes. What was the answer? The EC decided to try to unify standards and to tear down as many barriers as possible to the movement of people and goods among member nations.

In 1985, the EC began the long process of introducing what it called a "single internal market"—a "Europe without borders." The Community set a deadline of January 1, 1993, for completing this next major step.

The move to a single market stirred a great deal of controversy. Labor unions in countries like Germany and the Netherlands were skeptical. They enjoyed wage rates even higher than those in the United States. Their fear was that the single market would allow companies to shift factories to countries like Portugal and Greece, where average wages were less than a third as high.

To reassure workers, the EC proposed a "social charter." Among its provisions were community-wide standards for such matters as working hours and pensions. The "social charter," in turn, drew fire from small-business owners and from leaders like Margaret Thatcher, a Conservative, who was Britain's prime minister at the time. Thatcher was an outspoken critic of "big government." She declared: "European unity is the device through which the regulators and socialists hope to expand their grip on the Continent."

On the other hand, multinational companies and Europeans in many walks of life favored the move to a single market. Said one Italian merchant banker: "Economic union will not only make life easier, but we can't do without it."

Comecon: Unity Communist-Style. While Western Europe was working out new forms of economic and political cooperation, the Communist world was attempting to do the same. However, the satellite nations' trading bloc, called **Comecon**, was dominated by the Soviet Union, rather than being a cooperative effort among member states.

Comecon, known officially as the *Council for Mutual Economic Assistance*, came into existence in 1949. It was devised by the Soviet Union as a means of tying the economies of the satellite nations to the centrally planned Soviet economy. The Soviet Union dominated Comecon throughout its existence. Much of the trade within the organization was two-way trade between the Soviet Union and the other members, with comparatively little among the smaller members.

A key function of Comecon was to decide in which products each country would specialize. For example, East Germany became Comecon's chief producer of factory robots. Bulgaria specialized in computers. Czechoslovakia made tanks and explosives. The Soviet Union, for its part, supplied a wide range of raw materials, especially oil and gas. Massive pipelines ran from the oil and gas fields of Siberia to the major cities of the satellite nations.

By selling its oil and gas at relatively low prices, the Soviet Union could argue that it was helping its allies to build up their economies. However, people in the satellite nations generally believed that Comecon did more for the Soviet Union than it did for them. For example, the toothpaste and lamps and canned meats supplied by the satellites helped the Soviet Union to fill the gaps in its own consumer economy. At the same time, links to the inefficient Soviet economy tended to bog down the satellite economies. If the Soviet Union fell behind in its deliveries of raw materials, factories in other countries had to cut back production. Because of the centrally planned Comecon system, they were not free to find more dependable suppliers in other nations.

As time passed, leaders of the satellite nations became more and more critical of Comecon. Meanwhile, changes in the world at large were undermining the Soviet Union's ability to control its satellites—and its will to do so.

THE COLLAPSE OF COMMUNISM

As early as 1968, satellite nations began to try ways of loosening up their economic systems. Political change quickened. By the 1980s, protest movements were gaining strength in Poland and elsewhere.

166

Meanwhile, the Soviet Union entered a period of reform and self-doubt. Mikhail Gorbachev came to power in the Soviet Union in 1985. He tried to jump-start the lagging Soviet economy. Gorbachev also began allowing fresh breezes to blow through the political life of the Soviet Union. Reform in the Soviet Union undermined communism in the satellite nations. By 1989, when East Germany was forced to open the Berlin Wall, the old Communist empire was so shaky that it could no longer stand. In one country after another, Communist rule collapsed. At the end of 1991, the Soviet Union itself dissolved, with its 15 separate republics claiming the right to go their own ways as independent nations.

In the following pages, we'll take a step-by-step look at how the collapse of communism in Europe came about.

The Beginnings of Economic Reform.   Hungary was the first satellite nation to try to shake off the heavy hand of centralized control. Its leaders adopted consumer-oriented reforms in 1968, aimed at raising living standards and putting more food on people's tables. This program of economic reforms was officially known as the *New Economic Mechanism,* or NEM. Unofficially, it came to be called **goulash communism,** after a prized Hungarian beef stew.

Unfortunately for Hungarians, goulash communism contained more communism than goulash. True, Communist rules were relaxed to permit small-scale private businesses. Factory managers gained more leeway in running their factories. For the average Hungarian, this did mean more polite service at such newly privatized businesses as restaurants. But after a growth surge in the early 1970s, the economy returned to its old stagnation. One problem was that central planners kept setting the rules for industry, refusing to give up power to individual factories. A second problem was a recession that hit Europe as a result of rapid oil price rises in the mid–1970s. The recession undercut Hungary's efforts to boost exports to non-Communist countries.

Gorbachev: *Glasnost* and *Perestroika*.   Meanwhile, the Soviet economy also was struggling to overcome stagnation. Under Leonid Brezhnev, the Soviet Communist party leader from 1964 to 1982, feeble efforts to reform the economy made little headway. When Mikhail Gorbachev came to power in 1985, the Soviet economy was in a bad way indeed.

Gorbachev moved quickly to introduce changes. He announced a two-part program to reform both the political and the economic life of the Soviet Union. *Glasnost* (openness) was to be the rule in politics.

Gorbachev began to end the tight censorship of the Soviet press and to allow more open discussion of the problems of Soviet society. In economic life the new byword was *perestroika* (restructuring).

Gorbachev's political reforms proved more successful than his economic ones. By 1989 the Soviet Union was a much more open, freer society than it had been before. His attempts at economic reform had little impact.

A New Road for Eastern Europe. While Gorbachev's reforms were loosening up the Soviet Union, the Soviet leader was busily mending international fences. He met President Ronald Reagan, and later George Bush, to negotiate new limits on nuclear and conventional arms. The Soviet leader said he wanted an end to the Cold War. He encouraged the same kinds of reforms in the satellites as in the Soviet Union. Finally, as their Communist governments collapsed one by one, he let it be known that the Soviet Union would not try to stop the process.

Even before Gorbachev's announcement, however, the eastern European countries had begun to free themselves from the Soviet orbit. Poland held free parliamentary elections in June. Soon after, Tadeusz Mazowiecki (TAH-day-oos mah-zoh-VYETS-kee), a leader of the anti-Communist labor union Solidarity, took office as prime minister. He was the first non-Communist head of government in eastern Europe in more than four decades. Hungary also began moving toward multiparty democracy. Bulgarian protesters forced the country's Communist leader to resign.

The most dramatic event of all came in early November, when East Germany reversed its hard-line policies and opened all its borders— including the Berlin Wall. Television newscasts showed a flood of happy Germans bashing holes in the hated wall and dancing through the streets of Berlin. The unforgettable scenes thrilled viewers all over the world. They brought home in vivid images the immensity of the changes that were taking place. The wall, the most haunting symbol of Europe's division into hostile blocs, had fallen. Within a year, East Germany and West Germany were reunited as one German nation, independent and democratic.

As they struggled to build democratic systems, the nations of eastern Europe began to tear down their Communist-style economies. They moved toward free-market economic systems in which private companies and individuals, not government officials, would make the key decisions. Each firm would set its own prices. Each company would decide for itself what products or services to sell. Because it had no role to play

168

A crowd gathers to celebrate as a crane begins the final dismantling of the Berlin Wall. The event took place three months after the wall's gates first opened.

in this new world of private enterprise, Comecon, the Soviet-led trading group, dissolved in June 1991. Soon after, the Soviet-dominated Warsaw Pact military bloc also went out of existence.

The Soviet Union Disappears.   Meanwhile, in the Soviet Union, *glasnost* and *perestroika* were creating an explosive mixture. Rival leaders gained office at the local and regional level. One of the most popular was Boris Yeltsin, leader of the Russian republic—by far the largest republic, holding half of all the people in the Soviet Union. Some republics were demanding outright independence. The earliest to do so were the three Baltic republics, Lithuania, Latvia, and Estonia, which had been annexed by the Soviet Union against their will during World War II.

In August 1991, Communist hard-liners tried to take over the Soviet government and kick Gorbachev out. The coup failed, and Gorbachev returned to his Kremlin office. But Gorbachev was no longer the master of the Soviet Union. Power had shifted to the leaders of the separate republics, and especially to the Russian leader, Boris Yeltsin. In the aftermath of the coup, Soviet leaders did the unthinkable. They banned the Communist party, which had ruled the Soviet Union since 1917.

The republics now demanded full independence. Within weeks, the three Baltic republics had formalized their separation. All of the other republics soon followed—even Russia. In December 1991, 11 of the 15 former republics (all except Georgia and the Baltic states) signed an agreement to form a much looser association, called the Commonwealth of Independent States. Acknowledging that the Soviet Union no longer existed, President Gorbachev resigned his empty post.

Effects on Europe. The disappearance of the Soviet Union raised both hopes and worries in the former Communist nations of eastern Europe. On the bright side, there was the possibility of closer relations between these countries and the two sizable ex-Soviet republics just to the east, Ukraine and Belarus. Ukraine, especially, was rich in minerals and in agricultural lands. On the dark side, however, lay several difficult questions. How would the demise of the Soviet Union affect the economies of its former satellites? What would it mean for the region's stability? An example of possible instability was Moldova, just east of Romania (and once part of it), where Romanian-speaking and Russian-speaking people clashed.

Trade relations had already been disrupted by Gorbachev's economic reform efforts and by eastern Europe's turning away from centrally-run Communist-style economies. The Soviet economy was in such chaos that supplies virtually ceased flowing to Europe. As you have read, industries in the former satellites depended heavily on Soviet supplies. With those supplies shut off, many factories had to operate short shifts or shut down completely.

The Shrinking of Yugoslavia. Europeans got a glimpse of the dangers of ethnic flareups as Yugoslavia split into five separate nations. First formed in 1918, Yugoslavia had become a federation of six distinct republics after World War II. But ethnic rivalries simmered just beneath the surface. Yugoslavia's ethnic mix was explosive because none of the republics except Slovenia was **homogeneous**, that is, made up of a single ethnic group. Each of the others had large ethnic minorities intermingled with the most prominent group.

Yugoslavia's breakup began when Slovenia and Croatia withdrew in the summer of 1991. Macedonia and Bosnia-Herzegovina declared independence later that same year. In 1992, the two remaining republics, Serbia and Montenegro (mahn-tuh-NEG-roh), announced that they would remain in a shrunken Yugoslav federation. They said they would not try to annex any parts of the republics that had seceded.

However, civil war flared up in areas of the withdrawing republics where rival ethnic groups lived close together. The most bitter enmities were between Serbs and Croats and between Serbs and the Muslim

170

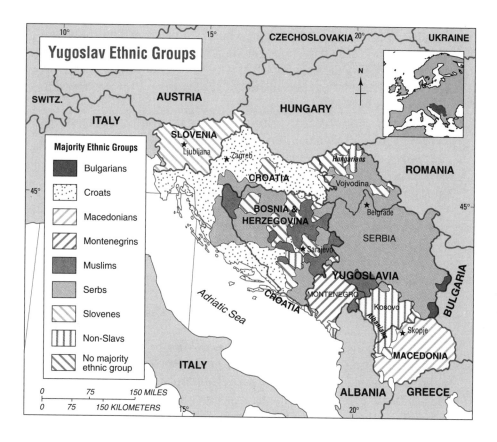

Yugoslav Ethnic Groups

Majority Ethnic Groups

- Bulgarians
- Croats
- Macedonians
- Montenegrins
- Muslims
- Serbs
- Slovenes
- Non-Slavs
- No majority ethnic group

0   75   150 MILES
0   75   150 KILOMETERS

SWITZ. ITALY AUSTRIA HUNGARY CZECHOSLOVAKIA UKRAINE ROMANIA BULGARIA GREECE ALBANIA ITALY

SLOVENIA — Ljubljana — Zagreb — CROATIA — Hungarians — Vojvodina — BOSNIA & HERZEGOVINA — Belgrade — Sarajevo — SERBIA — YUGOSLAVIA — CROATIA — MONTENEGRO — Kosovo — Albanians — Skopje — MACEDONIA

Adriatic Sea

Slavs of Bosnia-Herzegovina. Each of these groups nursed memories of atrocities committed against them in the past. The United Nations and the European Community tried to keep localized battles from expanding into full-scale civil war. But many thousands of people died.

THE NEW EUROPE: WHAT SHAPE WILL IT TAKE?

The breathtaking changes in eastern Europe raised many new questions for the continent as a whole. How would the changes affect the European Community? Would the move toward European unity now speed up? Would it slow down? How big could the European Community grow and still keep its vigor and purpose? And what would happen to the number two trading group, EFTA?

Linking the EC and EFTA. Eager to promote as much trade as possible among European nations, the European Community and EFTA

171

decided in 1991 to work together. The 12 EC nations and the seven EFTA nations formed a "super common market" that they named the **European Economic Area, or EEA.** The agreement forming the EEA had to be ratified by the parliaments of all 19 nations. It was planned to go into effect in 1993.

The EC and EFTA remain in place as separate organizations. However, their 19 member nations have promised to promote the free movement of goods, services, capital, and people across European borders. The EFTA nations will adopt many EC rules—for example, rules on labor practices, social policy, consumer protection, and the environment. At least initially, however, EFTA nations will still have looser ties with one another than EC nations have.

The EEA was expected to boost the already heavy trade among EC and EFTA nations. It may also lead to new political institutions, such as a new European court of justice and a 19-nation council of ministers.

Helping Eastern Europe Make a New Start. The industrial nations of Europe, North America, and Japan worked out a plan to help the former satellites and the former Soviet republics to build free-market economies. In 1990, the United States, Japan, Britain, and others created a European Bank for Reconstruction and Development. They pledged some $12 billion to the bank, whose purpose was to make loans to help with the conversion from communism to capitalism. Most of the loans were to help private investors take over companies once run by Communist governments.

EC Debate: "Wider" or "Deeper"? Within the EC, the 12 member nations began a debate over future growth. Two opposing positions emerged. On the one hand, some nations said the EC should open its arms to new European members, doubling or even tripling its membership. They favored a "wider" community under existing rules. On the other hand, some nations said it was more important to "deepen" the EC. They said the existing rules did not go far enough in merging the policies and the finances of EC nations. In this view, the EC should take further steps toward a "united Europe" before adding large numbers of new members.

Britain was the leading supporter of a "wider" community. Prime Minister Margaret Thatcher declared, "I do not believe in a federation of Europe, a United States of Europe." She and her successors wanted the EC to concentrate on promoting trade and not to interfere with British sovereignty by "meddling" in political and monetary matters.

France, on the other hand, backed a "deeper" community. French leaders saw a "united Europe" with strong federal institutions as the best means of tying German loyalties to western Europe. Recalling the trouble Germany had caused in the 1930s, France wanted a way to keep Germany from trying to throw its weight around again. German leaders too seemed interested in "deepening" the EC.

Creating a European Currency. Supporters of a "deeper" community won a round in 1991, when EC leaders agreed to create a new European currency by 1999 at the latest. The decision meant that new coins and bills with a new name (still to be chosen) would replace the francs and marks and guilders used in EC nations in the past. But it also meant far more. For in order to create a money that people could trust—a money that would have a stable value—EC nations would have to turn over to a central European authority many decisions traditionally made by each nation for itself. This was a major new step toward a United States of Europe.

Margaret Thatcher and her successor, John Major, continued to oppose Britain's signing away its powers over money. So the EC nations offered Britain a compromise. Any EC nation would have the right not to take part in the new monetary system.

These decisions came in a formal treaty drawn up by EC leaders at Maastricht (MAHS-trihkt), the Netherlands. The EC leaders at Maastricht also agreed to try to work out a common EC foreign policy, and to do so by majority vote. Sensitive to British feelings, the European leaders avoided using the word *federal,* to which the British objected so strongly. But the Maastricht treaty was a step toward federalism nonetheless.

Considering New Members. Steps to "widen" the European Community went on simultaneously with the steps to "deepen" it. EFTA nations like Sweden, Austria, and Finland seemed to be on the fast track to membership. By the middle or late 1990s, the European Community will probably have expanded to 15 or more members.

The former Communist nations of eastern Europe (and other nations, like Turkey, Cyprus, and Malta) have also sought to join the EC. They seemed unlikely to be admitted soon. Nonetheless, Jacques Delors, who served as president of the European Commission in the late 1980s and early 1990s, envisioned an eventual membership of 35 nations. He saw an expanding community as a way of attaining the twin goals of peace and the continuing vitality of Europe.

REVIEWING THE CHAPTER

I. Building your Vocabulary

In your notebook, write the term from the list below that best completes each sentence. (The list contains one extra term.)

sovereignty	goulash communism	Comecon
Warsaw Pact	*glasnost*	*perestroika*

1. Mikhail Gorbachev's policy of allowing greater political freedom in the Soviet Union was called _____.

2. Trade between the satellite nations and the Soviet Union was carried out under an organization called _____.

3. An early effort by a satellite country to reform its Communist economic system was called _____.

4. Britain has been reluctant to give up any of its _____ by giving more power to the European Community.

5. Mikhail Gorbachev tried to cure the ills of the Soviet Union's sluggish economy through a policy called _____.

II. Understanding the Facts

In your notebook, write the letter of the word or phrase that best completes each of the following sentences.

1. A major difference between the EC and EFTA is that EFTA:
   a. promotes expanded trade among its members.
   b. has more members.
   c. has a common tariff on all imports entering EFTA from the rest of the world.
   d. does not proclaim political unity as one of its goals.

2. "Goulash communism" included efforts to:
   a. sell off major industries to private owners.
   b. hold elections in which many political parties could compete.
   c. give factory managers more control over their factories.
   d. abolish the alliance between the Soviet Union and its satellites.

3. Gorbachev urged the Communist governments of eastern Europe to:
   a. send food aid to the Soviet Union.
   b. put down any attempts to change the Communist system.
   c. make reforms similar to *glasnost* and *perestroika*.
   d. discontinue their trade with the Russian government of Boris Yeltsin.

4. The Maastricht treaty:
   a. laid the groundwork for a common currency.
   b. created the European Coal and Steel Community.
   c. created the European Economic Area.
   d. provided for the creation of a "single internal market" within the European Community.

III. Thinking It Through

In your notebook, write the letter of the word or phrase that best completes each of the following sentences.

1. The Commonwealth of Independent States resembled the United States in 1776 because of its:
   a. two-party system.   c. powerful legislature.
   b. weak central government.   d. expanded system of courts.

2. "Deepening" the European Community would mean that:
   a. member nations would give up more power to the EC.
   b. Europeans would have to learn a common language.
   c. the EC would grant membership to former Soviet satellites.
   d. the EC would forget about political unity.

3. A key reason for joining a "common market" would be to:
   a. protect industries that have trouble competing.
   b. sell more products to other nations.
   c. insulate its economy from problems in other nations.
   d. increase its population.

4. If you were a factory worker, you might expect the EC's "single internal market" to affect you in what way?
   a. It would make it harder for you to move to a new job.
   b. It would raise the prices of products you buy.
   c. It would complicate crossing borders when you travel.
   d. It would lower your wages.

INTERPRETING A CARTOON

Examine the cartoon below. Then answer the questions.

1. Why do you suppose the cartoonist has labeled the two panels "Before" and "After"? Before and after what?

2. What do the letters U.S.S.R. in the top panel stand for?

3. Which countries in Europe west of the U.S.S.R. are not shown in the top panel?

4. What point does the cartoon make?

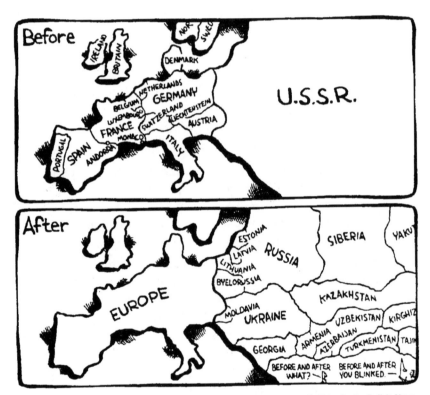

By Toles for the Buffalo News

DEVELOPING CRITICAL THINKING SKILLS

1. Evaluate the European Community from the perspective of United States interests. In what ways might the existence of EC benefit the United States? In what ways might it hurt the United States?

2. Provide arguments for and against giving greater powers to the European Parliament. Discuss how the Community might change if its parliament gained more power.

3. How did membership in Comecon affect the economies of the satellite nations? In your opinion, did the satellite countries gain or lose by belonging? Explain your reasoning.

4. Compare the European Bank for Reconstruction and Development to the Marshall Plan. What similarities and differences can you find?

ENRICHMENT AND EXPLORATION

1. Using library resources, find out more about the European Community and the European Free Trade Association. Create charts showing each group's structure and purposes. Highlight differences and similarities between the two groups.

2. Imagine that you are an American business owner interested in selling your product in Europe. You have a limited marketing budget, so you must concentrate either on EC countries or on EFTA countries. Write a report telling which group of countries you will choose and explaining your reasons.

3. Ask volunteers to prepare and perform a skit illustrating what happens when someone crosses an international border. Have the volunteers portray travelers, customs inspectors, and passport control officers. They should demonstrate the inconvenience of traditional border inspections. Then have them replay the crossing as it might occur within the European Community's borderless "single market."

4. Consult an almanac or the economics section of a newspaper to find the names of currencies used in European Community countries and their current value in United States dollars. Portray this information in a chart. Use separate columns for the names of countries, the names of currencies, and the value in dollars. Add a fourth column showing how much of each nation's currency a worker earning the equivalent of $400 a week would receive. (For example, if a British pound sterling is worth $1.70, the worker would earn 400 divided by 1.7, or 235 pounds sterling per week.)

5. Imagine that each state in the United States of America printed its own special money, like the nations of Europe. Write a short story describing a person's experiences on a journey across several states.

8 *Northern Europe*

Northern Europe spans some 1,500 miles (2,400 km.) from Iceland in the gray North Atlantic to Finland, which borders on Russia. Located at the same high latitudes as Alaska, Northern Europe is a region of long winters and short summers. Snowy winters give people plenty of opportunity to practice winter sports. Many world class skiers and ice skaters hail from this region.

The nations of Northern Europe are either very new to democracy or quite experienced in its ways. For example, the Baltic nations of Estonia, Latvia, and Lithuania are still struggling to build democratic institutions after having been under Soviet domination for half a century. Iceland, on the other hand, tried democracy at a very early date. It claims to have been the first nation in the world to have set up a parliament, in about A.D. 930. The region's other countries, Sweden, Norway, and Denmark— together called the Scandinavian nations—and Finland, also have long traditions of democratic rule.

THE REGION

Although Northern Europe lacks valuable resources, its people have turned the resources they have to good advantage. The region boasts some of the highest standards of living in the world. However, it also has some of the highest taxes. The taxes help to pay for government programs that provide people with health and pension benefits.

Land and Sea.   Almost anywhere you go in Northern Europe, you'll find seacoasts dotted with fishing villages. Morning and evening, you can see fishing boats setting out to sea or returning with a day's catch. You might even see a large whaling vessel setting off for distant waters.

178

Some Facts About Northern European Countries

COUNTRY	CAPITAL CITY	POPULATION (millions)	AREA (square miles)	PER CAPITA INCOME (U.S. dollars)	LIFE EXPECTANCY AT BIRTH
Denmark	Copenhagen (koh•puhn•HAY•guhn)	5.1	16,631	$ 24,500	72 M 79 F
Estonia	Tallinn (TAHL• ihn)	1.5	18,370	6,240	NA
Finland	Helsinki (HEL•sing•kee)	5.0	130,119	15,000	71 M 79 F
Iceland	Reykjavik (RAY•kyuh•veek)	0.3	39,709	24,031	75 M 81 F
Latvia	Riga (REE•guh)	2.7	25,400	NA	NA
Lithuania	Vilnius (VIHL•nee•oos)	3.6	25,174	3,000	NA
Norway	Oslo (AHS•loh)	4.3	125,049	17,900	73 M 80 F
Sweden	Stockholm (STAHK•hohm)	8.6	173,800	15,700	74 M 81 F

NA = Not Available
M = Male
F = Female

Sources: 1992 Information Please Almanac; World Almanac and Book of Facts, 1992

Besides offering food, the sea influences the region's climate. Mild sea breezes make summers cooler and winters milder than they would otherwise be, given the region's high latitude. The sea also provides a handy highway for travel—and for shipping raw materials and the products of industry.

Northern Europe contains rugged mountains and jutting peninsulas. Mountains fill much of the interior of Norway and most of the western part of Sweden. Those two countries occupy the massive Scandinavian peninsula that curves out of Europe, dividing the Arctic Sea in the north from the North Sea in the west and the Baltic Sea in the southeast. Most of the land suitable for farming is in the south of the peninsula and near the coasts. In the mountains and in the north are forests that provide wood and other products.

A small church overlooks a fiord, a long, deep-water inlet on the coast of Norway. Norway's many beautiful fiords are popular ports of call for cruise ships.

Denmark occupies a number of islands and another peninsula that juts north from Germany. Denmark is relatively flat, as are the Baltic nations of Estonia, Latvia, and Lithuania. A much larger proportion of their lands is suitable for farming.

Iceland is an island far to the west of the other nations of the region. Although Iceland does contain extensive ice fields, its name is somewhat misleading. Mild ocean currents help to keep the winter temperatures in Reykjavik (RAY-kyuh-veek), the nation's capital, at about the same level as temperatures in New York City.

The People. The people of Northern Europe tend to be similar to one another in appearance and background. In the Scandinavian countries and Iceland, people speak languages related to a Germanic tongue called Old Norse. The Icelandic language has changed little over the centuries. Icelandic school children can still read ancient Norse literature, provided the spelling is updated. The Swedish, Norwegian, and Danish languages have evolved much more and so bear less resemblance to Old Norse.

180

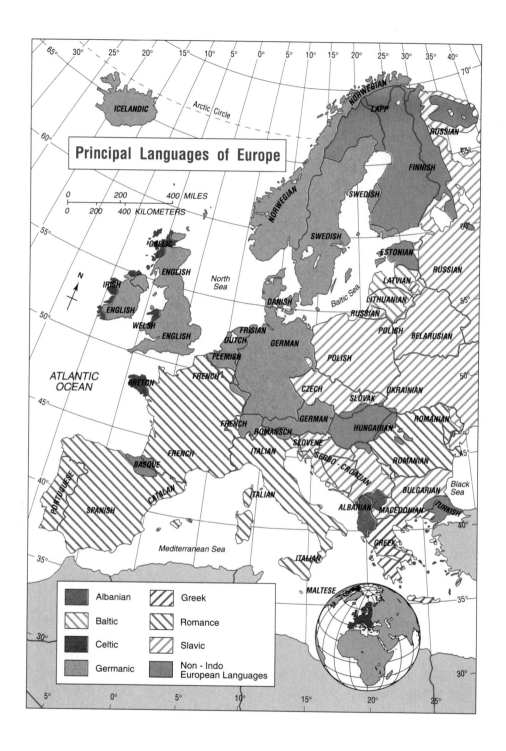

Principal Languages of Europe

In Latvia and Lithuania, people speak what are called Baltic languages, which are most closely related to Slavic languages like Russian and Polish. Finns and Estonians speak similar languages that are related to no others in Europe except Lapp and, distantly, to Hungarian.

Northern Europe was deeply affected by the Protestant Reformation, and in all but two countries most of the people are Lutherans. Most Lithuanians and about half the Latvians are Roman Catholics. Other Christians in the region include members of the Eastern Orthodox and Baptist churches. There are also Muslims who have immigrated from southern Europe and southwest Asia since the 1960s. The Jewish population of the region is small.

In rural areas, many people still follow a traditional way of life as farmers, herders, and foresters. Many of the Lapp people of northern Finland, Sweden, and Norway herd reindeer for a living, moving around with their herds. (*Lapp* comes from a Finnish word meaning *nomad.*) The reindeer graze on lichens that grow in the cold northern lands. A 1986 accident at a nuclear power plant in Chernobyl, in Ukraine, spread radiation into Scandinavia. High doses of radiation collected in lichens, making the meat and milk of the reindeer inedible for many months. The incident seriously disrupted the lives of the Lapps.

Urban life in Northern Europe dates back to prehistoric towns in what are now Sweden and Denmark. A large proportion of the region's population lives in towns and cities today. Major cities have all the modern conveniences, from electronic banking to cable television. The largest cities of the region are three of the capital cities: Stockholm (STAHK-hohm), Sweden (population 1,435,000); Copenhagen (koh-puhn-HAY-guhn), Denmark (population 1,358,000), and Riga (REE-guh), Latvia (population 915,000). Other capitals with populations of more than 450,000 are Vilnius (VIHL-nee-oos), Lithuania; Tallinn (TAHL-ihn), Estonia; Helsinki (HEL-sing-kee), Finland, and Oslo (AHS-loh), Norway. The whole country of Iceland contains only 255,000 people, and Reykjavik, the capital, has fewer than 100,000 inhabitants.

Regional Cooperation. The nations of Northern Europe have many political and economic ties with one another. For example, the governments of Denmark, Norway, and Sweden are joint owners of an international airline known as S.A.S. (Scandinavian Airlines System). Since regaining their independence, the Baltic nations of Estonia, Latvia, and Lithuania have tried to work together, too. However, that effort is still in its infancy. One problem is that the three Baltic nations produce similar goods and thus must compete with each other for customers.

A canal and buildings in Copenhagen, the capital and largest city of Denmark. The city is also its nation's commercial and cultural center and its largest port.

Of the eight nations in the region, only Denmark has been a member of the European Community (EC). Four nations—Sweden, Finland, Norway, and Iceland—joined the rival European Free Trade Association (EFTA). Eager not to be shut out of the EC's expanding markets, Sweden and Finland have applied for EC membership. Other Northern European nations may also join.

Three of the countries in Northern Europe—Denmark, Norway, and Iceland—have long been allies of the United States. All three are members of the North Atlantic Treaty Organization (NATO). Under the domination of the former Soviet Union for half a century until 1991, the Baltic nations had Soviet troops stationed within their borders. Sweden and Finland, in contrast, remained neutral throughout the entire Cold War.

SWEDEN: THE WELFARE STATE

Sweden has long been noted not only for its neutrality, but also for its generous system of social services. Ever since the 1930s, Sweden has been a leading example of the welfare state. A welfare state is a country in which government programs cushion people against hardship by such means as paying for their health care and supplying them with money when they lose jobs or retire. Sweden combines the welfare state with a capitalist economy.

The Swedish People. In the 1600s and 1700s, Sweden was a great power, ruling a vast area around the rim of the Baltic Sea. This Swedish empire included present-day Finland, Estonia, and Latvia. In 1638, Sweden started a North American colony in what is now Delaware. In time, Sweden lost its empire and resigned itself to living within its present boundaries. Indeed, Sweden gained a reputation as a peace-loving state. During the 1900s, the Swedes remained neutral throughout the two world wars and the Cold War. They have been strong supporters of the United Nations.

The Swedish people are remarkably homogeneous, or alike. Most come from families that have been Swedish for generations. Almost everyone in the country speaks Swedish, although small minorities of Lapps and Finns speak their own languages. In recent years, people from such African and Asian countries as Turkey, Iraq, and Nigeria

A tree-lined road separates a meadow, in the foreground, from a wheatfield in the background. Most of Sweden is flat, gently rolling countryside.

have moved to Sweden and taken up Swedish citizenship. Sometimes such "new Swedes" have faced mistreatment and hostility. But the government has worked to end discrimination.

Over the centuries, many Swedes have emigrated to other countries. Some 1.3 million went to North America. A large proportion of those emigrants settled in Wisconsin and Minnesota. The Swedish influence is reflected in place names such as Stockholm, Wisconsin, and Malmo, Minnesota. Many Americans carry on Swedish customs, such as having a young girl light the family Christmas tree.

Children in Sweden study English from the early grades, and most adults can speak at least some English. Many Swedes speak other languages as well. Because Swedish law assures workers at least five weeks of paid vacation each year, Swedes have time to travel. Many Swedish tourists head for the sunny beaches of Southern Europe, Africa, and the Caribbean.

The Economy.   Sweden's vast forests, extensive mineral supplies, and plentiful water power have allowed it to build up a strong industrial economy. Sweden did not acquire large-scale industries until late in the 1800s. Because of this late start, it did not develop the grimy industrial cities and slums of the early Industrial Revolution. Swedish industries are scattered around the country, mainly in small to middle-sized cities.

Forestry products are among Sweden's leading exports. Besides timber and pulp, the nation sells such manufactured goods as furniture, paper, and matches.

As early as the Middle Ages, Swedes cut down trees to make charcoal. With the charcoal, they smelted iron. Sweden became one of the world's leading sources of iron. By the 1800s, coal had largely replaced charcoal in the production of iron and steel. But Sweden had almost no coal or other fossil fuels, so it turned to electricity produced by hydroelectric dams. Sweden remains a major producer of iron and steel, specializing in high-quality alloys and stainless steel. Sweden also has major metal-using industries. Its factories turn out products that range from precision instruments and axe blades to ships and warplanes.

Lacking coal, Sweden has depended heavily on hydroelectric and nuclear power. For a time it produced more nuclear power per person than any other country. However, Swedish citizens worried that nuclear power was unsafe. Swedish citizens voted in a referendum to close down all nuclear power plants by 2010. Finding a new source of non-polluting energy will be a major challenge.

CASE STUDY:

Scandinavian Design

Simple, practical, and inexpensive lines of Scandivanian furniture and housewares have become popular around the world. Modern artists and designers wanted to make everyday factory-made items, such as dishes and glasses, as beautiful as handmade works of art. Elizabeth Gaynor explains the background of the movement:

> Scandinavian design and architecture came into their own in the modern era. Feeling the effects of the Industrial Revolution nearly a century after southern Europe and the United States, the Nordic [Scandinavian] countries learned from the failings of other nations. . . . Products reflected values: objects must relate to human proportions and comfort . . . , needs . . . , and beauty.[1]

Poul Henningsen, a Danish designer and architect and one of the leaders of this movement, urged other craftspeople and artists of the 1920s to join him:

> Dear craftsmen friends! How can you expect us to go on respecting you, while this swindle continues in the name of art? . . . We have no proper tumblers [drinking glasses], plates, . . . spoons, knives, or forks, while richer homes are flooded with trash and rubbish at fantastic prices! Think a little, and consider your obligations to make things for the delight of your fellowmen in their daily life! Throw away your artists' berets and bow ties and get into overalls. Down with artistic pretentiousness! Simply make things which are fit for use: that is enough to keep you busy and make lots of money![2]

---

[1] Elizabeth Gaynor. *Scandinavia: Living Design*. New York: Stewart, Tabori, and Chang, 1987.
[2] Connery, Donald S. *The Scandinavians*. New York: Simon and Schuster, 1966.

1. How did industrialization change furniture and housewares?

2. What values does Elizabeth Gaynor find reflected in Scandinavian products?

3. Why does Henningsen tell artists to wear overalls instead of berets and bow ties?

Swedish farmers grow a variety of grains, potatoes, and sugar beets. Dairy farms produce milk and cheese. Most of these products are consumed within Sweden. A modest fishing industry, operating mainly out of ports along the west coast, supplies the nation with herring and cod.

Sweden's Government. The Swedish people are deeply devoted to democracy—and to their king. That is not so contradictory as it sounds, for the Swedish king is a constitutional monarch who reigns but does not govern. The nation's government is headed by a prime minister, who appoints the cabinet. The prime minister is responsible to the *Riksdag*, as Sweden's **unicameral** parliament is called. A unicameral parliament is one that has a single chamber.

Sweden's system of government is designed so that a wide range of political opinions can be heard. National elections are held every three years. Under a system of **proportional representation**, a political party wins seats in proportion to its share of the votes in each of the country's 28 electoral districts. Thus, if a party wins one third of the votes in a district, it gets one third of that district's seats. In addition, some members are elected "at large," by all of the voters of the country. Any party receiving at least 4 percent of the total votes is guaranteed one or more seats in parliament. As a result, while many parties have seats in the *Riksdag*, most of the time, no single party has a majority. That means that Swedish governments are usually **coalitions**, or alliances of two or more parties.

Ever since the Great Depression of the 1930s, Sweden's dominant party has been the Social Democratic party, which is backed by Sweden's powerful labor unions. The Social Democrats regularly win from 35 to 50 percent of the vote. They headed the Swedish government for 53 of the 59 years from 1932 until 1991. In 1991, the voters handed them a stinging defeat. A coalition of four parties from the center and right took control in 1991.

The Ombudsman. Swedes who believe that the government is treating them unfairly can appeal to a special official called the **ombudsman** (AHM-buhdz-muhn) (literally, "representative"). The ombudsman serves as a watchdog to protect the public against big government. This popular function, which originated in Sweden in 1809, has been adopted by a number of other countries, among them Norway, Finland, and New Zealand. The idea of the ombudsman has begun to spread to the United States. For example, the *Washington Post* newspaper has an ombudsman who checks into complaints about the newspaper's reporting.

The Middle Way. The Swedish form of welfare state has often been called the "middle way"—an alternative path between capitalism and socialism. Unlike pure capitalism, Sweden's middle way provides a safety net for people who might be threatened by economic change. However, unlike socialism, the Swedish system leaves control over production in the hands of private companies. Sweden boasts some of the largest privately owned enterprises in Europe. Swedish companies such as Volvo (automobiles) and Electrolux (household appliances) have factories and customers in many parts of the world.

For the average Swede, the welfare state means both high taxes and generous benefits. Economists rate the "tax burden" of a nation according to what proportion of the nation's total output the government collects in taxes. Sweden has consistently ranked at the top when compared with other industrial nations. Its tax burden reached 68 percent of national output before dropping below 60 percent in the 1980s. (For the United States, the figure is about 30 percent.) However, businesses—especially large firms—get tax breaks that encourage them to reinvest part of their earnings. That helps to keep Swedish industry competitive.

A man in a fish market holds up two large fillets. Fish—fresh, smoked, or pickled—is an important part of the diet in all Scandinavian countries.

In return for their high taxes, Swedes get a variety of social benefits. For example, Swedes do not have to worry about the economic consequences of losing a job or suffering a serious illness. The state welfare system pays a laid-off worker almost full pay for up to 300 days. Social security pays a generous portion of medical and dental bills. Workers lose only a small percentage of pay when illness (their own or a child's) keeps them away from their jobs. One result of Sweden's comprehensive social services is an infant death rate that is significantly lower than in the United States.

Rethinking the Welfare State.   The economic troubles of the 1990s were worrisome ones. Factories closed, unemployment rose, and government revenues declined. Was Sweden's economic slump merely temporary—or was the nation losing its competitive edge in a changing world? Many Swedes believed the nation faced long-term problems. Some said the nation could no longer afford its high-tax ways.

Swedish leaders have begun to trim back social benefits. They do not want to give up the welfare state, but they realize that the degree of government spending in the past cannot be kept up in periods of sustained recession. Furthermore, once Sweden joins the European Community, people from other community nations will be free to move to Sweden. They can take jobs in Sweden and apply for social benefits. Sweden is concerned that this will place a permanent economic burden on taxpayers.

FINLAND

Sweden's eastern neighbor, Finland, shares many of Sweden's characteristics—but not all. Finland, too, is a modern industrial nation that offers extensive social benefits to its people. But while Sweden's eyes turn west, toward the rest of Europe, Finland's eyes turn east, toward Russia. The entire Finnish population of 5 million about equals the population of the single Russian city of St. Petersburg, which lies 100 miles southeast of Finland's border. The Finns have never been able to forget the Russians and the part they have played in Finland's past.

Historical Ties to Sweden and Russia.   Finland's history as an independent nation is relatively brief. For many centuries it was a part of Sweden. Even today, about one Finn in every 12 speaks Swedish at home. Swedish and Finnish have equal recognition as official languages.

In 1809, after a Russian victory over Sweden, Finland fell under Russian rule. Following the chaos of Russia's Bolshevik revolution of 1917, Finland became an independent nation for the first time—but not without fighting a brief civil war. During the civil war, Germany helped the winning side and Russia helped the losing side. Finland became a democratic republic, with an elected president and parliament.

The start of World War II in 1939 found Finland and its Baltic neighbors, Estonia, Latvia, and Lithuania, pinched between two mighty powers. To the southwest was Nazi Germany. To the east was the Soviet Union. Soviet troops marched into all four nations. While the Soviets were able to occupy and annex the three Baltic states, Finland put up a strong resistance. In the Winter War of 1939–1940, crack Finnish ski troops battled against the invading Soviet army. The Soviets were able only to seize a part of Finland known as southern Karelia and to place a naval base on Finland's southern coast. Most of Finland remained unoccupied by foreign troops.

The German Nazis used Finnish territory in their attack on the Soviet Union in 1941. Finland then resumed its war against the Soviet Union. It managed to reoccupy the lost Finnish lands and take some Soviet land as well. However, the Soviet Union recaptured all the lands before the war ended. In a treaty signed in 1947, Finland accepted the loss of southern Karelia and agreed to pay reparations, or war damages, valued at several hundred million dollars. An estimated 400,000 Finns moved out of the lost territories into Finland.

"Finlandization."   Aware of its precarious position in the shadow of the Soviet Union, Finland adopted a cautious policy throughout the Cold War. Officially neutral, the Finnish government leaned over backward to avoid antagonizing Soviet leaders. It signed a friendship treaty with the Soviet Union in 1948 and renewed it every eight or ten years. On various occasions, the Soviet Union applied pressure and forced changes in Finnish policy. This situation led to the coining of a new word, **Finlandization**, describing the situation of a small nation that carefully avoids doing anything that might anger a larger neighbor.

While pacifying the Soviets, Finland managed to keep its independence and its democratic institutions. It joined the United Nations, cultivated ties with its Scandinavian neighbors, and became a member of the European Free Trade Association. It also gained unique advantages as a trading partner of the Soviet Union. Finnish companies grew rich selling products that ranged from shoes and clothing to giant icebreakers to the Soviets. (Icebreakers are ships that plow through winter ice and clear a path so other ships can reach ice-bound ports.) In exchange, the Soviet Union supplied Finland with much-needed oil, gas, and other raw materials. Finland also traded heavily with such western nations as Sweden, Germany, and Britain.

The Finnish Economy.   Like Sweden, Finland has a capitalist economy, although its companies are much smaller than Sweden's. Finland is a major exporter of forest products such as sawn timber, newsprint, paper, and plywood. The need to pay war reparations to the Soviet Union spurred the development of metal-fabricating and engineering industries after World War II. Today most of Finland's people work in manufacturing or service industries, with fewer than 10 percent in agriculture or forestry. The country has many dairy farms, with a large proportion of farmland producing hay and fodder for animal feed.

Multiparty Government.   Like Sweden, Finland uses a system of proportional representation that favors the multiplication of political parties. As many as 10 parties may hold seats in parliament at any one time. The three largest groups are the Center party, the Social Democratic party, and the Conservative party. Over the years they have alternated in power, forming coalitions with one another and with smaller parties. Finland's president, elected for a term of six years, has considerable power. The president can temporarily veto bills passed by parliament and can dissolve parliament and call new elections.

Finnish folk dancers perform in Helsinki. Elaborate costumes are essential to many folk dances, whose traditions are passed from one generation to the next.

Eyes on Russia.   The end of the Cold War and the breakup of the Soviet Union put an official end to Finlandization. In 1992, Russia and Finland signed a new friendship treaty promising to treat one another as equals. Finland then felt free to apply for membership in the European Community—a step Finland had earlier avoided, fearing the Soviet Union would see it as an unfriendly act.

But the economic turmoil that resulted from the Soviet Union's breakup caused considerable hardship for Finland. Finnish exports dropped sharply. Hundreds of Finnish firms went bankrupt. Unemployment soared.

The Finnish people still keep a wary eye to the east. Russia remains a gigantic and unpredictable neighbor. Political unrest in Russia, or the adoption of hard-line policies by Russia's government, would seriously affect Finland. While some Finns have urged their government to demand a return of the Karelian lands seized by Russia in World War II, the government has acted with caution. It has, however, said it would encourage Finnish companies to develop business with Russian Karelia.

THE BALTIC STATES

The three Baltic nations—Estonia, Latvia, and Lithuania—were part of the Russian empire before gaining their independence at the end of World War I. They enjoyed barely 20 years of independence before the Soviet Union annexed them in 1940. For the next 51 years, they were part of the Soviet Union.

During that time the three republics underwent great changes. Picturesque old cities grew into modern centers of industry. Communist authorities abolished small family farms, replacing them with large state farms (where farmers were paid employees of the government) and collective farms (where farmers pooled their lands and shared machinery). The texture of the population changed too, as large numbers of Russians moved into the Baltic region.

Since regaining their independence in 1991, the Baltic nations have been struggling to forge a new life. They are not finding the task easy.

Land and People.   All three nations have extensive areas of farmland and forest. Mineral resources tend to be scarce. However, Estonia has the good fortune to possess oil shale, or oil-bearing rock that can be crushed to produce fuels. Estonia's oil shale is converted to gas. A pipeline carries the gas westward to Estonia's capital, Tallinn, and east-

Estonians in Tallinn gather signatures in favor of voting to secede from the Soviet Union, August 1989. Two years later the nation regained its independence.

ward to the Russian city of St. Petersburg. All three Baltic nations have deposits of peat—pressed organic matter that is formed in swampy areas where plants like grasses and mosses die and accumulate over the centuries. Power plants burn the peat to produce electricity.

The current borders of the Baltic nations are a result of centuries of push-and-shove among the nations of the region. One of the three nations, Lithuania, was once a strong military power. In the 1300s and 1400s, Lithuanian armies drove east almost to Moscow and south as far as the Black Sea. Then, for centuries, Lithuania and Poland were joined together, and upper-class Lithuanians spoke mainly Polish. During Lithuania's brief interlude of independence between the world wars, its present capital, Vilnius, was part of Poland.

Russian influence on the region was strong under the old czarist empire and during the time the area was part of the Soviet Union. In the 1960s the Communist authorities built factories on the outskirts of Latvia's capital, Riga, and brought in ethnic Russians to work in the factories. One result is that Riga and other Latvian cities now have more Russian inhabitants than Latvians. Indeed, Russians make up a significant portion of the total population in all three Baltic nations—32 percent in Latvia, 27 percent in Estonia, and 8 percent in Lithuania. Many, if not most, of those Russians cannot speak the local language.

Citizenship and Government. In 1991, after each Baltic republic had regained its independence, one of the first questions facing the new legislatures was, Who will be entitled to citizenship? Some wanted to restrict citizenship to people who had lived in the country in 1940 and their descendants. Others favored citizenship for all who were residents in 1991, when independence was reclaimed. Still others proposed a language test, restricting citizenship to people who could speak Estonian, Latvian, or Lithuanian. The issue of citizenship had far-reaching implications. Not only would it determine who could vote, but also who could own property and hold public office.

All three of the Baltic nations set out to write democratic constitutions that would provide new institutions of government. New political parties formed and announced their platforms, though political power remained in a state of flux. However, each of the Baltic nations hoped to improve on the record of the period between World Wars I and II, when all three suffered military coups and periods of authoritarian rule.

Untangling Economic Ties. Under Soviet control, the economies of the Baltic states became closely intertwined with the economies of other Soviet republics. The Soviet republics supplied oil, grain, and industrial raw materials at prices that were low by world standards. In return, the Baltic nations shipped eastward such products as textiles, consumer goods, meat, and fish.

Such interdependence had many advantages. The Baltic nations enjoyed standards of living much higher than those in the rest of the Soviet Union. But there were also disadvantages. For example, Baltic factories depended on Soviet supplies of raw materials. The coming of independence in 1991 coincided with economic turmoil in Russia and other former Soviet republics. Many Baltic factories could no longer get the supplies they needed. They tried desperately to find new suppliers in Europe and elsewhere. Meanwhile, living standards in the Baltic republics dropped while competition for supplies became fierce.

Under Soviet rule, industries in the Baltic republics were owned and run by the state. Post-independence governments set out to **privatize** major industries—that is, sell them off to private investors. But few Estonians, Latvians, or Lithuanians had enough money to buy a big factory. So the new governments sought to interest foreign investors in them as well.

Hope for the Future. Serious challenges lay ahead for the reborn Baltic nations. But leaders remained confident that they could meet the challenges. They recalled how, in the fading days of Soviet rule, hundreds of thousands of Estonians had poured into Tallinn's Song Festival Arena. They had stayed for a week, singing lustily day and night in a show of determination to regain Estonia's independence. With that same spirit, the Baltic peoples are building a new life, restructuring their economies, and attempting to develop strong and lasting democratic institutions of government.

OTHER COUNTRIES OF NORTHERN EUROPE

The remaining countries of Northern Europe have much in common with Sweden. They share Sweden's Scandinavian culture and Lutheran religion. They share Sweden's prosperity. And they share its long commitment to democracy. Unlike Sweden, Finland, and the Baltic nations, they have all been allies of the United States within NATO.

Norway. Sharing the Scandinavian peninsula with Sweden, Norway has much the same rugged terrain and climate. However, offshore oil and gas deposits have allowed Norway to become an exporter of energy. Norway's industries make such products as steel, ships, and skis. The country is a constitutional monarchy like Sweden.

Denmark. Situated on a number of islands and a peninsula that juts north from the European mainland, Denmark is separated from Norway and Sweden by two narrow straits. Ships must pass through those straits to go from the Atlantic Ocean into the Baltic Sea. Denmark is a major exporter of agricultural products such as ham, bacon, and cheese, and has many modern industries. Denmark occupies only one ninth as much land as Norway, but its population of 5.1 million is slightly larger. It, too, is a constitutional monarchy.

Iceland. If you could move the state of Kentucky into the North Atlantic, fill it with volcanoes, and sprinkle glaciers and icebergs around, you would come up with something like Iceland. Fishing and whaling are the traditional occupations of Icelanders. More recently, Iceland has dammed its rivers and used hydroelectric power for aluminum smelting, which requires large amounts of energy. Iceland is a republic, with an elected president and a parliament.

REVIEWING THE CHAPTER

I. Building Your Vocabulary

In your notebook, for each term in Column A, write the best description in Column B.

Column A	*Column B*
1. coalition	a. a watchdog to protect the public
2. unicameral	b. policy of a small nation trying not to anger a larger neighbor
3. Finlandization	c. a system of electing people to parliament that gives many parties seats
4. ombudsman	d. an alliance of parties to run a government
5. proportional representation	e. (a legislature) having one chamber

II. Understanding the Facts

In your notebook, write the letter of the word or phrase that best completes each of the following sentences.

1. Which of the following is *not* a characteristic of Sweden's welfare state?
   a. Negotiations between labor unions and employers are highly centralized.
   b. Most major industries are owned by the government.
   c. Taxes are very high.

2. Sweden is a major exporter of:
   a. petroleum and fish products.
   b. aluminum and textiles.
   c. forest products and steel.

3. During World War II, Finland:
   a. fought alongside the Allies against Nazi Germany.
   b. went to war against the Soviet Union.
   c. remained neutral and uninvolved.

4. The Baltic country that was once joined to Poland and whose people are mainly Roman Catholics is:
  a. Estonia   **b.** Latvia   **c.** Lithuania.

III. Thinking It Through

In your notebook, write the letter of the word or phrase that best completes each of the following sentences.

  1. One possible reason for Sweden's not having applied sooner to join the European Community (EC) is that:
  a. Sweden wanted to remain neutral in the Cold War.
  b. Sweden was not much interested in foreign trade.
  c. Sweden's standard of living was lower than that of EC nations.

  2. The "Finlandization" of Finland came about mainly because:
  a. the Soviet Union wanted to take land away from Finland.
  b. Finland was a small, weak nation next to a large, strong one.
  c. the Finns favored the Russians over the Swedes.

  3. A possible reason for Sweden's low infant death rate may be that:
  a. all Swedes have access to free or low-cost medical care.
  b. something about Sweden's climate gives babies immunity to disease.
  c. not many babies are born in Sweden.

  4. A common problem shared by Finland and the Baltic states is that:
  a. they have no resources upon which to build a modern economy.
  b. all their ports are closed by ice during the winter.
  c. their economies became heavily dependent on trade with Soviet republics.

DEVELOPING CRITICAL THINKING SKILLS

1. Evaluate the pros and cons of Sweden's welfare state. If you were a Swede, would you want to make changes in the welfare state? Explain. In your opinion, what lessons should the United States draw from Sweden's experience with its welfare policies? Explain your reasoning.

2. The multiparty political system of Sweden is quite different from the two-party system of the United States. How does the Swedish voting system contribute to the multiplication of political parties? Would you favor or oppose a multiparty system for the United States? Why?

3. How has the presence of large numbers of Russian inhabitants affected the Baltic nations? Discuss three approaches to determining citizenship in the Baltic republics, giving arguments for and against each approach.

INTERPRETING A GRAPH

The bar graphs below show the percentage of the gross domestic product (GDP) in various countries that is collected by the government in taxes. Study the graphs and then answer the questions that follow.

1. Which of the Northern European countries for which data is provided has the lowest taxes? Which country has the highest taxes?

2. How many times higher is the proportion of GDP taken by taxes in Sweden than in the United States?

3. Which of the countries collect more than one half of GDP in taxes? Which collect between one third and one half of GDP in taxes?

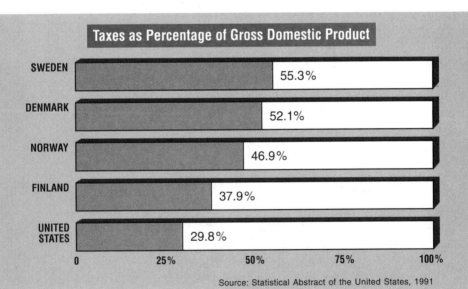

Taxes as Percentage of Gross Domestic Product

SWEDEN	55.3%
DENMARK	52.1%
NORWAY	46.9%
FINLAND	37.9%
UNITED STATES	29.8%

0   25%   50%   75%   100%

Source: Statistical Abstract of the United States, 1991

INTERPRETING A CHART

Study the chart on page 179. Then answer the following questions.

1. What country of Northern Europe has the largest population? The smallest?

2. Rank the three Baltic republics in order of population, from most to least populous.

3. Which country, Denmark or Sweden, has the greater density of population (that is, people per square mile)?

4. How many years is a newborn male in Iceland expected to live? A newborn female?

5. Leaving out Latvia, rank the countries of the region according to the average income of their people, from richest to poorest.

ENRICHMENT AND EXPLORATION

1. Prepare a class program on the cultural contributions of Northern Europe to the world. Divide the class into three groups. Have one group work on music, one on literature, and one on art and architecture. The program should include recordings of music by Northern European performers or composers, readings from literature, and photographs of art and architecture.

2. Research and write a report on the role of the ombudsman in Sweden and other countries. Include ways in which the concept of ombudsman has been put into practice within the United States.

3. Use your school library to find out more about Alfred Nobel and the Nobel prizes he established. Make a bulletin board display showing the achievements of recent Nobel prize winners.

4. Using almanacs and other resource books, make a chart showing infant death rates (also called *infant mortality*) in the United States, Northern Europe, and other parts of the world. Find information about the various factors that contribute to high death rates among infants, and include it with your chart.

5. Make a bulletin board display of newspaper and magazine clippings about recent developments in Estonia, Latvia, and Lithuania. Include information about how people of Baltic heritage in the United States have reacted to developments in the Baltic region.

9 Western Europe

In 1066, when Duke William wanted to take his army of Normans from France across the English Channel to England (see page 61), he had to build a vast armada of ships. Today's travelers have it much easier. Ferries and airplanes crisscross the channel at frequent intervals. After 1993, passenger and freight trains can speed back and forth through the underwater **Chunnel** (channel tunnel) connecting southern England with northern France.

Britain and France are the anchors of Western Europe. For centuries the British were separated by the English Channel from the rest of Europe. They turned their backs to Europe and instead built an empire in Asia, Africa, and the Americas. During those same centuries, France built its own overseas empire in many of the same regions. Britain and France were more often enemies than friends.

Times have changed. Since the end of World War II, Britain and France have had to give up their empires. In the 1950s, France was one of the founding members of the European Community. Britain became a member in 1973, and since then its links to the continent have grown close. Britain has "joined Europe" in more ways than one.

THE REGION

Western Europe contains four independent countries besides Britain and France. The Republic of Ireland is an independent nation on an island within the British Isles. On the European continent, northeast of France, lie three other small nations—Belgium, the Netherlands, and Luxembourg. All six of Western Europe's nations belong to the European Community. All but Ireland belong to NATO, the North Atlantic Treaty Organization.

200

The Six Countries. The countries of Western Europe vary greatly in size and shape. France is by far the largest, occupying about four fifths as much territory as Texas. The *United Kingdom of Great Britain and Northern Ireland,* as Britain is officially known, is roughly the size of Oregon. It is less than half as large as France. All of the region's other countries are smaller yet. The smallest, Luxembourg, would fit comfortably within Rhode Island.

Many of the countries of Western Europe have been pieced together over the years from smaller territories. The United Kingdom contains four distinct parts: England, Wales, Scotland, and Northern Ireland. France is a patchwork of ancient kingdoms and duchies with such historic names as Normandy, Burgundy, and Aquitaine (AK-wuh-tayn). Other countries of the region also have provinces and other subdivisions with distinctive histories and outlooks.

You should note that the name Ireland applies both to an island and to a republic. They are not the same. The republic of Ireland occupies about five sixths of the island of Ireland. The remaining sixth, called Northern Ireland, is part of the United Kingdom.

Some Facts About Western European Countries

COUNTRY	CAPITAL CITY	POPULATION (millions)	AREA (square miles)	PER CAPITA INCOME (U.S. dollars)	LIFE EXPECTANCY AT BIRTH
Belgium	Brussels (BRUS • uhlz)	9.9	11,781	$ 17,000	70 M 77 F
France	Paris (PAR • is)	56.7	211,208	14,600	72 M 80 F
Great Britain	London (LUHN • duhn)	57.5	94,247	14,300	72 M 78 F
Ireland	Dublin (DUHB • luhn)	3.6	27,136	8,900	72 M 78 F
Luxembourg	Luxembourg (LUHK • suhm • burg)	0.4	999	17,200	71 M 78 F
Netherlands	Amsterdam* (AM • stuhr • dam)	15.0	16,041	18,000	74 M 81 F

M = Male
F = Female
*Amsterdam is the Netherlands' official capital, but the seat of government is The Hague.

Sources: 1992 Information Please Almanac; World Almanac and Book of Facts, 1992

The Land.   Large areas of Western Europe are lowlands, with relatively flat land that is ideal for farming. Indeed, half of the Netherlands is so flat and low that it lies below sea level. (The name *Netherlands* means *Low Country*.) By building dikes to hold back the sea, the people of the Netherlands, known as the *Dutch*, have been able to expand their country's area over the years.

There are beautiful highland areas in western and northern Britain, in Ireland, and in central and southern France. By and large, these highlands are ancient mountains, worn down over the centuries into gentle slopes and valleys. Western Europe's most rugged terrain lies in France. It is found in the Pyrenees Mountains of the southwest, along France's border with Spain, and in the Alps of the southeast, along the French–Swiss and French–Italian borders.

The principal river of the region, and of Central Europe as well, is the Rhine (see page 6). The Rhine starts in Switzerland and flows north through Germany. For about 100 miles it forms the border between Germany and France. The Rhine enters the North Sea at the Dutch port of Rotterdam, which handles more freight than any other port in Europe. Other important rivers include the Thames in England and the Seine, Loire, Garonne, and Rhône in France (see pages 7–9). Canals link major rivers, and barges use the waterways to move bulky products like coal and iron.

Although Western Europe lies at high latitudes, almost all of it is closer to the equator than Northern Europe. Northern Scotland is at roughly the same latitude as Denmark (58° N). That line of latitude passes through North America at about the middle of Canada's Hudson Bay. Southern France is at about the same latitude as Boston (between 42° and 43° N).

The climate of the region is somewhat milder than these northerly latitudes might suggest. The reason is that warm waters, originating thousands of miles away in the Caribbean Sea, sweep north and east across the Atlantic in a pattern known as the Gulf Stream. The warm waters help to moderate the temperature of the air that sweeps off the Atlantic over Western Europe. That is why British winters are mild and have much more rain than snow. Temperatures around London rarely dip as low as 20° F. (–7° C.), and Britain's southwest coast may go an entire winter without frost.

The People.   The main languages spoken in Western Europe are English (in Britain and the Republic of Ireland), French (in France, Luxembourg, and southern Belgium), and Dutch or Flemish (in the

Much of England is gently rolling countryside. Here the green fields and meadows of Shropshire, a county in western England, stretch into the distance.

Netherlands and northern Belgium). (See map, page 181.) Some people in Luxembourg speak a Germanic tongue called Luxembourgish.

Belgium is sharply divided along linguistic lines. The two parts of Belgium are Flanders, where people speak Flemish, and Wallonia, where people speak French. The Flemish speakers and the French speakers of Belgium have a history of quarreling over almost everything. Even Belgium's political parties have split into Flemish-speaking and French-speaking halves. But somehow the country manages to muddle through. The nation's capital, Brussels, although it lies 20 miles inside Flanders, is officially bilingual.

The ethnic mixture of Western Europe has been shaped by centuries of conquest and intermarriage. Celtic (KEL-tik) peoples who dominated the region before Roman times still live in the region today. In the British Isles, they include the Irish, the Scottish, and the Welsh. In France, they include the Bretons—the people of Brittany, in France's northwest. Many people of Celtic heritage proudly speak their traditional languages (whether Irish, Scottish Gaelic, Welsh, or Breton) instead of English or French. If you visited places like Wales or Ireland, you could hear Celtic languages spoken on the streets and on radio and television.

The Economy. Western Europe is richly endowed with natural resources. Vast coalfields underlie various parts of Britain, and another major coal region stretches from Belgium into northeastern France. In the same general areas iron, copper, and other valuable minerals are found. While miners have been digging out the coal and metals for centuries, reserves of oil and gas have been tapped only recently. The main

203

sources lie beneath the North Sea, off the east coast of Scotland and England. Smaller oil and gas supplies are found off Ireland's coast and in the continental countries.

The region's mineral wealth has been both a blessing and a curse. It has been a blessing because the plentiful coal and iron allowed the region (especially Britain) to take the lead in the Industrial Revolution. That, in turn, brought economic prosperity to many areas. The negative part is that mining and burning of coal took a heavy toll on the environment. The cities of Britain in the 1800s were among the grimmest and dirtiest the world has ever known. So depressing were the sooty buildings of Birmingham, England, that Queen Victoria ordered the shades drawn on the windows of the royal train whenever she passed through. Vigorous efforts in recent years have scrubbed away much of the soot and begun to attack other forms of environmental pollution.

Today, all the countries of Western Europe have industrial economies with high standards of living. Even Ireland, the poorest land in the region, ranks among the world's top 30 countries in per capita income.

Customers browse at one of the famous bookstalls along Paris's River Seine. Part of the medieval cathedral of Notre Dame can be seen in the background.

Many Attractions.   Of the 7 million or so Americans who visit Europe each year, a large proportion stop in Western Europe. The region boasts an almost endless array of attractions. It has prehistoric monuments, ancient battlegrounds, and palaces dripping with history. It has art museums, concert halls, dance halls, and cabarets. It has luxurious restaurants, sporting events, and holiday resorts.

Many of the chief attractions are in the national capitals. Those are: London, England (population 9.1 million); Paris, France (2.1 million); Brussels, Belgium (1 million); Amsterdam, the Netherlands (695,000); Dublin, Ireland (550,000); and Luxembourg (80,000). Besides being the capital of Belgium, Brussels is the principal seat of the European Community.

GREAT BRITAIN: NEW REALITIES

For two or three centuries, the British Empire stretched far and wide, bringing Britain prosperity and power of immense proportions. "The sun never sets on the British Empire" was a popular expression in the 1800s. It was true, for when it was nighttime in Britain, it was daylight in some other part of the empire. London, at the center of the empire, became a political and financial center of world renown. Britain led the world in trade. Its ships "ruled the waves."

Two world wars and changes in technology undercut British power. Today the British Empire is gone, succeeded by a commonwealth of equal and independent nations. Though British people earn more today than ever before, other nations have surged ahead. Among the six nations of Western Europe, Britain ranks fifth in per capita income (see chart on page 201).

The United Kingdom.   The United Kingdom of Great Britain and Northern Ireland has a long and complex history. Three of its four parts, England, Scotland, and Wales, lie on the island of Great Britain. The fourth part, Northern Ireland, is, appropriately, in the northern part of the island of Ireland. The core of the kingdom is England—a land invaded in turn by Celts, Romans, Jutes, Angles, Saxons, Frisians, Vikings, and Normans. After the Norman Conquest of 1066—the last successful invasion of Great Britain—English kings began to build up their power. In the 1300s, they attached Wales, in the west of the island, to England. In 1707, the two kingdoms of England and Scotland, which had had the same monarch since 1603, joined to form the kingdom of Great Britain.

A conquered Ireland was attached in 1801, creating the United Kingdom of Great Britain and Ireland. In 1921 the Irish Republic, which makes up most of the island, gained its independence. However, Britain retained control of Northern Ireland. Those are the boundaries the United Kingdom has today.

Most of the people in the United Kingdom are Protestants. In England and Wales, the Church of England (or Anglican Church) is the official church. The official Church of Scotland is Presbyterian. Roman Catholics are a minority in all parts of the United Kingdom. There is a small Jewish population. In recent decades there have been many Muslim immigrants from Pakistan and other Islamic countries.

Pomp, Pageantry, and Parliamentary Rule. The roots of the British monarchy reach far back into history. The monarchs of long ago held great power. But their power was limited by such documents as the Magna Carta of 1215 and the Bill of Rights of 1689. The colorful pageantry of royal ceremonies gives Britons a link to the past and to one another. But the monarch is now a figurehead.

In today's British system, supreme power rests in the hands of Parliament. Britain has no written constitution, so there are no constitutional restraints on Parliament, such as those that apply to the U.S. Congress and President. Fortunately, moderation prevails in British politics, and Britons enjoy most of the freedoms Americans take for granted. But not all. For example, British law imposes limits on the rights of criminal defendants in terrorism cases. In addition, the authorities have wider powers than in the United States to label government documents "secret" and thereby stop the press from reporting about them.

The Two Houses of Parliament. Britain's Parliament is made up two chambers. The lower chamber, the **House of Commons**, is democratically elected. It wields most of the lawmaking power. The weak upper chamber, the **House of Lords**, is not elected. It can amend bills, and it can delay them for one year. But the lower chamber can then pass the bills into law, and the House of Lords has no further say.

The House of Lords is a relic of ancient times. Some of its members are dukes, barons, and others with hereditary titles. Since 1958 its members also have included people who have been named "life peers" for their accomplishments in politics, business, religion, or the arts. Life peers hold seats in the House of Lords until they die, but their seats do not pass on to their descendants.

206

Britain's Parliament meets in this building on the River Thames in London. The chimes of its clock tower, "Big Ben," are imitated by clocks throughout the world.

Britons have long debated the value of the upper chamber. Some scorn it as "an old folks' home" or "a living obituary column," because most of its 1,200 members are elderly. Only a smattering of the members are women, and only a few hundred members take an active part in deliberations. The Labor party has proposed turning the House of Lords into a second elected house. However, defenders of the upper chamber see it as a protector of British liberties. By amending or delaying legislation, it serves as a counterweight to the immense powers of the prime minister and the House of Commons.

British Politics. British members of parliament—that is, of the House of Commons—are called MPs. They are elected in winner-take-all elections in 650 single-member districts. The system of proportional representation is not used. One result is that Britain has essentially a two-party system, with a handful of minor parties. Most of the time, one party has a majority of seats in the House of Commons. Therefore, it can name a prime minister on its own, without coalition rule.

The leader of the majority party becomes prime minister. He or she forms a government by appointing a slate of ministers, all of whom are members of the House of Commons or the House of Lords. The government stays in office until the next election or until it loses a vote of confidence in the House of Commons. The prime minister will also be replaced if the majority party chooses a new leader. For example, in 1990, when the Conservatives held a majority in the House of Commons, party officials chose John Major to replace Margaret Thatcher as party leader. Major automatically took over as prime minister.

The timing of British elections is not fixed, like the every-four-years presidential elections in our own country. Parliamentary elections must be held at least once every five years. But the prime minister can call an election at any time during those five years. Prime ministers try to pick times when public opinion is running in their favor, to improve their chances of victory.

Most of the drama of British government takes place in the House of Commons. Opposing parties sit on facing benches, with an empty aisle between. By ancient tradition, the aisle is the width of two sword blades plus one foot. No one draws a sword in Parliament these days, but verbal darts are something else. The MPs seem quite unruly by U.S. standards. They heckle and jeer their opponents, even the prime minister. If things seem to be getting out of hand, an official bellows "Order! Order!" Traditionally, this official, the **speaker** of the House of Commons, has worn an elaborate wig. (That's why we call an important person a "bigwig.") But in 1992, a woman took over the job for the first time. She gave up the wig for a less formal appearance.

MPs may hoot and shout, but when it comes to voting, British political parties are much more disciplined than American parties. Prime ministers can usually count on support from their party's MPs. Thus, when the British government submits an important bill to the House of Commons, the bill is almost certain to become law.

Political Parties.   The leading parties are the Conservative (or Tory) party and the Labor party. The Conservatives are generally considered pro-business. They favor individual enterprise and limited government. The Laborites draw strong support from British labor unions and working-class voters. Labor traditionally called for socialism, including public ownership of major industries, but it no longer does so. Conservatives have generally worked closely with the United States on foreign policy, while Labor has been more critical of U.S. actions.

Up to the 1920s, the Conservatives alternated in power with another party, the Liberal, or Whig, party. But Labor replaced the Liberals as Britain's second major party. The Liberal party has evolved into the Liberal Democratic party, which is a small, centrist third party today.

Regional Nationalism.   Scottish, Welsh, and Irish factions also have representation within the British party system. Scotland elects 72 MPs to the House of Commons, Wales 38, and Northern Ireland 17.

Small parties like the Scottish National party speak for people who want independence from Britain. Backers of the SNP range from the movie actor Sean Connery to James Mill, a paper-mill worker. Running for a local council seat in a recent election, Mill told a reporter: "I'd rather be out riding my motorcycle. But I see all these other countries in Europe getting their independence and I can't help but say, 'Hey, we want a bit of that too.'"

To fend off the drive for Scottish independence, Britain's Labor party has proposed creating a Scottish parliament. Within Scotland, the new body would take over certain powers from the British Parliament, such as the power to set taxes. Such a handing down of power to a lower level of government is called **devolution**. The Conservative party has opposed devolution.

Northern Ireland already has its own parliament, sitting in the Belfast suburb of Stormont. But violent unrest broke out in Northern Ireland in 1969, and the British government suspended the regional parliament three years later.

In earlier times, British rulers tried to stamp out local languages and cultures. Today, many people are trying to nurture the Welsh, Irish, and Scottish Gaelic languages, and to keep alive the old Celtic traditions. If you traveled through Wales, you would see road signs in Welsh. Many children attend Welsh-language schools, and almost one person in five in Wales can speak the Welsh language. In Scotland, however, fewer than one person in 50 can speak Gaelic.

The British Class System. The British are very aware of social differences revealed by a person's way of speaking. As Irish playwright George Bernard Shaw once remarked, "It is impossible for an Englishman to open his mouth without making some other Englishman despise him." Britain has three main social classes: working, middle, and upper. The working class and the middle class are roughly equal in size. Basically, working-class people work with their hands and middle-class people do not. Only about two people in 100 qualify as upper class. Upper-class people owe their status largely to inherited wealth or titles.

Education. Various aspects of the British educational system help to perpetuate the class system. For example, secondary-school students are directed onto two "tracks." A "grammar-school" track (mainly for the middle class) leads to university. A "general-school" track (mainly for the working class) leads directly to a job or to a postsecondary technical school. A second means by which the class system is maintained is an extensive system of private schools. (Confusingly, the British call these "public" schools. The British term for schools operated by local governments is schools.) Most children of the upper class attend tradition-steeped public schools, such as Eton, Harrow, and Charterhouse. The "old school ties" resulting from such an education knit a network of friendships that helps to hold Britain's upper class together.

However, other aspects of the educational system undermine the class system. For example, government grants permit some students from poorer families to attend select private schools. Scholarships help students from working-class families to pay tuition to British universities. Two British universities, Oxford and Cambridge, are among the world's most respected institutions of higher learning.

The Welfare State. In the late 1940s, as the sun was beginning to set on the British Empire, Britain embarked on a new course at home. It became a welfare state much like Sweden. Medical care became free or nearly so, and the government offered generous social benefits of many sorts. In those days Britain still ranked as Europe's greatest trading nation, and perhaps its richest.

But British industry took a beating during the 1960s and 1970s. Other nations offered cheaper manufactured goods. Many British steel mills and coal mines had to shut down. Unemployment rose sharply. Social ills such as drug addiction spread. So did slums.

Margaret Thatcher, a Conservative who served as prime minister from 1979 to 1990, diagnosed the problem as "too much government." Thatcher trimmed back government programs. She sold off government shares in such industries as airlines, telephones, water and gas supply, auto manufacturing, and oil. She worked to hold down taxes.

The Thatcher government revised but did not end the welfare state. For example, it introduced free-market principles to public housing. The government encouraged residents of public housing to buy the apartments they had been renting, and thus become homeowners.

Thatcher and her successor, John Major, also revamped the National Health Service (NHS). The NHS is the branch of government that administers medical care. Britons can use NHS doctors and hospitals at little or no cost—but they may have to wait a year or more for elective surgery (that is, surgery for conditions that are not life-threatening). Britons who can afford private medical care get quicker service at the many nonpublic health facilities. Per capita spending on health care is about one third as much as in the United States.

Adapting Britain's Economy. Thatcher, Major, and other British leaders have tried to adapt to the world's changing conditions. They have encouraged new, high-tech industries like electronics. They have stressed service industries such as banking and insurance. (The insurance organization known as Lloyd's of London underwrites policies throughout the world.)

By entering the European Community in 1973, Britain sought to end its economic decline and avoid being shut out of the wider European market. But Britain's relations with the EC have been prickly. British leaders have worked to slow the EC's drive toward fuller monetary and political union, fearing a loss of British sovereignty and a weakening of British ties to the Commonwealth.

IRELAND

Because of its lush green pastures and natural beauty, Ireland is called the "Emerald Isle." But life in Ireland has seldom been easy. In the 1840s, for example, a failure of the potato crop caused a famine that killed 500,000 Irish and forced more than a million to emigrate, mainly to the United States. More recently, political violence has seldom been far away.

The Irish refer to the political violence that has simmered in Northern Ireland since 1969 as "the Troubles." If you asked people to explain the causes of the Troubles, you would hear many answers—often conflicting. Some would mention British colonialism and the Irish struggle for self-rule. Some would dwell on religious differences between Roman Catholics and Protestants. Still others would draw attention to social differences that divide rich from poor and middle class from working class. All of these contribute to the Troubles. But before we discuss them, let's get an overview of the two parts of the island—the republic of Ireland, and Northern Ireland.

The Land. Ireland is rainy, even more so than England. Almost all of Ireland has rain at least 175 days a year (every second day), and some parts of western Ireland get rain two days out of three. The rain makes the grass grow, so Ireland's many cows and sheep can eat heartily. But farmers have a hard time growing crops such as grain, which require dry weather for harvesting. So most Irish farmland is meadows and pastures.

Ireland's physical layout features a large central plain surrounded by hills and low mountains. About one seventh of the land is marshy. Thus, conditions for the formation of peat are ideal. Peat bogs provide fuel for Irish homes and power stations.

The People.   The island of Ireland contains 5.2 million people. Of those, 3.6 million live in the republic and 1.6 million in Northern Ireland. Religious differences between the two parts of the island are sharp. In the republic, the overwhelming majority is Roman Catholic. In Northern Ireland, on the other hand, Protestants outnumber Catholics two to one. Many of the Protestants are the descendants of English, Scottish, and Welsh settlers.

At the time of Irish independence in the 1920s, Northern Ireland chose to remain part of the United Kingdom. Northern Ireland is sometimes called **Ulster,** because it includes six of the nine counties of the old Irish province of that name.

Ireland has a high birth rate, and economic opportunities are limited. Therefore, many people leave. Millions of settlers came from Ireland to North America in the 1800s, and hundreds of thousands of workers have gone to other European countries in recent decades. While emigration has allowed Ireland to supplement its income and avoid overpopulation, it has been painful for Irish families. Mary Robinson, elected president of the republic in 1990, declared that she "would always have a candle" lit in the presidential mansion in memory of those who had left Ireland.

The Economy.   Both the republic and Northern Ireland have many farmers, although year by year the number shrinks. In the republic at the start of the 1990s, one worker in every six was on a farm.

Tourism is important in both Northern Ireland and the republic. The two parts of the island have struggled to develop other industries. Modest oil supplies have been discovered beneath Irish territorial waters, and oil companies are trying to find more. Offshore wells supply the republic with generous quantities of natural gas.

"The Troubles."   The turmoil in Northern Ireland began after demonstrations in 1968 by Roman Catholics demanding greater civil rights and economic opportunities. Riots broke out. Soon, extremists in both Catholic and Protestant communities resorted to violence. A paramilitary (military-style) organization called the Irish Republican Army (IRA) launched a campaign of terror. Its goal: to break Northern Ireland's ties with Britain and unite it with the republic of Ireland. The IRA drew its name from the leading Irish nationalist organization fighting the British in the 1910s and 1920s. Most of its members were Catholics. On the Protestant side, paramilitary groups called the Ulster Volunteer Force and the Ulster Freedom Fighters also resorted to terror.

212

Looking out for snipers, British troops dash across the street in a troubled area of Belfast, the capital of Northern Ireland, in 1981.

The IRA set off bombs—in Northern Ireland, in England, even at British army bases on the European continent. Often the bombs killed innocent people. Shootings and assassinations multiplied on both sides. By the 1990s, the Troubles had taken some 3,000 lives.

The republic of Ireland publicly denounced the IRA and deplored the violence. Like Britain, it forbade the publication or broadcast of statements by the paramilitary groups or their political wings.

In 1985, Britain and the republic of Ireland signed a formal promise to work together to restore peace to Northern Ireland. Under this Anglo-Irish Agreement, Britain and Ireland began holding regular meetings to discuss possible solutions. Many **Unionists**, those who wish to maintain the union with Great Britain, object to giving the republic a say in Northern Ireland's affairs. They see it as the first step to a takeover of Northern Ireland by the republic. However, the British government has said it will not permit unification unless Northern Ireland's voters agree.

The Troubles have seriously disrupted Northern Ireland's economy, as businesses refrain from investing in the troubled region. Many people are jobless, especially in Catholic neighborhoods. Northern Ireland's political parties have been trying to find a compromise that might restore peace so that people can resume normal lives.

CASE STUDY:

The Irish "Troubles" in Poetry

Irish poets and songwriters have written many verses from many points of view about the "Troubles." The following poem by Seamus Heaney is about British troops on Irish soil.

The Toome Road

One morning early I met armoured cars
In convoy, warbling along on powerful tyres,
All camouflaged with broken alder branches,
And headphoned soldiers standing up in turrets.
How long were they approaching down my roads
As if they owned them? The whole country was sleeping.
I had rights-of-way, fields, cattle in my keeping,
Tractors hitched to buckrakes in open sheds,
Silos, chill gates, wet slates, the greens and reds
Of outhouse roofs. Whom should I run to tell
Among all of those with their back doors on the latch
For the bringer of bad news, that small-hours visitant
Who, by being expected, might be kept distant? . . .
O charioteers, above your dormant guns,
It stands here still, stands as vibrant as you pass,
The invisible, untoppled omphalos.

From "The Toome Road," in *Field Work*, by Seamus Heaney. New York: Farrar, Strauss, & Giroux, 1979.

1. The speaker in the poem contrasts the warlike military equipment of the soldiers with the peaceful agricultural equipment of his farm. What are some examples of each?

2. *On the latch* means with doors unlocked. Why do people have their back doors on the latch? What will the speaker tell them?

3. The omphalos is a stone marking the central point of the world. What is the speaker saying about the place where the poem takes place? To whom is he saying it? Explain.

214

FRANCE: THE FIFTH REPUBLIC

On the continent, France went through its own time of troubles in the late 1950s. Bitter disputes set one group of French citizens against another. Finally, Charles de Gaulle stepped forward. De Gaulle was a general who had led Free French forces during World War II (see page 148) and had then retired. Called to power in 1958 at the age of 67, de Gaulle put down a revolt and averted civil war. He gave the French a new constitution and new political institutions. Because de Gaulle's constitution is the fifth since the French Revolution of 1789, the present framework of government is called the **Fifth Republic**.

De Gaulle and Algeria. In May 1958, France was in turmoil. Its colonial empire had begun to crumble, first in Indochina, then in North Africa. Now, in the North African territory of Algeria, Islamic nationalists were fighting a guerrilla war for independence. A million French settlers in Algeria were terrified that France would withdraw its 500,000 troops and abandon them. In Paris, the government leaders were unable to take decisive action as one weak government succeeded another.

The crisis came to a head on May 13, when a band of soldiers and civilians seized power in Algeria. Their goal: to keep Algeria French. Too weak to put down the revolt, and fearful of civil war in France itself, the French politicians turned to de Gaulle. Parliament agreed to give him exceptional powers for six months. On June 1, de Gaulle took office as **premier**, the French equivalent of prime minister.

Three days later, in the Algerian capital of Algiers, Charles de Gaulle stood on a balcony, ramrod straight, with a look of grim determination on his face. Before him, a delirious crowd chanted, "Al-gé-rie fran-çaise" (AL-ZHAY-REE-FRAWN-SEZ)—"French Algeria." The crowd, mostly French settlers, saw de Gaulle as the man who would keep Algeria French. Slowly and dramatically, de Gaulle raised his arms. "I have understood you," de Gaulle shouted—and the crowd roared back its approval. But de Gaulle's actions would disappoint the settlers.

For de Gaulle understood that France could no longer cling to the past, that its colonial empire was doomed. Even Algeria, which technically was considered a part of the French nation, could not be held against the will of most of its 10 million people. By fits and starts, de Gaulle worked out a settlement with Algeria's Muslim rebels. In 1962, French voters approved Algerian independence, and French settlers began streaming back to France. De Gaulle also set in motion a process that led to the independence of French colonies elsewhere in Africa.

Charles de Gaulle, speaking to a group of reporters, makes a point in the emphatic way that was typical of him.

Only a man of de Gaulle's towering moral stature could have pulled it off. In 1940 he had won the respect of his fellow citizens by rallying the French to continue battling the German Nazis, even after the French government and armed forces had surrendered. But respect did not necessarily mean love. Many people objected to his stubbornness and to his drive to return France to "greatness." Still, those very characteristics permitted de Gaulle to leave his mark on France.

A Strong Presidency. Referring to one of France's many political parties, de Gaulle once scoffed: "Oh, yes, that party with six members and seven tendencies!" The remark summed up de Gaulle's dislike of the Fourth Republic's "regime of the parties," in which governments rose and fell through a succession of wobbly coalitions. He shaped the constitution of the Fifth Republic to assure stability and order in government. Voters approved the constitution in a referendum in the fall of 1958.

Today in France, power centers in the presidency. De Gaulle held the position himself from 1959 to 1969. His "Gaullist" political party remained strong even after de Gaulle stepped down. In 1981, the voters elected François Mitterand (mee-tehr-RAWN), a Socialist. He won re-election in 1988.

In the past, election procedures allowed many small parties to flourish. Under the Fifth Republic, the rules favor larger and more powerful parties. Often, one party or another has a majority in the National Assembly, without having to piece together a coalition with other parties. The principal parties are the Socialists, the Gaullists, the Centrists, and the Communists.

What Role for France?   De Gaulle's determination to maintain French "greatness" made for difficult relations with the United States and other NATO allies. De Gaulle withdrew French troops from the unified NATO command. He made sure France developed its own nuclear striking force. Even after de Gaulle's retirement, France continued to take an independent line in foreign and defense policy.

While the era of French colonialism in Africa has come to an end, France maintains close trading ties with its former possessions. French troops remain in many African countries at the invitation of host governments. Meanwhile, French rule persists in such far-flung territories as New Caledonia and French Polynesia in the Pacific, Réunion (ray-oo-NYAWN) in the Indian Ocean, Guadeloupe (gwah-duh-LOOP) and Martinique (mahr-tuh-NEEK) in the Caribbean, and French Guiana in South America.

As a founding member of the European Community, France has been working to shape Europe's future. It has insisted on EC rules that allow generous subsidies for farmers. As a result, France turns out mountains of butter and other products, which it then sells at bargain prices on world markets. The United States has often protested against such policies, which make it harder for American farmers to sell their own products overseas.

THE BENELUX NATIONS

In 1948, Belgium, the Netherlands, and Luxembourg formed a **customs union** known as Benelux, from the first letters of each country's name. Within a customs union, member nations allow products to move back and forth across borders without taxes or tariffs. The Benelux nations later removed other barriers to the movement of goods, people, and capital across their common borders. These were important steps. They helped to set the pattern for the wider European Community that now includes the Benelux nations plus nine others.

Belgium, the Netherlands, and Luxembourg remain separate nations with distinct identities. All three are democratic monarchies. Belgium and the Netherlands are kingdoms. The current sovereigns are King Baudouin (boh-DWAN) I of the Belgians and Queen Beatrix of the Netherlands. Little Luxembourg is a **grand duchy**. That means its sovereign is a grand duke or duchess—currently Grand Duke Jean. In each country, voters elect a parliament that chooses the prime minister who heads the government.

Belgium. Because of its strategic location between Germany and France, Belgium played a key role in both world wars. German troops smashed through Belgium to attack France in 1914. Again in 1940, the Germans invaded and occupied the country. The occupation increased differences between Flemish-speaking and French-speaking Belgians, as many in the French community accused the Flemish of collaborating with the Germans.

Once a colonial power like France, Belgium freed its African colonies in the 1960s. However, it still maintains close economic ties with Zaire (zah-IHR) (the former Belgian Congo) and other former possessions.

Under Belgian law, eligible citizens are *required* to vote in elections. If they do not, they are subject to fines.

Netherlands. People sometimes refer to the Netherlands as *Holland*, although North and South Holland are only two of the 12 Dutch provinces. The two Hollands contain the largest cities of the nation, Amsterdam and Rotterdam. Because of the brisk trade encouraged by its location at the mouth of the Rhine, the Netherlands earns the highest per capita income in Western Europe. Roman Catholics outnumber Protestants by a small margin.

Like France, the Netherlands retains a small portion of its former colonial empire. In Southeast Asia, the Dutch East Indies have become the independent nation of Indonesia. But the Dutch still control two territories, Aruba and the Dutch Antilles, in the Caribbean.

Luxembourg. Tiny Luxembourg owes its existence to European power politics. Over the centuries it has passed from independence to foreign domination and back. Its foreign masters have included Burgundy, Spain, France, Austria, and (during the world wars) Germany. Dutch kings for a time served double duty as grand dukes. Since 1890, except for the world wars, Luxembourg has had its own ruling family.

Despite its small size, Luxembourg has much farmland and many industries. Iron mines gave Luxembourg the basis for a strong steel industry. Many international banks are based in Luxembourg, as are some of the offices of the European Community. The people are mainly Roman Catholics.

REVIEWING THE CHAPTER

I. Building your Vocabulary

In your notebook, write the term from the list below that best completes each sentence. (The list contains one extra term.)

House of Commons   devolution   grand duchy
House of Lords   premier   Fifth Republic

1. Under a policy of _____, Scotland would have its own parliament to decide local matters.

2. The government of France since 1958 has been called the _____.

3. The _____ can amend a bill but cannot keep it from becoming law.

4. A duke or a duchess heads the government of a _____.

5. The British prime minister is responsible to the _____, which is elected by the British people.

II. Understanding the Facts

In your notebook, write the letter of the word or phrase that best completes each of the following sentences.

1. The only Western European nation that is not a member of NATO is:
   a. Ireland.   b. Luxembourg.   c. France.

2. Rotterdam is a major port at the mouth of the:
   a. Thames River.   b. Rhône River.   c. Rhine River.

3. The Welsh, Scottish, Irish, and Breton people are:
   a. descendants of the ancient Romans.
   b. under British rule.
   c. members of Western Europe's Celtic minority.

4. Roman Catholics are in the majority in:
   a. Ireland.   b. Northern Ireland.   c. Scotland.

5. During World War II, Charles de Gaulle was:
   a. chief of staff of the French army.
   b. president of France.
   c. leader of the Free French forces that fought alongside the Allies.

III. Thinking It Through

In your notebook, write the letter of the word or phrase that best completes each of the following sentences.

1. Britain's per capita income would be lower than it is if:
   a. many British steel mills had not closed down.
   b. Britain could not tap oil from under the North Sea.
   c. the British Empire had not broken up.

2. An argument in favor of keeping the House of Lords is that:
   a. most of its members have excelled in business, government, or the arts.
   b. its members tend to be older and wiser than MPs.
   c. it serves as a check on the powers of the prime minister and the government.

3. A possible reason for a British prime minister to call a general election three years after the last election is that:
   a. the economy is booming and people are happy.
   b. elections are always held at three-year intervals.
   c. the queen wants a change of government.

4. Charles de Gaulle's chief accomplishments after assuming power in 1958 were to:
   a. increase French leadership in NATO and form closer ties with Great Britain.
   b. end the war in Algeria and give France a more stable political system.
   c. put down a rebellious military and start a new political party.

5. By resorting to armed force, the IRA hopes to:
   a. win independence for Northern Ireland.
   b. unite Northern Ireland and Ireland.
   c. establish a Catholic government in Ireland.

DEVELOPING CRITICAL THINKING SKILLS

1. Describe environmental difficulties faced by the Dutch and the Irish. How have the two peoples responded to those difficulties?

2. Imagine that you are a citizen of Great Britain. What part do you play in choosing the people who run the nation's government? How would the role of a citizen of the United States be different?

3. Within Great Britain and the republic of Ireland, government policy bars members of the IRA and Protestant paramilitary groups from being quoted in the press or interviewed on radio or TV. Do you think this is a wise policy? Why or why not?

4. What resemblances can you see between the Troubles in Northern Ireland today and the turmoil in France in 1958? What differences? Do you think the way the French responded to their difficulties would have any relevance to the people of Northern Ireland? Explain your reasoning.

ENRICHMENT AND EXPLORATION

1. Find out more about the way the Dutch have created new land by building dikes to hold back the sea. Make an oral or written report.

2. Use encyclopedias and other library resources to find about art, music, or literature in one of the countries of Western Europe. Assemble the information into a classroom display. You might want to add a musical dimension, using recordings of musical works by composers and performers.

3. Watch a session of the House of Commons on C-SPAN. If possible, brush up on British affairs beforehand by reading a recent British magazine (such as *The Economist*) or newspaper (such as the *Manchester Guardian Weekly* or *The Times* of London).

4. Hold a classroom debate on the situation in Northern Ireland. Divide the class into four groups. Have the groups take the perspective of (a) Protestants in Northern Ireland, (b) Catholics in Northern Ireland, (c) people in England, and (d) people in the republic of Ireland. Brainstorm ways in which tensions could be reduced and a peaceful solution reached.

5. Make a classroom display of newspaper and magazine articles about France. Include information about French tourist attractions, French ways of making a living, and current events.

10 *Central Europe*

Imagine that the borders of nations could be observed from space, like the colored lines on maps. Imagine further that a camera high above the earth's surface has filmed Central Europe over many centuries. Now the film is being shown in speeded-up motion—100 years of history every minute. What a kaleidoscope of movement the camera shows! You notice at once the wild swings in the borders of Germany, Central Europe's largest state. Small, big, bigger, smaller. Now split; now united. Now spilling far to the east and south; now drawing back to the north and west. Pulled together as a nation for the first time only in 1871, Germany has kept the mapmakers busy by repeatedly changing its shape ever since.

At times in the past, Germany has dominated Central Europe by means of military conquest. Today, Germany is Europe's economic powerhouse. Its influence over Central Europe is now economic and cultural, rather than military.

THE REGION

Two historic empires—both Germanic—have cast their shadows over the region known as Central Europe. The first of these was the empire of the Habsburg dynasty, called Austria–Hungary from 1867 until its collapse at the end of World War I. Austria–Hungary ruled over most of Central Europe south of Germany. Centered in Vienna, it controlled areas inhabited by a wide variety of people of German, Hungarian, Slavic, and other backgrounds. The second dominant empire was Germany, formed around the old state of Prussia with its capital at Berlin. It was Prussia that gathered all the other German states except Austria into a German Reich (empire) in 1871. The Reich's borders enclosed not only present-day Germany but much of present-day Poland and smaller parts of several other countries.

222

Some Facts About Central European Countries

COUNTRY	CAPITAL CITY	POPULATION (millions)	AREA (square miles)	PER CAPITA INCOME (U.S. dollars)	LIFE EXPECTANCY AT BIRTH
Austria	Vienna (vee • EN • uh)	7.7	32,275	$ 13,600	71 M 79 F
Croatia	Zagreb (ZAH • greb)	4.8	35,132	NA	NA
Czechoslovakia	Prague (PRAHG)	15.7	49,374	7,878	68 M 75 F
Germany	Berlin* (buhr • LIHN)	78.7	137,838	24,980	73 M 81 F
Hungary	Budapest (BOO • duh • pest)	10.4	35,919	6,108	65 M 73 F
Liechtenstein	Vaduz (vah • DOOTS)	.03	61	15,000	NA
Poland	Warsaw (WAWR • saw)	38.2	120,727	4,565	66 M 74 F
Slovenia	Ljubljana (LOO • bluh • nah)	2.0	12,584	NA	NA
Switzerland	Bern (BURN)	6.8	15,941	17,800	74 M 82 F

NA = Not Available
M = Male
F = Female
*While Berlin is Germany's official capital, most government offices are still in Bonn.

Sources: 1992 Information Please Almanac; World Almanac and Book of Facts, 1992; New York Times

The peace treaties that ended World War I broke Austria–Hungary into many separate nations. The treaties returned Poland to the map as an independent state. Germany's crushing defeat in World War II redrew the map again. Germany lost a large territory to Poland and the Soviet Union. The remainder was divided into four occupation zones and later into two nations, East and West Germany. Further change took place in 1990, when the two German republics were reunited, marking an end to the Cold War.

Central Europe today contains nine nations. Five of them—Austria, Hungary, Czechoslovakia, Slovenia, and Croatia—were once part of Austria–Hungary. Germany and Poland lie to the north. Finally, west of

Austria lie two mountainous nations that take great pride in their political neutrality. One is Switzerland, somewhat larger than Maryland. The other is Liechtenstein (LIK-ten-steyen), so small it could squeeze within the borders of Washington, D.C. Liechtenstein is a **principality**—a state headed by a prince.

The Land. Central Europe contains two large plains or lowlands, plus extensive mountains. The lowlands have provided land for farming—and for the maneuvering of armies. The mountains have served to cut ethnic groups off from one another. Because of this isolation, more different groups have been able to take root.

The largest lowland is in the north, along the North Sea and the Baltic Sea. It is part of the Great European Plain, which stretches from France deep into Russia. The northern half of Germany and most of Poland lie on this plain. Another lowland flanks the Danube River, which winds its way southward and eastward through Central Europe toward the Black Sea. Hungary occupies the largest part of this lowland.

The village of Alpach nestles in its Alpine valley in western Austria. Villagers farm the surrounding fields, some of which are on steeply sloping mountainsides.

Central Europe contains two main mountain ranges, the Alps and the Carpathians. The Alps reach as far north as southern Germany. Austria, Switzerland, and Liechtenstein are mainly Alpine countries, that is, located in the Alps. Slovenia and Croatia, too, have Alpine sections. The Carpathians rise in Czechoslovakia and southern Poland. After leaving Central Europe in the east, the Carpathians loop through Ukraine and Romania.

The People. The inhabitants of Central Europe are mainly of Germanic and Slavic background. Germanic peoples live mainly in the west and north but are scattered throughout the region. Slavs live in the east and south. A third group, the Magyars or Hungarians, lives mainly in Hungary.

Germans trace their ancestry to tribes that lived in the forests of northern Europe before and during Roman times. Those early tribes included Franks, Alemanni, Saxons, and Bavarians. Some of today's German states bear the names of those ancient tribes. Over the centuries, German settlers ranged over much of Central Europe and east as far as the Volga River, in Russia. An estimated 2 million "Volga Germans," whose ancestors moved to the Volga in the 1760s, still live in Russia and Kazakhstan. Other German communities are scattered through Poland, Czechoslovakia, Romania, and nearby countries. Most of the German-speaking people of Czechoslovakia were expelled after World War II, however, as were many of those in Poland.

The main concentrations of German-speaking people today live in Germany and Austria. Liechtensteiners and two thirds of the people of Switzerland also speak German. (See map, page 181.)

Slavic people, or Slavs, speak a number of different but related languages. The largest group of Slavic speakers live outside Central Europe. They are the Eastern Slavs, who include Russians, Ukrainians, and Belarusians. Within Central Europe, Slavs are divided into Western and Southern Slavs. The Western Slavs include Poles, Czechs, and Slovaks. The Southern Slavs include Slovenians and Croats, as well as Serbs, Macedonians, and Bulgarians. From 1918 until 1991, Slovenians, Croats, Serbs, and Macedonians were united in a South Slavic federation known as Yugoslavia. (In Slavic languages, *Yugo* means *South*.) The federation splintered when the Slovenian, Croatian, and other republics broke away as independent nations.

Hungarians or Magyars speak a language that is distantly related to Finnish and Estonian. Many countries around Hungary, especially Romania, have Hungarian-speaking minorities.

Religion.   The Roman Catholic Church has a very strong presence in Central Europe. Catholicism is the dominant religion in every country. Only in Germany and Switzerland do Protestants come anywhere near equality in numbers. (Both Germany and Switzerland were centers of the Protestant Reformation that began in the 1500s.) Hungary and Czechoslovakia also have Protestant minorities.

Christianity has played a political and social as well as a religious role in the region. By translating the Bible into local languages, early missionaries helped to determine which alphabet a nation used in its writing. This is most noticeable in independent Croatia and in Serbia (part of Yugoslavia), where the people speak a common language known as Serbo-Croatian. Croats write the language in the Roman alphabet (the one we use). That's because they adopted the Roman Catholic form of Christianity. Serbs use the Cyrillic alphabet (the one that Russians and Ukrainians use). That's because they adopted the Eastern Orthodox form of Christianity.

Until World War II, Central Europe had a large Jewish population. Cities like Warsaw, Berlin, Vienna, and Budapest held thriving Jewish communities. However, prejudice against Jews was widespread. The German Nazi leader Adolf Hitler exploited that prejudice in a campaign to eliminate all Jews. German armies conquered all of Central Europe during World War II. In what is known as the Holocaust, Hitler's followers murdered an estimated 6 million Jews in Nazi death camps. Today, only a tiny remnant of Central Europe's Jews remains.

Hitler's victims also included millions of Slavs and Gypsies. Gypsies are an ethnic group who live in many parts of Europe, including Central Europe. Many Gypsies are nomads. They speak a language, Romany, that is related to the major language family of India.

The Economy.   A visitor to Warsaw, Poland's capital, often notices a brown haze settling over the city. The haze comes from the smokestacks of factories. It is a sign of the heavy industry that is spread through much of Central Europe.

The presence of valuable mineral resources has encouraged industrial development in the region. Germany, where rich deposits of iron and coal are located together, became an industrial powerhouse in the late 1800s. Other parts of the region, especially Czechoslovakia, began their industrial development in the early 1900s. Poland and Hungary did not really get started until after World War II.

While free market systems have long prevailed in the western part of the region, they have only recently been revived in the east. Eastern

226

Germany, Poland, Czechoslovakia, Hungary, Slovenia, and Croatia all had command-style Communist economies from the late 1940s until the early 1990s. Decisions about what to produce and what prices to charge were made by central planners, not by the push and pull of market forces. Now, all that has changed. Communist governments have fallen. Democratically elected leaders are struggling to breathe new life into stagnant economies by selling state-run companies to private owners.

Farm life varies greatly from one place to another. Small, independently operated farms are common in the western areas. In former Communist states, some people operated private farms while others worked on large state-run farms. They held specialized jobs: tractor driver, bookkeeper, technician. Now, private farming is expanding in the former Communist states.

GERMANY: FROM TWO GERMANYS TO ONE

Germany's reunification of 1990 gave Germans a new identity—and a new set of jokes. One joke told of an encounter between an East German and a West German. Exhilarated by the fall of the Berlin Wall, the East German shouted out the slogan of East Germans who had campaigned for reunification: "Down with the Wall! We are one people!" The West German shot back: "So are we!"

One People or Two? In the months after reunification, it did indeed appear that the "one" German people was really two. It seemed that East and West Germans had formed habits that set them apart and made reunification more difficult than many had anticipated.

But then, western and eastern Germany had had separate histories long before the Cold War and the split into rival states. Western Germany was the core area of the ancient German states. In the period from about A.D. 600 to 1100, what is now eastern Germany was inhabited mainly by Slavic peoples. Then Germans moved eastward, conquering and absorbing the Slavs. In time, peasants in the east (in the area called Prussia) became landless laborers. Over them stood a landowning class called **Junkers** (YOONG-kuhrz). Many farm people in the west, on the other hand, gradually came to own their own farms and had considerably more freedom. Thus, the societies of eastern and western Germany developed differently.

The Cold War era added new differences. East Germany became a Communist state. The lands of the Junkers were taken over by the state.

Some of the old estates became collective farms, where farm workers supposedly shared ownership but actually worked under Communist party direction. Others became state farms, under government ownership and control. Industries, too, were placed under state ownership. Government officials in Berlin, the East German capital, made decisions about what and how much to produce. The managers of shops and factories had no need to build markets for their products and little incentive to cut costs. Thus, many East German industries became outmoded and inefficient.

Today the united German government is striving to restore the free market and build up the economy of eastern Germany. It hopes to raise the living standards of easterners to the level enjoyed by westerners. But differences between the two parts of Germany will no doubt remain strong for many years to come.

The Land. Today's Germany is relatively small when compared to the Germanys of the past. The Germany of 1871 was 40 percent larger. The Germany of 1937 was 30 percent larger. Those earlier Germanys extended farther to the east, across much of present-day Poland. When Germany lost World War II, it had to give up much land. Some of the millions of Germans forced out of the "lost" territories in 1945 still hope to return some day. However, the German government has solemnly promised to accept the current borders.

Germany's land can be divided into three main areas. In the north is a lowland, part of the Great European Plain. Soil there is relatively poor and mineral resources are limited. But transportation routes are handy and travel is easy. Major cities include Berlin (population 3.4 million), Hamburg (1.6 million), Bremen, and Hannover.

The best lands are in a central section of hills and valleys. Excellent soils occur along the borders between the lowlands and the hills. Deposits of coal, iron, and potash (used for chemicals and fertilizers) are found in this section. So are Germany's main centers of mining and industry—the Ruhr Valley, the Saarland (SAHR-land), and areas in Saxony. Major cities include Frankfurt, Cologne, Düsseldorf (DEE-suhl-dawrf), Dresden, and Leipzig

Finally, in the south, is a mountainous region where the Alps begin to rise. Munich, the capital of the German state of Bavaria, lies in this section. Munich is Germany's third largest city, with 1.2 million inhabitants.

Germany benefits from the presence of major rivers and canals that allow cheap and easy transport of raw materials by boat. The main

A view of Munich. The gate at center right is part of the city's medieval fortifications. The twin towers of Munich's cathedral are visible in the distance.

avenue of transport is the Rhine, along with its tributaries such as the Ruhr, the Main (MEYEN), and the Mosel (MOH-zul). Germans have a deep attachment to the Rhine and its legends. For example, the composer Richard Wagner based a cycle of operas, *The Ring of the Nibelung* (NEE-buh-loong), on a medieval German epic about the Rhine. The epic tells of a race of dwarfs called the Nibelungs and the theft of a treasure that they kept in the Rhine.

The great cathedral city of Cologne and the former West German capital of Bonn are located on the Rhine. Other major German cities lie along other rivers. Berlin, for example, is on the Spree River. Hamburg is on the Elbe. Bremen is on the Weser. All of those rivers flow northward. However, the Danube River, which rises in Germany's south, flows southeastward into Austria on its journey toward the Black Sea. The Rhine and Danube have been connected by a canal, allowing the transport of goods all the way across Central Europe.

The Economy. Taking advantage of extensive resources and a well disciplined work force, Germany has become the industrial powerhouse of Europe. Its economy is almost twice the size of France's economy. Germany ranks alongside the United States and Japan among the world's three top exporting nations. Like Japan, it often has a large trade surplus, selling more abroad than it buys.

229

Like Sweden, Germany began the industrial revolution long after England did. This had important consequences. For one thing, infant German industries could take advantage of a spreading rail system. Trains could bring raw materials like coal and iron to the factory door. This meant that factories could more easily be situated in existing cities, rather than near out-of-the-way coalfields. Many of Germany's industrial cities, including Cologne, Frankfurt, and Munich, developed around medieval trading towns.

Germany's (and Europe's) greatest concentration of industry is in the Ruhr coalfields north of Cologne. The bituminous (hard) coal of this region is used in steel-making. Softer brown coal, or **lignite,** which is mined around Cologne and Leipzig, is used to heat homes and make electricity. Iron is mined near Brunswick, in central Germany. Large deposits of potash and other raw materials for the chemical industry are found in what used to be East Germany. Also present is uranium, used in producing nuclear reactions.

A heavy dependence on brown coal contributed to high levels of air pollution, especially in East Germany, during the 1970s and 1980s. Careless handling of other industrial materials, such as uranium, polluted ground water. Cleaning up the pollution will require years of effort and lots of money.

Besides industries based on coal and iron, Germany has many lighter industries such as electronics and optics. German cameras and optical instruments have a longstanding reputation for quality. Engineering is another German specialty. Germany's auto industry turns out such cars as the Volkswagen ("people's car"), Mercedes, Porsche, Audi, and BMW. Auto travel is fast and easy in Germany. In the 1930s, Germany pioneered in the construction of superhighways, or autobahns, along medieval trade routes.

Government.   Germany's present democratic form of government has evolved out of a tortured past. Germany went from a collection of independent states (before 1871) to a powerful empire (1871–1918) to a weak republic (1919–1933) to a Nazi dictatorship (1933–1945). Finally, Hitler's Third Reich came crashing down in defeat at the end of World War II.

For the four and a half decades from 1945 until 1990, Germany little resembled its former self. At first it was split into four zones of occupation. Each of the major Allies of World War II—the United States, the Soviet Union, Britain, and France—occupied one zone. In 1949, three zones became West Germany and the Soviet zone became East Germany. West Germany (Federal Republic of Germany) became a parliamentary democracy. East Germany (German Democratic Republic) became a Communist dictatorship.

Germany's 1990 reunification looked very much like an annexation by West Germany of East Germany. By and large, West German laws remained in effect. The West German parliament merely swore in 144 new members who had been elected by East German voters.

Germany is a parliamentary republic organized along federal lines. As in the United States, power is shared between a central or federal government and separate state governments. Germany has 16 states, five of which are in the former East Germany.

The federal government is led by a prime minister, known as the **chancellor**. The president is a relatively powerless official, indirectly elected to serve for five years. The chancellor is elected by the **Bundestag** (BOON-des-tahg), or lower house of parliament, and usually is the head of the party with the largest number of seats.

The 662 members of the Bundestag are popularly elected under a complex voting system in which voters cast two ballots apiece. A party must win at least 5 percent of the national vote before it can enter the Bundestag. The two dominant parties are the conservative Christian Democrats and the left-leaning Social Democrats. One or the other usually forms a coalition with a centrist third party, the Free Democrats. Smaller parties like the environmentalist Greens and the anti-immigrant Republicans also attract some votes.

An upper house, the **Bundesrat** (BOON-des-raht), represents the 16 states, with each state's delegates voting as a bloc. The Bundesrat can veto any law passed by the lower house that affects the powers of the states. In practice, it has a voice in about half of all laws.

The West German government had its capital at Bonn, a sleepy provincial town on the Rhine. A German joke says that Bonn is half the size of a Berlin cemetery—and twice as dead. Over a 12-year period, most operations of government will move to the new capital, the much bigger eastern metropolis of Berlin. (Berlin served as Germany's capital from 1871 to 1945.) The Bundesrat, however, voted to remain in Bonn.

Foreign and Military Policy. Germany has the largest military force in Europe, outside the Commonwealth of Independent States. What role will Germany play in the Europe of tomorrow? Will it strike out on its own? Or will it be closely allied to the United States? Will it return to the aggressive posture of the Hitler years? Or will it use its immense economic power in the interest of peace and prosperity? At the time of reunification, Chancellor Helmut Kohl assured the world of Germany's

A typical snack in Bavaria, in southern Germany, consists of several kinds of sausages and smoked meats served with bread, pretzels, and cucumber slices.

peaceful intentions. "Germany will not go it alone," he proclaimed. "There will be no unilateral [one-sided] nationalism and no 'restless Reich.'"

During the Cold War years, the major powers stationed hundreds of thousands of soldiers in the two Germanys. West Germany joined the North Atlantic Treaty Organization (NATO), while East Germany joined the Soviet-led Warsaw Pact. With the end of the Cold War, the Warsaw Pact collapsed. But NATO remains strong, and the new Germany is a key member of NATO. Even leaders of the former Soviet Union accepted this status. Apparently, they thought membership in NATO would help to keep Germany "tame."

Under the 1990 accords by which the major powers relinquished their occupation rights, Germany accepted limits on the size of its armed forces. It agreed not to acquire nuclear, biological, or chemical weapons. It agreed to its present borders. The accords provide that only German forces (and not soldiers from other NATO countries) can be stationed in the former East Germany. But at least some NATO troops will remain in western Germany.

Besides belonging to NATO, Germany is a leading member of the European Community. Along with France, it has been pushing the EC along the road to greater unity.

Daily Life.   Some people picture oompah bands when they think of Germany. Others see foaming mugs of beer or goosestepping soldiers. All those have been a part of Germany, although the goosestep (a high-kicking parade march borrowed from France by the Prussian army in 1726) has now been dropped.

Pork and potatoes are traditional German foods, as are cabbages, from which Germans make their famous *Sauerkraut* (sour cabbage). German butcher shops offer sausages (*Würste*) in endless variety. Some are for frying, some for spreading on bread. A German style of fast-food restaurant sells *Würste* and fried potatoes. Customers stand at counters while they eat. At home, German cooks often prepare sweet-sour dishes like *Sauerbraten,* a kind of beef pot roast.

Rich desserts are also a German tradition. German cities abound in pastry shops and cafes. There, people can indulge their taste for cakes, cookies, and custards.

If you visited Berlin, you would find a great variety of restaurants, shops, museums, and concert halls. From 1961 until 1989, an ugly barrier of concrete and metal, the Berlin Wall, divided the city into Communist and non-Communist halves. Communist authorities put up the wall to stop people from fleeing to the West. Over the years some 200 people were shot and killed while trying to sneak across. Today, Berlin is a single city again. New construction and colorful shops are ending the drabness that once characterized the eastern part of the city.

Women in Germany have traditionally stayed home to look after children and keep house. However, throughout Germany but especially in the east, women have broken away from the old pattern. Like American women, they have entered professions and taken jobs in industry and government. German teenagers are less likely than Americans to hold after-school jobs. They have less reason to save money for college, because college tuition is free. But in other ways, German teenagers seem much like Americans. For example, they like the heady beat of rock music, and they're just as eager to make friends and have a good time.

EAST CENTRAL EUROPE: RECOVERING FROM COMMUNISM

The eastern countries of Central Europe fell under Soviet domination at the end of World War II. Local Communist parties, backed by the Soviet Army, seized power. During the Cold War, the countries were often called satellite nations. Like satellites orbiting the earth, they were unable to escape the powerful larger body nearby.

Reform programs introduced by Soviet leader Mikhail Gorbachev after 1985 helped to bring the Cold War to an end. Beginning in 1989, the Communist governments of eastern Europe collapsed. New governments took power. They have been struggling to create democratic political systems and to move from centrally controlled to free-market economies.

Our examination of east Central Europe will start with Poland. Then we will look at Czechoslovakia and Hungary.

Poland's Land and People. Poland has assumed various shapes over the centuries. At times it united with Lithuania to form a huge kingdom. At other times it has vanished from the map, swallowed up by Germany, Austria, and Russia. Today Poland is a sizable nation. In area and population, it is second only to Germany in Central Europe.

Poland's land lies mainly on the Great European Plain, where it can be readily invaded by foreign armies. In the south, the land slopes upward to the Silesian Plateau and the Sudeten and Carpathian Mountains.

Most of the people of Poland are Polish-speaking Slavs. But almost a million people of German origin live within Polish borders. Relations between Polish-speaking and German-speaking people are sometimes tense. Polish nationalists have protested against the fact that German companies have taken over many Polish firms since 1990.

Poland's capital, Warsaw, lies on the Vistula River, which flows north into the Baltic. Warsaw once had a sizable Jewish population, but the Jewish ghetto as well as much of the rest of Warsaw was destroyed in fierce battles during World War II. Today, Warsaw boasts many modern buildings. It has a population of 1.6 million. Poland's second big river, the Oder, and a tributary, the Neisse (NEYE-suh), make up the Oder-Neisse Line. That line serves as Poland's western border with Germany.

Poland Finds Solidarity. In the years after World War II, Poland built a solid industrial base. Its coal mines and steel mills supplied markets in Poland and around the world. Its textile mills made clothing for Poles, Russians, and others. Its shipyards busily turned out ships. The Polish standard of living rose, but not so rapidly as many Poles wished. Every few years, demonstrators would take to the streets. They protested against price rises or against political repression in general.

Lech Walesa, leader of the labor union Solidarity, attacks Poland's Communist government in a speech to striking shipyard workers in Gdansk, 1988.

In the 1970s, shipyard workers at Gdansk and other Baltic ports began to organize a more effective opposition movement. In 1980, they created a new trade union called **Solidarity**. Led by a shipyard electrician named Lech Walesa (LECK vah-WEN-suh), Solidarity organized strikes that won major concessions from the government in 1980.

This was highly unusual in a Communist country, but Solidarity was helped by Poland's powerful Roman Catholic Church. The church had a tradition of promoting Polish nationalism and speaking out against communism. Its effectiveness had been increased in 1978, when a Polish cardinal became pope, or spiritual leader of all the world's Roman Catholics. As Pope John Paul II, he visited Poland and spoke out for human rights and religious causes.

The Polish government cracked down and declared martial law in 1981, but Solidarity remained strong. The Polish leader, General Wojciech Jaruzelski (VOY-chek yah-roo-SHEL-skee), ordered Walesa arrested. But Jaruzelski had to ease up as the 1980s wore on. Freed from prison, Walesa and other Solidarity leaders resumed their drive for change. Finally, in the face of growing unrest and a declining economy, Jaruzelski permitted free parliamentary elections in 1989. Solidarity won a landslide victory. The following year, Polish voters elected Walesa president. Poland joined the ranks of Europe's democratic nations.

"Shock Therapy."   The transition to democracy and capitalism brought hard times for the Polish people. The government decided it was better to jump into icy water than to walk in slowly. So it administered "shock therapy." At the start of 1990, it removed all price controls, opened Poland's borders to imports, and began selling state-run businesses. The good news was that products began to appear on empty shop shelves. Bananas, soap, and hundreds of other scarce items suddenly became plentiful. But there was bad news, too. Many businesses shut down, unable to stand the competition of the free market.

Many Poles lost their jobs. People found that living standards were falling. They demanded relief, but the government stuck to its plan. The plan had won the approval of international agencies and governments that had lent Poland billions of dollars. Abandoning the plan would have jeopardized the outside assistance Poland was getting.

Unhappiness with shock therapy muddied the Polish political picture. Solidarity split into factions. Twenty-nine parties, many of them critical of the government's plan, won seats in parliament. Leaders had trouble assembling enough votes to form coalitions that could govern effectively. Poland's political system remained in flux as the parliament worked on a new, democratic constitution. President Walesa proposed strengthening the powers of the president. But many Poles remembered how a powerful president had become a right-wing dictator in the 1920s. They didn't want that to happen again.

Poland's experience showed how hard it could be to make the transition to a free society. Czechoslovakia and Hungary faced similar problems.

Czechoslovakia: Land of the Czechs and Slovaks.   Poland's neighbor to the south, Czechoslovakia, is a federation of two groups, the Czechs and the Slovaks, created in 1918. Both peoples are Western Slavs, but they have slightly different languages and traditions. The more rural Slovaks, who are outnumbered two to one, resent what some call "Czech domination." The end of Communist rule brought a national debate over Slovak proposals to end the federation or perhaps convert it into some sort of looser confederation.

As a federation, Czechoslovakia has a central government that controls national affairs. It also has two lower-level governments, the Czech and Slovak republics. The national capital, Prague (population 1.2 million), is also the capital of the Czech republic. The Slovak capital is Bratislava (brah-tih-SLAH-vuh) (430,000).

Czechoslovakia has a strong industrial base, dating to the 1920s. Slovakia has been a leading producer of armaments such as tanks and automatic weapons. Czech and Slovak factories also produce automobiles, construction equipment, and many more products. The Czech city of Plzen (PULL-zen) is famous for its light "pilsner" beer.

From Prague Spring to Velvet Revolution.   During four decades of Soviet domination, Czechoslovaks kept alive a spirit of resistance. That spirit blossomed into the "Prague Spring" of 1968, when liberal Communists led by Alexander Dubcek ousted hard-liners in the Czechoslovak Communist party and began a program of reforms. But the reforms were short-lived. In August 1968, Soviet-led Warsaw Pact troops stormed into Prague. They restored hard-line, pro-Soviet Communists to power.

A more lasting change occurred in 1989. Massive protest demonstrations brought down the Communist government that fall. This **Velvet Revolution**, so called because it was carried out with no deaths or even injuries, put the noted Czech playwright Václav Havel in the presidency. Under the Communists, Havel had spent more than five years in prison for his campaigns against abuses of human rights.

Like the Poles, the Czechoslovaks decided to restore free enterprise as quickly as possible. They began to **privatize** state-owned companies, that is, to transfer government property to private ownership. As part of this process, the government offered stock (ownership shares) in the

Two smiling women in Czech folk dresses display a photograph of Václav Havel on the day he was elected president of Czechoslovakia, December 1989.

CASE STUDY

Straight Talk from President Havel

Until 1989, playwright Václav Havel of Czechoslovakia was one of the leaders of the Czech movement for human rights, opposing the Communist regime. In December 1989, the regime fell, and Havel became president. In his first speech as president, on New Year's Day, 1990, he described the state of the country after 40 years of communism.

> My dear fellow citizens,
>
> For forty years you heard from my predecessors on this day different variations on the same theme: how our country flourished, how many million tons of steel we produced, how happy we all were, how we trusted our government, and what bright perspectives were unfolding in front of us.
>
> I assume you did not propose me for this office so that I, too, would lie to you.
>
> Our country is not flourishing. . . . Entire branches of industry are producing goods which are of no interest to anyone, while we are lacking the things we need. A state which calls itself a worker's state humiliates and exploits workers. Our obsolete economy is wasting the little energy we have available. . . . We have the most contaminated environment in Europe. . . .
>
> But all this is still not the main problem. The worst thing is that we live in a contaminated moral environment. We fell morally ill because we became used to saying something different from what we thought. We learned not to believe in anything, to ignore each other, to care only about ourselves. . . .
>
> We had all become used to the totalitarian system and accepted it as an unchangeable fact and thus helped to perpetuate it. . . .
>
> Let us not be mistaken: the best government in the world, the best parliament and the best president, cannot achieve much on their own. . . . Freedom and democracy include participation and therefore responsibility from us all.

"New Year's Address," Václav Havel. From *Open Letters: Selected Writings, 1965-1990*. New York: Knopf, 1991.

1. List three problems Havel says face Czechoslovakia.

2. Why does Havel say that the Czechs and Slovaks themselves were corrupted during the years of totalitarian government?

companies to the public. It even helped people to buy the stock. For about $37, a person could buy a book of coupons from the government. The coupons could then be traded for stock shares, often worth far more. People could later sell the stock, if it increased in value. Or they could keep the stock and share in any profits a company made.

Hungary: Land of the Magyars. The people known as Magyars have lived in Hungary for 1,100 years. Set apart from their Germanic and Slavic neighbors by language and history, they have created a nation distinctly their own. Until recent times, Magyar life was essentially rural. Today many Magyars live in cities and work in factories.

Budapest, the capital (population 2.1 million), is actually two cities, Buda and Pest. They flank the Danube River in central Hungary. Many of Hungary's industries are located there. Among the factories are textile mills, steel mills, and pharmaceutical plants.

Hungary's farms were among the most successful farms in all the satellite nations. Today they win praise for their meats, fruits, and wines, many of which are exported. Since the nation lies mainly on a plain, it has much land that is suitable for farming.

Hungary was the scene of a major uprising against Soviet control in 1956. Soviet troops crushed the revolt with heavy loss of life. About

The Danube River flows between Buda, on the left, and Pest, on the right. The two cities were joined in 1873 to form the single city of Budapest, Hungary's capital.

20,000 people died. Another 200,000 people fled the country, many of them emigrating to the United States. During the 1970s and 1980s, Hungary's Communist regime adopted many economic reforms. These made the Communist system less rigid and more efficient. Since the downfall of communism in 1990, Hungary has become a parliamentary democracy. Like its neighbors to the north, it has moved to restore a free-market economy.

SLOVENIA AND CROATIA: REJOINING CENTRAL EUROPE

Although they have often been ruled by outsiders, Slovenia and Croatia have maintained their own distinct identities. Both were part of the Austro-Hungarian empire. They largely escaped rule by the Turks, who controlled areas just to the south for hundreds of years. From 1918 to 1991, Slovenia and Croatia were part of Yugoslavia. Both were mainly Roman Catholic, while southern parts of Yugoslavia were inhabited mainly by Eastern Orthodox Christians and Muslims. Slovenes and Croats used the Latin alphabet, unlike Yugoslavia's Serbs. What's more,

A steep and narrow street leads to the sea in the Croatian seaport of Dubrovnik. The historic city was badly damaged by Serbian attacks in 1991.

Slovenia and Croatia got an early start at building industry. That was thanks to deposits of oil, bauxite, mercury, and other natural resources. Good rail links to the markets of Austria and Hungary also helped. Slovenia and Croatia enjoyed a far higher standard of living than other sections of Yugoslavia.

In 1991, Slovenia and Croatia withdrew from the Yugoslav federation. Fighting broke out between Croatian forces and armed bands formed by Serbs living within Croatia. The Yugoslav army went to the Serbs' aid. Some 10,000 people died in a seven-month war, which heavily damaged many Croatian cities. After a ceasefire in 1992, United Nations peacekeepers moved in. Negotiations began in search of a formula that might satisfy both the 4.3 million Croats and the 500,000 Serbs living in Croatia.

Slovenia. Tucked away in the northwest corner of Yugoslavia, Slovenia had an easier time establishing its independence. It has a large number of industries and a high standard of living. The capital, Ljubljana (LOO-bluh-nah), has some 250,000 inhabitants. Most of the people are Slovenes, with small minorities of Italians and Hungarians.

Croatia. Bigger than Slovenia, Croatia has an irregular shape. A long, thin area of Croatia extends southward along the coast of the Adriatic Sea. This rugged region, known as Dalmatia, has many resorts. Its beaches and winter sun attract tourists from all over the world. Much of the remainder of Croatia lies on a sweeping plain. The capital, Zagreb (ZAH-greb) (population 765,000), is on the Sava River, which flows southeastward until it joins the Danube at Belgrade, the Yugoslav capital.

Hostility between Croats and Serbs has flared before in history. During World War II, Nazi sympathizers created a puppet state in Croatia that murdered hundreds of thousands of Serbs and Jews. Many Serbs joined a Communist-led partisan movement that fought on the side of the Allies against the Croatian state. Each side accused the other of atrocities, and the bitterness has lasted ever since.

THE NEUTRAL NATIONS

The remaining countries of Central Europe are Switzerland, Austria, and Liechtenstein. All remained neutral during the Cold War. All are prosperous nations with high standards of living. All are mountainous countries with snowy passes and ski resorts.

Switzerland. Switzerland, somewhat larger than Maryland, is a loose confederation of local units called **cantons.** The cantons enjoy a great deal of local autonomy, or self-rule. This system has helped to preserve peace among Switzerland's three major language groups—German (the largest), French, and Italian. A fourth language, Romansch, is spoken in one small area of the country.

Switzerland's largest cities are Zurich (population 345,000), Basel (BAH-zuhl) (170,000), and Geneva (juh-NEE-vuh) (165,000). The capital city, Bern, has 135,000 people. Switzerland is noted for precision engineering of products like watches. It also produces chemicals, heavy equipment, and fancy chocolates.

Switzerland has been so determined to remain neutral that it has refused to join the United Nations. However, it takes part in many UN agencies. It is a member of EFTA, and in 1992 it broke with tradition by applying for admission to the European Community.

Austria. Once the center of a powerful empire, Austria today is a small country the size of Indiana. United with Germany by Hitler in 1938, it fought as part of Germany during World War II. When the war ended in 1945, it was, like Germany, divided into four occupation zones. Ten years later, in 1955, the occupying powers withdrew. In return, Austria agreed to remain neutral, following the example of Switzerland.

Austria glories in a proud musical tradition that has included such composers as Wolfgang Amadeus Mozart (MOH-tsahrt), Joseph Haydn (HEYE-duhn), Franz Schubert, and Johann Strauss (STROWS). Austria's capital, Vienna (population 1.5 million), has a famous opera house and many concert halls. Music festivals at Salzburg, Mozart's birthplace, draw performers and music lovers from many countries.

Vienna sits on the Danube River and is Austria's leading center of industry. It is also the headquarters of the International Atomic Energy Agency. Austria has long been a member of the European Free Trade Association, or EFTA. Like Switzerland, it has applied for membership in the European Community.

Liechtenstein. Scarcely larger than a postage stamp itself, Liechtenstein draws a tidy fraction of its income from the sale of stamps to collectors around the world. The capital city is Vaduz (fah-DOOTS) (population 4,900). The capital is dominated by a medieval castle, the home of Prince Hans Adam. Liechtenstein has a variety of small industries in fields like electronics and pharmaceuticals. It is Europe's largest manufacturer of dentures.

Chapter 10:
CHECKUP

REVIEWING THE CHAPTER

I. Building Your Vocabulary

In your notebook, for each term in Column A, write the best description from Column B. (There is an extra item in Column B.)

Column A	*Column B*
1. Junkers	a. countries dominated by the Soviet Union during the Cold War
2. principality	b. country whose sovereign is a prince
3. canton	c. self-governing unit in Switzerland
4. Bundesrat	d. German pot roast
5. *Sauerbraten*	e. lower house of the German parliament
	f. members of landowning class in Prussia

II. Understanding the Facts

In your notebook, write the letter of the word or phrase that best completes each of the following sentences.

1. The largest ethnic groups in Central Europe are the:
   a. Germans and Magyars.   c. Germans and Poles.
   b. Slavs and Magyars.   d. Slavs and Germans.

2. A key distinction between Croats and Serbs is that:
   a. they use different alphabets to write the same language.
   b. Croats are of German heritage and Serbs are Slavic.
   c. Croats are mostly Christians and Serbs are mostly Muslims.
   d. at one time Croats were ruled by Turkey and Serbs were ruled by Austria.

3. A Central European country that was not under Communist rule was:
   a. Poland.   b. Hungary.   c. Austria.   d. Slovenia.

4. Germany's economic power is roughly equivalent to that of:
   a. France.   b. Russia.   c. Japan.   d. Taiwan.

5. One disadvantage of Poland's location is that:
   a. it has no outlet to the sea.
   b. there are few natural barriers to help defend against foreign invaders.
   c. most of the land is too mountainous to farm.
   d. it has no Slavic neighbors.

III. Thinking It Through

In your notebook, write the letter of the word or phrase that best completes each of the following sentences.

1. One fact that is not a consequence of the historical differences between western and eastern Germans is that:
   a. easterners have lower incomes than westerners.
   b. westerners have more experience with democracy.
   c. pollution is a serious problem in eastern Germany.
   d. the Ruhr Valley has abundant deposits of coal and other minerals.

2. One feature of Germany's government that is not related to its federal form is:
   a. the voting system in the Bundesrat.
   b. the existence of 16 state governments.
   c. the fact that the Bundestag chooses the chancellor.
   d. the distribution of powers between the Bundestag and the Bundesrat.

3. As a member of NATO, Germany:
   a. will not have to maintain its own army.
   b. will remain an ally of the United States.
   c. will gradually lower its tariffs.
   d. is barred from acquiring nuclear weapons.

4. Which of the following statements is closest to the truth?
   a. The restoration of democracy in the satellite nations in recent years has brought a host of new problems.
   b. The people of the satellite nations made little effort to resist Soviet domination.
   c. Living standards in the satellite nations declined between 1945 and 1990.
   d. The former satellite nations had little trouble creating free-market economies after 1989.

INTERPRETING GRAPHS

The circle graphs below show the percentage of West German and East German workers in various occupations at the time the countries merged in 1990. Study the graphs and then answer the questions that follow.

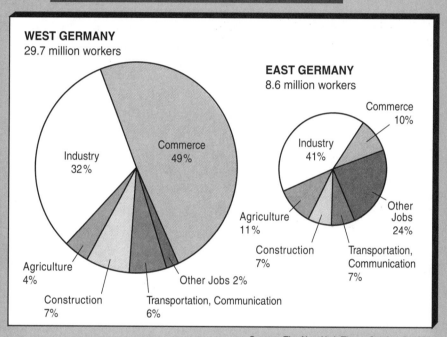

West German and East German Work Force, 1990

WEST GERMANY
29.7 million workers

Industry 32%

Commerce 49%

Agriculture 4%

Construction 7%

Transportation, Communication 6%

Other Jobs 2%

EAST GERMANY
8.6 million workers

Commerce 10%

Industry 41%

Agriculture 11%

Construction 7%

Other Jobs 24%

Transportation, Communication 7%

Source: *The New York Times*, October 3, 1990

1. Which Germany had the larger proportion of its workers in agriculture? Which had the larger proportion in industry?

2. In which Germany was a majority of workers employed in commerce, transportation, and communication?

3. Which Germany had more workers in construction? Explain your reasoning.

4. How many workers did Germany have? What percentage of them lived in West Germany? What percentage lived in East Germany?

DEVELOPING CRITICAL THINKING SKILLS

1. Describe the historical causes of differences between western and eastern Germany. How do such differences affect Germany today?

2. In what ways is the political system of Germany similar to that of the United States? In what ways is it different?

3. What factors contributed to Solidarity's success in bringing change to Poland? Explain the process by which Poland shook off its Communist system.

4. What difficulties did the former satellite nations experience during the transition from Communist-style command economies to free-enterprise market economies? Describe the transition policies of two such countries.

ENRICHMENT AND EXPLORATION

1. Using historical atlases or history books as a source, draw a series of maps showing the borders of Central Europe in 1871, 1914, 1920, 1943, 1960, and today. Write an explanation of the changes.

2. Find information about the life of a composer, writer, or architect from Central Europe. Write a two-page paper describing that person's life and achievements.

3. Use library sources to find more about the causes and results of industrial pollution in Central Europe, especially in the former East Germany. Make an oral report describing the problem and what is being done about it.

4. Draw up a menu for a typical German meal. Consult cookbooks, encyclopedias, and other sources for guidance. Class members who have family members or friends of German ancestry might ask them for favorite recipes. For extra credit, prepare such a meal at home under adult supervision, and describe your experience in a brief paper or oral report. (Alternatively, base the meal on the cuisine of another Central European ethnic group.)

5. Consult newspapers and magazines to collect information about recent developments in Poland's economic life. Are jobs easy to get? How well do people live? Imagine that you are a teenager living in a major Polish city. Write a letter to an American friend describing how economic developments have affected your day-to-day life.

11 Southern Europe

Southern Europe is often looked upon as the birthplace of European civilization, and therefore as the seedbed of our own way of life. We look to Athens, in the Greece of the 500s B.C., for the first example of democracy. We trace many of our legal concepts to the Roman republic that flourished from 509 to 27 B.C. Because of this heritage, references to Greece and Rome abound in our literature. It is not only the American poet Edgar Allan Poe who dreams of being "brought . . . home,"

> To the glory that was Greece,
> And the grandeur that was Rome.

However, Southern Europe is much more than Greece and Rome. The region stretches from the stormy shores of the Atlantic to the balmy beaches of the Black Sea. Within that span are ten full-sized nations and five "mini-states." From most to least populous, the full-sized nations are Italy, Spain, Romania, Portugal, Greece, Yugoslavia, Bulgaria, Bosnia-Herzegovina, Albania, and Macedonia. The "mini-states" are Malta, Andorra (an-DAWR-uh), Monaco, San Marino, and Vatican City.

THE REGION

During the Cold War, the region split into a western half (allied with the United States through the North Atlantic Treaty Organization) and an eastern half (ruled by Communist governments). The western nations —still in NATO—are Portugal, Spain, Italy, and Greece. The Communist nations were Romania, Bulgaria, Albania, and Yugoslavia. Of these, only Yugoslavia retains a Communist government today.

Some Facts About Southern European Countries

COUNTRY	CAPITAL CITY	POPULATION (millions)	AREA (square miles)	PER CAPITA INCOME (U.S. dollars)	LIFE EXPECTANCY AT BIRTH
Albania	Tirana (tuh•RAHN•uh)	3.3	11,100	$ 1,200	72
Andorra	Andorra La Vella (an•DAWR•uh lah VAIL•yuh)	0.5	175	NA	NA
Bosnia-Herzegovina	Sarajevo (sah•rah•YEH•voh)	4.1	19,741	NA	NA
Bulgaria	Sofia (SOH•fee•uh)	9.0	42,823	5,710	68 M 74 F
Greece	Athens (ATH•uhnz)	10.0	50,961	5,605	75 M 80 F
Italy	Rome (ROHM)	57.7	116,500	18,420	73 M 80 F
Macedonia	Skopje (SKAW•pyeh)	1.9	9,928	NA	NA
Malta	Valletta (vah•LET•ah)	0.4	122	5,645	74 M 78 F
Monaco	Monaco–Ville (MAHN•uh•koh VEEL)	0.03	1	NA	NA
Portugal	Lisbon (LIZ•buhn)	10.4	35,550	6,900	71 M 78 F
Romania	Bucharest (boo•kuh•REST)	23.4	91,700	3,445	67 M 73 F
San Marino	San Marino (sahn mah•REE•noh)	0.02	24	NA	NA
Spain	Madrid (muh•DRIHD)	39.0	194,884	10,100	74 M 80 F
Vatican City	Vatican City (VAT•ih•kuhn)	0.001	0.2	NA	NA
Yugoslavia*	Belgrade (BEL•grayd)	9.9	39,440	NA	NA

NA = Not Available
M = Male
F = Female
*Serbia and Montenegro

Sources: 1992 Information Please Almanac; World Almanac and Book of Facts, 1992; New York Times

As you read in the previous chapter, the Central European republics of Slovenia and Croatia have broken away from Yugoslavia. So, too, have the republics of Bosnia-Herzegovina and Macedonia. Of the six original republics, only Serbia and Montenegro remain as parts of Yugoslavia. Yugoslavia, Bosnia-Herzegovina, and Macedonia are considered to be part of Southern Europe.

Land and Sea.   Travelers in the countryside of Southern Europe would be wise to take mountain boots and a canteen. There are mountains almost everywhere. Elevations exceed 15,000 feet (4,570 meters) in the Italian Alps and 11,000 feet (3,350 meters) in Spain's Pyrenees and Sierra Nevadas. Without a canteen, a hiker could run out of water, because water is scarce in most of Southern Europe. Farmers have used irrigation for centuries.

Look at the map facing page 1. You'll see that Southern Europe is composed of three major peninsulas. From west to east, they are the Iberian peninsula (Portugal and Spain), the Italian "boot" (that's its shape), and the Balkan peninsula, containing several countries. The arms of the Mediterranean that divide the peninsulas have names of their own. Can you find the Tyrrhenian Sea? The Adriatic Sea? The Aegean Sea?

Most of the land in all three peninsulas is mountainous. Flatlands occur in river valleys or on high plateaus. The nation with the greatest proportion of level lowland is Romania.

Many of the region's nations include Mediterranean islands. Majorca (muh-JAWR-kuh) is part of Spain. Sardinia and Sicily are parts of Italy. Crete, Rhodes, and dozens of smaller islands are parts of Greece. Malta, south of Sicily, is an independent island nation.

Two Maltese fishermen prepare their boat to go to sea. Behind their harbor are the church and houses of a small town on the south shore of Malta.

The vast Mediterranean Sea serves as a unifying link, providing a pathway for travel from one nation to another. Also, its warm waters help to moderate the climate of all the lands it touches. For example, Italy's capital, Rome, lies farther north than New York City. Yet Rome's maximum temperatures in January average 54° F (12° C) compared to New York's 37° F (3° C).

The deep blue color of the Mediterranean has inspired poets and lovers for centuries. The color is due to the high salt content of the Mediterranean's water. That, in turn, is due to high evaporation caused by the dryness of the climate. The Mediterranean region is noted for its hot, dry summers, with most of the year's rain falling in winter. In the United States, such a climate is found only in southern California.

People and Culture. The imprint of the past shows up throughout Southern Europe today. Almost the entire region once fell under Roman rule. In later centuries, Moors (Berbers and Arabs from northern Africa) invaded and conquered much of the Iberian peninsula. The Ottoman Empire ruled the entire Balkan Peninsula at one time, and Turkey stills holds its southeastern corner.

A visitor to Cartagena (kahr-tuh-HAY-nuh) ("New Carthage"), on Spain's Mediterranean coast, can find evidence of a succession of rulers—Carthaginians, Romans, Goths, Byzantines, Moors. Spain's name comes from a Phoenician word, *span*, meaning "far-away land." Spain's dominant language comes from Rome, and much of its music and food from the Moors. Similarly varied influences can be found at Sofia (SOH-fee-uh), Bulgaria. Founded by the Romans, later ruled by Byzantines and Turks, Sofia is today the capital of an independent Slavic state. Its Christian churches and Muslim mosques recall two of the strands in its past.

Slavs are the principal inhabitants in the southeastern portion of Southern Europe, in Bulgaria, Yugoslavia, Bosnia-Herzegovina, and Macedonia. The Romanians, who live north of Bulgaria, trace their language and heritage to the Romans, who conquered the lower Danube Basin in the 100s A.D. That's why they call their country Romania. The Albanians have their own distinct background. They trace their ancestry to a people, the Illyrians (ih-LIHR-ee-uhnz), who lived in the western Balkans long before the Roman empire. (See map, page 181.)

Over the centuries, Greeks and Romans roamed far and wide. The Greeks live mainly within Greece today. But they once had colonies and outposts through much of Southern Europe, western Asia, and northern Africa. The Romans were among the ancestors of today's Italians.

St. Peter's Basilica in Vatican City, in the western part of Rome, is the world's largest church. The dome was designed by Michelangelo and completed in 1590.

They spoke the Latin language. The languages spoken today in Italy, Spain, Portugal, France, and Romania all grew out of Latin. Because of their Roman origins, all these are called **Romance** languages.

The dominant religion in Southern Europe is Christianity. Rome has been a principal center of Christianity, in the form of Roman Catholicism, since the 300s A.D. Most people in Italy, Spain, and Portugal are Roman Catholics. The equally ancient Eastern Orthodox branch of Christianity developed in the Byzantine Empire and its capital of Constantinople. The two churches became permanently separated in A.D. 1054 (see page 46). The distinctive onion-shaped domes of Orthodox churches grace villages and cities throughout the Balkan peninsula. During the centuries of Turkish rule, most people in Albania plus many in Yugoslavia and Bulgaria became Muslims. Albania has the largest percentage of Muslims among European nations today.

The Economy. Southern Europe is the poorest of all Europe's regions. It has the fewest industries and the greatest percentage of people living in poverty. In many of the eastern parts of the region, economic life has been greatly disrupted by the turmoil that followed the collapse of Communist systems.

The bustling industries of northern Italy stand out as exceptions to the general poverty. Cities like Milan (mih-LAN), Rome, and Turin

251

(TOOR-ihn) throb with energy. Standards of living there are among the highest in Europe. In fact, Italy's per capita income exceeds Britain's. Other countries that are well on their way to building up industry are Spain, Portugal, and Greece. Italy, Spain, Portugal, and Greece benefit from membership in the European Community.

The agricultural and mineral resources of Southern Europe are scattered. Because so much of the land is mountainous, good farmland is scarce. The dryness of the climate poses further problems for farmers. As for minerals, mines in Southern Europe turn out such products as iron and gypsum, but energy minerals (coal and oil) are in short supply. Therefore, the region has to import most of its fuel. Romania's modest oil output is the biggest in the region. Spain is the biggest coal producer.

ITALY: TWO ECONOMIES, TWO CULTURES

Visit a village of southern Italy, and you could easily believe you had gone back a century in time. Villagers might get their water from a pump. They might plow with horses instead of tractors. Most would live in the simplest of conditions. On the other hand, if you visited a village in northern Italy, you'd find life much more modern. There would be tractors in the fields, running water in the homes, and fine homes with shiny motorcycles or cars outside.

Italy is one country, but it is split into two unequal parts, a prosperous north and a lagging south. The poverty of the south has pushed a steady stream of people to emigrate to other countries. Over the decades many southern Italians have left—for the United States, Canada, Argentina, Australia, and elsewhere. Italy's government has tried to even out the north-south differences, but it has made little headway. Many northerners resent the money the government has poured into southern development. Aid to the south has become a touchy political issue.

The Land.   The Italian "boot" is lumpy with mountains. In the far north rise the Alps, which separate Italy from France, Switzerland, and Austria. A chain of lower but still rugged mountains, the Appenines, forms the backbone of Italy's "boot." An extension of the Appenines reappears across the water in Sicily. Italy contains scattered volcanoes, such as Vesuvius (vuh-SOO-vee-uhs), Etna, and Stromboli (STRAWM-boh-lee). Vesuvius, in the south near Naples, is famous for an eruption in A.D. 79 that buried the cities of Pompeii and Herculaneum. Etna, in Sicily, had a major eruption as recently as 1992.

Belching thick clouds of smoke and great streams of molten lava, Mount Vesuvius forces people to flee from their homes near Naples, in southern Italy, in 1944.

The mountains and hills of Italy yield a variety of minerals, including mercury, sulphur, and a little coal and oil. But quantities tend to be limited. One of Italy's best-known resources is the exquisite marble that is quarried at Carrara (kuh-RAHR-uh) near Florence. Sculptors and builders in Italy and throughout the world have long prized Carrara marble for its fine color and texture.

Italy's chief lowland is the wide North Italian Plain, through which runs the Po River. The Po starts in the Alps and flows southeastward across northern Italy, emptying into the Adriatic Sea south of Venice. Two of Italy's most important industrial cities are located on this plain. They are Milan (population 1.5 million) and Turin (1 million). Farmers grow such crops as wheat, rice, and corn and raise herds of dairy cattle on the heavily-irrigated lands of the North Italian Plain. Farther south, smaller lowlands squeeze between the Appenines and the shores of the Mediterranean.

Many major cities lie in the mountains and hills of central Italy. The capital, Rome (population 2.8 million), flanks the Tiber River. Genoa (730,000) is a major seaport. Other central Italian cities include Bologna (buh-LOHN-yuh) (440,000) and Florence (435,000).

The poorest and driest lands occur in the hilly terrain of southern Italy. Farmers eke a poor existence out of the thin soil. They grow crops such as beans, olives, citrus fruits, and wine grapes, using irrigation wherever possible. The metropolis of southern Italy is Naples (population 1.2 million).

The People.   Throughout the Italian peninsula, people speak a common Italian language, although with many regional accents. For this the Italians can thank the towering influence of such writers of the 1300s as Dante. Dante's *Divine Comedy* helped to give Italy a single language to unify the earlier dialects.

Only in a few parts of Italy do people speak other languages. In the northeast, on lands acquired from Austria after World War I, some people speak German. In the northwest, some people speak French. An overwhelming majority of Italy's people belong to the Roman Catholic Church.

Governments: They Come and Go.   Like Germany, Italy is a relative latecomer to the world stage. Its various parts first unified in 1861, forming a constitutional monarchy under King Victor Emmanuel. The kingdom did not take control of Rome away from the church until 1870. From the 1920s to the early 1940s, Italy had a fascist government under dictator Benito Mussolini. It sided with Hitler's Germany in World War II—until 1943, when Mussolini was overthrown and Italy joined the Allies. After the war, Italians abolished the monarchy and created a democratic republic.

Italy's head of state is a president, elected by legislators. But the president is a figurehead. Most power is in the hands of a prime minister, elected by parliament. Parliament consists of two houses, the Chamber of Deputies and the Senate, and each house must approve all bills. Elections are held at least every five years.

With several political parties splitting the vote, the Italian republic seems to have turned governing into a game of musical chairs. A new prime minister comes to power about once every 11 months, as coalitions dissolve and form again. But Italy's government is not really as unstable as it would seem. In fact, the same politicians turn up again and again in positions of power. In the course of 50 successive governments from 1945 into the 1990s, only 18 men held the position of prime minister.

Under a system of proportional representation, more than a dozen parties hold seats in parliament. Over the years, the two largest parties have been the Christian Democrats, who are conservative and Catholic, and the Communists, leftist and anti-Catholic. Those parties' share of the votes has been slipping. In 1991, hoping to win wider support, the Communists revamped the party and adopted a new name, the Democratic Party of the Left. The Christian Democrats usually hold a dominant role, forming coalitions with smaller parties.

Italy's Economic Vitality. Governments might rise and fall, but for many years Italy's economy headed steadily upward. After World War II, Italy became one of Europe's economic "miracles." Its growth rate led the continent during the 1980s, ranking second only to Japan in the world at large.

In many parts of the world you can find such Italian products as fashionable silks, high-quality shoes, and Fiat automobiles. Occasionally you'll see a Lamborghini sports car. Step into almost any American shopping mall and you'll notice one of the shops of the Benneton chain, founded by three young members of an Italian family. Italian apparel turns up in many other stores as well. Each year, fashion buyers flock to Milan for showings of the latest styles offered by such Italian designers as Giorgio Armani and Gianni Versace. Milan rivals Paris as a center of world fashion.

Italy has all the basics of modern industry. It has vast steel mills, shipyards, machine-tool plants, textile mills, food processing plants. Companies like Fiat, Pirelli, and Olivetti are giant industrial firms. However, Italy's businesses are more likely than those in other industrial countries to be small and family-owned. That makes it harder for Italy's businesses to raise capital for expansion. A second weakness of Italy's economy is a relative lack of high-tech industries. Research centers at cities like Bari, on Italy's east coast, are trying to help Italy develop the industries of the future.

North and South. The biggest economic problem of all, however, is the gap between the prosperous north and the struggling south, which includes the islands of Sicily and Sardinia. Wages are lower in the south, and unemployment is higher. Even though many industries have been started in the south, often with government subsidies, few have prospered. The productivity (output per worker) of southern industries is barely half that of northern industries.

Food, Italian Style. Walk down almost any Italian street and you'll see a restaurant called a *trattoria* (trah-toh-REE-uh) where you can buy a simple meal. By studying the menu, you may be able to tell whether you are in the north or the south of the country. For the two halves of Italy are divided by a food boundary that is just as real as the economic boundary.

A traditional Italian meal starts with pasta. In the north, one common pasta dish is baked lasagna, made with layers of flat wide noodles sandwiched with sauce, cheese, and sometimes meat. Meat and cheese may also be pinched between layers of dough to form little packets called ravioli. Hard-noodle dishes like spaghetti and macaroni are more popular in the south. Sauces for pasta dishes come in endless varieties. As a reminder that you are never far from the sea in Italy, sauces often include seafoods like clams, tuna, anchovies, and squid.

Enjoying Life. Food is one of many aspects of life that Italians take the time to enjoy. Another is music. Performances at Milan's famed opera house, the Teatro alla Scala (SKAH-lah), are but one part of Italy's musical heritage. Melodies also float over the canals of Venice, where a person rowing a long narrow gondola may break into song to entertain the passengers. Florence and other cities hold annual music festivals. The beat of popular music thumps from speakers throughout the nation.

SPAIN AND PORTUGAL: THE IBERIAN TWINS

If you board a plane in Rome in late afternoon and fly westward toward the setting sun, by suppertime you can be in Madrid, the capital of Spain. Because the Spanish eat late—10 p.m. is about right—you'll have plenty of time to enjoy a leisurely meal at a sidewalk cafe. Start with a cold gazpacho soup blending tomatoes, cucumber, garlic, and olive oil. Then dig into a steaming chicken and seafood stew called a *paella* (pah-YEL-uh).

Spain shares the Iberian peninsula at the southwestern corner of Europe with its neighbor, Portugal. By far the larger of the two is Spain. It covers five times the area of Portugal and has four times more people.

In many ways, Spain and Portugal are twins. They share a common past that includes rule by Romans and Moors. Their people once spoke a common language, Latin. However, Portugal gained its own ruler in the 1100s, and separate languages evolved on different sides of the border. While both nations passed through a long period of dictatorship in the 1900s, they have had democratic governments since the 1970s. Spain and Portugal have joined the European Community and are trying to build fully industrialized economies.

Spain: Land and People. Most of Spain lies on a high, arid plateau fringed with mountains. Madrid is in the center of the plateau, 190 miles (306 km.) from the sea. That is farther inland than any other capital in Southern Europe. In the north, the Pyrenees cut Spain off from its neighbor, France. Only in the Ebro Valley of the northeast and the Andalusian Plain of the southwest do extensive lowlands occur.

Spain's difficult geography has isolated its regions and made for a variety of cultures and languages. The language we call Spanish is really the language of Castile (kas-TEEL), the area around Madrid. Most of Spain's people speak this Castilian Spanish. But in the north and east, large numbers of people prefer to speak their own local languages. In Catalonia, around Barcelona, people speak Catalan (KAT-uh-lan), another Romance language. In the Basque provinces around Bilbao (bil-BAH-oh), people speak Basque, which is unrelated to any other known language. In Galicia (guh-LISH-uh), at the northwestern tip of Spain, people speak Galician, which is similar to Portuguese.

Regional feeling is often strong. Indeed, a small Basque separatist movement has resorted to terrorism in a campaign for independence. Spain's governments have tried to accommodate regional feelings. They now allow the regions a great deal of autonomy in local affairs.

The running of the bulls through the streets of the city of Pamplona is a famous yearly event in Spain. It is part of the city's annual fiesta, or festival.

CASE STUDY:

Snacktime in Madrid

In Madrid and other Spanish cities, customers at cafes enjoy a sampling of *tapas*, or appetizers, before their dinner—or often in place of it. Some cafes offer as many as 50 *tapas*. Here are some of the choices:

1. Ham chunks garnished with red peppers
2. Pork with a sauce of olive oil, garlic, vinegar, and spices
3. Boiled potatoes garnished with parsley, mayonnaise and garlic
4. Broad beans with ham and sausage
5. Potato omelet
6. Fish in cognac sauce with crabmeat, carrots, and seasonings
7. Kidneys sauteed in white wine sauce . . .
8. Shrimp in hot olive oil with garlic, parsley, and red pepper
9. Chicken livers in meat sauce with egg slices
10. Salt cod with a Basque sauce . . .
11. Salmagundi of shellfish with hard-cooked egg
12. Red peppers sprinkled with garlic
13. Black olives marinated with onions and oregano
14. Fried bread crumbs
15. Salt cod stewed with garlic and cayenne
16. Tuna fish pies
17. Fried green peppers with red sausage
18. Stewed quail
19. Tripe stew
20. Snails in hot sauce
21. Pickled beets
22. Pigs' feet in tomato, olive oil, onion, and garlic sauce
23. Green peppers stuffed with chopped veal in meat sauce
24. Baby eels boiled in oil . . .
25. Small squid "in their ink"

Peter S. Feibleman and the Editors of Time-Life Books. *The Cooking of Spain and Portugal.* New York: Time-Life Books.

1. Make one general statement about the kind of ingredients used in the *tapas* listed above.

2. Compare *tapas* to typical American snack foods. List three differences.

Tolerance and Intolerance.   The leniency of today has not always been a feature of Spanish life. Spain has known periods of great tolerance, but also of great intolerance. During the 1200s, Christians, Jews, and Muslims lived in harmony in Iberia. Later, in a series of wars known as the *reconquista* (ray-kohn-KEES-tah) (reconquest), Spanish forces drove Moorish armies across the Strait of Gibraltar to Africa. A period of great intolerance followed. In 1492, Spain's rulers expelled all Jews and Muslims who refused to convert to Roman Catholicism. Most Spanish governments from that time through the end of the Franco dictatorship in the 1970s also treated dissenters harshly.

Republic or Monarchy for Spain?   As Franco grew old, an old question resurfaced: Should Spain be a republic (without a king) or a monarchy (with a king)? Franco himself preferred that Spain become a monarchy. He arranged for Juan Carlos, a member of the old ruling family, to become king after his own death, which occurred in 1975.

In the new democratic Spain, the king has served as a symbol of unity and a supporter of the rule of law. He stood firm when a group of army officers tried to seize power in 1981. The king has little real power, however. The government is headed by a prime minister who is responsible to the elected parliament. Socialists are Spain's strongest political group. Parties on the political right have been weakened by splits and by a tendency to focus on regional issues.

Spain's Economic Growth.   Since Spain joined the European Community in 1986, it has torn down its high tariff walls. The "opening to Europe" has given Spain's economy a boost. Car makers and other multinational companies have built new plants in Spain, to take advantage of its relatively lower wages. Cities like Madrid (population 3.2 million), Barcelona (1.8 million), and Seville (645,000) have experienced building booms.

Barcelona is in Catalonia, Spain's richest region. It has a proud tradition of modernism in art, industry, and even architecture. Visitors to Barcelona can gaze up at the knobby spires of the Church of the Holy Family, designed by Catalonian architect Antonio Gaudí. They can tour the immense stadium constructed for the 1992 Summer Olympics.

Tourism is one of Spain's busiest industries. Many tourists come especially to see bullfighting. Tourists also like the sunny beaches of places like the Costa Brava (northeastern Catalonia) and Majorca (off Spain's east coast). Portugal also gets visitors seeking sun and fun.

Portugal: Land and Climate. Hills and mountains cover most of Portugal, with lowlands in the west and south. Because of its location at the western edge of Iberia, Portugal receives more rain than most of Spain. Moist winds off the Atlantic give northern Portugal a rainy climate with short, cool summers. Southern Portugal, however, has the dry climate one would expect to find along the Mediterranean.

Hot, dry weather is ideal for the cork oak, which has a spongy bark to protect it against hot winds. The bark yields cork, as in bottle stoppers. Portugal is the world's leading producer of cork.

Portugal's Economy. Until quite recently, agriculture, forestry, and fishing were Portugal's main industries. Leading crops include wine grapes, cotton, and olives. Because Portugal's farms tend to be small and inefficient, Portugal imports about half its food.

Unlike Spain, Portugal has always been a trading nation, so it never erected high tariff barriers. Portugal has traditionally had close ties with Britain. The British drink large quantities of Portugal's famous port wine. British investors own many Portuguese businesses.

Portugal's top manufacturing industries produce textiles and shoes. Competition in such goods is fierce, so Portugal has been trying to develop a wider range of industries. The European Community has supplied money to help build new roads and railroads.

Portugal's capital and major city, Lisbon, has a population of 820,000. For centuries, Lisbon was the center of a far-flung Portuguese empire. The last vestiges of that empire vanished in the 1970s when two African colonies, Mozambique and Angola, won their independence.

Many decades of authoritarian rule under Antonio Salazar (sah-lah-ZAHR) also ended in the 1970s. Portugal is now a democracy. The nation has an elected president and a prime minister who answers to parliament.

THE BALKANS: CONFLICTING NATIONALISMS

To some outsiders, the Balkans, as the countries of the Balkan peninsula are called, seem always to be feuding. During the 1800s, quarrels in the Balkans were a constant concern of European diplomacy. Remember that it was the assassination of an Austrian archduke at Sarajevo, the capital of Bosnia-Herzegovina, that touched off World War I in 1914. These conflicts reflect the amazing ethnic variety of the region.

Land and People. A mountainous and difficult terrain divides the Balkan peninsula into many small natural regions. Peaks and plateaus help to isolate groups from one another. But the mountains are not an effective barrier against invasion, and invaders have often stormed into the peninsula. One such invader was the Ottoman Empire, based in what is now Turkey. The Muslim Turks ruled most of the peninsula for hundreds of years, and left their mark.

Stop for a cup of coffee at a cafe in Skopje (SKAW-pyeh), the capital of Macedonia. You'll be served the thick, syrupy Turkish version of the brew. Walk through the streets of Skopje looking for houses of worship. You'll see not only Orthodox Christian churches but also the minarets of Islamic mosques. You'll find Roman Catholic churches as well. Those three religions have many believers in the Balkans.

The peoples of the Balkan peninsula speak six major languages. The languages are Romanian, Albanian, Greek, Serbo-Croatian, Macedonian, and Bulgarian. Romanians and Albanians use our own Latin alphabet, but if you picked up a newspaper elsewhere in the area you might have trouble making out the letters. The Greeks have an alphabet of their own. Others in the region are South Slavs who use the same Cyrillic alphabet as the Russians.

Mixing It Up. If you tried to draw lines on a map to show divisions among ethnic groups within the Balkans, you'd soon give up in dismay. That's because the Balkan peoples often live jumbled together, rather than in distinct ethnic neighborhoods.

The scrambling of peoples in the Balkans has helped to produce the feuding and warfare for which the region is noted. Feelings of nationalism run high. Nationalist movements fought against the Turks and other conquerors. But often they have turned neighbor against neighbor.

The Cold War imposed a measure of stability on the Balkans. Communist governments ruled much of the region. They forcefully squelched nationalist quarrels. But the end of the Cold War brought a release of pent-up resentments. The old feuds of the Balkans flared up once again, with the greatest impact on Yugoslavia.

Yugoslavia. Born as a union of South Slavs in 1918, Yugoslavia entered the 1990s as a federation of six republics—Serbia, Macedonia, Croatia, Slovenia, Bosnia-Herzegovina, and Montenegro. As you read in the last chapter, the federation began to disintegrate in 1991. Once again, neighbor battled against neighbor.

A Serbian woman stands outside the remains of her house, which was completely destroyed in fighting betweens Serbs and Croats, July 1991.

The towering presence of one man had held Yugoslavia together after the bitter Croat-Serb clashes of World War II. That man was a Croat known by his Communist code name Tito. His real name was Josip Broz. During World War II, Tito led an anti-Nazi resistance group called the Partisans. After the war, Tito became the supreme national leader. He vigorously suppressed local nationalisms by concentrating power in Belgrade, the federal capital (and also the capital of Serbia). So long as Tito was alive, his Communist system kept Yugoslavia united. But after his death in 1980, the federation began a slow disintegration.

In 1991, four republics—Slovenia, Croatia, Bosnia–Herzegovina, and Macedonia—seceded and claimed the status of independent nations. They began experimenting with freely elected governments and free-market economies. But many Serbs who lived in those four republics resisted the moves to independence. They did not want to live under non-Serb rule. Fierce fighting broke out, not only in Croatia but in other republics as well. The Serbian minority groups got help from Communist leaders who retained power in Belgrade, and from the

Yugoslavian army, most of whose officers were Serbian. The fact that the Serbs often lived intermingled with other groups made a solution to the problem difficult, as did the wishes of minority groups, such as Albanians, who live within Serbia.

Albania.   The poorest country in Europe, Albania is about the size of Maryland. It hugs the eastern shores of the Adriatic, with Albanian-speaking people spilling over into neighboring Serbia and Macedonia.

During the Cold War, Albania had one of the harshest of all Communist systems. Its people eke a simple living out of the hilly and mountainous land. A newly democratic government has contracted with Western oil companies to explore possible offshore oil deposits that might help to finance an expansion of industry. Albania exports chrome, copper, hydroelectric power . . . and frogs.

Bulgaria.   Facing east onto the Black Sea, Bulgaria is a Slavic nation that historically has looked to Russia as a protector. It was a Russian victory over Turkey in 1878 that freed Bulgaria from Ottoman rule. To this day, about 10 percent of Bulgaria's population speaks Turkish. Under Communist rule, this Pennsylvania-sized nation built up industry and built nuclear plants to provide electric power. It produced many of the computers used in the Communist bloc. Democratic elections in the 1990s produced a non-Communist government. However, many voters still support the former Communists, who have regrouped in the new Bulgarian Socialist party.

Romania.   Lying north of the Danube River from Bulgaria, Romania has the largest population of any Balkan nation. It also occupies the largest area. The Carpathian Mountains separate lowland areas in the south and east from another lowland area, Transylvania, in the northwest. A large Hungarian minority lives in Transylvania, which probably is best known as the home of the fictional vampire Count Dracula.

Nationalist agitation has called into question Romania's eastern border with Moldova. Much of Moldova was part of Romania before becoming part of the Soviet Union in 1940. Moldova gained its independence in 1991. Two out of three Moldovans speak Romanian, and many of them wish to reunite Moldova with Romania.

The collapse of the Communist era in Romania was especially brutal. After deadly clashes between security forces and anti-Communist crowds, the army supported a popular uprising in 1989. The corrupt and brutal Communist ruler, President Nicolai Ceausescu (chow-SHESSkoo), and his wife, who was also a high official, were executed. Many of the Ceausescus' associates remained in power during the transition to a more democratic system.

Greece. The one Balkan country that did not fall under Communist rule was Greece, at the southern tip of the peninsula. However, Greece did go through a period of repressive military rule from 1967 to 1974. A referendum in 1974 abolished the Greek monarchy, and today Greece is a republic. The main power is in the hands of a prime minister, who is responsible to an elected parliament.

Greece occupies a "mini-peninsula" that extends south from the main Balkan peninsula. Besides a mountainous main section, the nation includes dozens of islands that are scattered through the Ionian and Aegean Seas. Greek mythology has familiarized the world with many of the place names, such as Mount Olympus, home of the Greek gods.

Say the word "Macedonia" to Greeks and they will assume you are speaking of the northern section of their country, around the port city of Salonika (sal-uh-NEE-kuh). Historically, the name Macedonia has applied to a region that includes parts of Greece and Bulgaria. Macedonia was once a powerful kingdom, the base from which Alexander the Great launched his conquest of Greece and the Persian empire in the 300s B.C. Greek nationalists object to the use of the name Macedonia by Slavs, claiming it to be a Greek place and name.

Despite its past cultural glory, modern Greece has known widespread poverty. Efforts to build up industry gained strength when the European Community admitted Greece to membership in 1981. However, Greece has been slow to open its economy to outside influences. Two thirds of the economy is under government ownership or control. The main industries are centered around the capital, Athens (population 3 million), the nearby port of Piraeus, and Salonika.

Greece has been a close military ally of the United States ever since 1947, when President Truman sent aid to help crush a leftist rebellion. Greece became a member of NATO. During the Persian Gulf War of 1991, the United States used the Greek island of Crete as a supply base.

FIVE SMALL COUNTRIES

No survey of Southern Europe would be complete without a glance at five "mini-states" tucked into odd corners of the region. Most of these states trace their origins to feudal times. Except for Vatican City, whose nationhood dates to 1929, they owe their existence to historical quirks and sometimes to out-of-the-way locations.

Andorra. Perched high in the Pyrenees Mountains between Spain and France, Andorra has transformed itself from a land of simple farmers into a thriving tourist resort and trading center. Since the 1400s it has been a co-principality (a land ruled by two princes), ruled jointly by a Spanish bishop and the president of France. By ancient tradition, Andorrans still pay the bishop an annual tribute of seven hams, 14 chickens, and 28 cheeses. The co-princes must approve any new laws passed by a 28-member parliament. Andorra has no constitution and no income tax. Workers are not allowed to form trade unions. Only about 10,000 of the 50,000 people living in Andorra are Andorran citizens.

Monaco. Monaco is known to gamblers the world over as the site of a famed casino at Monte Carlo. Occupying less than one square mile, Monaco is an **enclave** on the southern coast of France, near the border with Italy. An enclave is a small, separate territory within the borders of a bigger land. Monaco is a principality with a single sovereign, Prince Rainier (ren-YAY) III. The prince rules with the aid of an elected National Council of 18 members. Besides gambling, Monaco has a smattering of light industries.

Malta. A strategically situated island in the central Mediterranean, Malta has a long history as a naval base. A line of naval powers from Phoenicia and Rome down to Britain has controlled Malta. Malta became independent in 1964 and is now a republic within the Commonwealth of Nations. The nation includes Malta and four other islands, occupying less land all told than the city of Philadelphia. Christianity came to Malta in A.D. 58, when the apostle Paul was shipwrecked on his way to Rome. Today almost all the nation's 400,000 people are Roman Catholics. Political power has swung between a leftist, anti-clerical party and a rightist, pro-Catholic one.

San Marino. Covering less than one fifth as much territory as Malta, San Marino claims to be the smallest republic in the world. Officially styled the Most Serene Republic of San Marino, it is a mountainous enclave in eastern Italy, 12 miles inland from the Adriatic Sea. According to one tradition, a Christian stonecutter named Marino founded the country in the 300s A.D. when he fled from persecution in Rome. Another tradition tells of a foreign army that got lost in the fog

*The capital city of San Marino, also called San Marino,
climbs the side of Mount Titano to the castle at its peak.
The city is surrounded by a medieval stone wall.*

when trying to invade San Marino in the 1500s. The would-be invaders could not find the country, gave up, and went home.

Millions of tourists visit San Marino each year to admire its medieval fortress and buy cut-rate perfumes, furs, and electronic goods imported from other countries.

Vatican City. The smallest of all mini-states is Vatican City, a tiny remnant of the Papal States, which once included much of central Italy. As the spiritual and administrative ruler of the Roman Catholic Church, Pope John Paul II is also the ruler of Vatican City. Like other independent states, the Vatican sends diplomats to serve as ambassadors in foreign nations.

Vatican City's 109 acres include exquisite gardens, libraries, church offices, and church courts, as well as museums and places of worship. Many papal ceremonies take place in the massive sanctuary of St. Peter's Basilica, which adjoins the papal palace near one edge of Vatican City. Nearby is the Sistine Chapel, where art lovers can gaze up at Michelangelo's masterly fresco on the vaulted ceiling. Classical Greek sculptures and other famous art works are also among the Vatican's many treasures.

Chapter 11:
CHECKUP

REVIEWING THE CHAPTER

I. Building Your Vocabulary

In your notebook, for each term in Column A, write the letter of the best description in Column B. (There is an extra item in Column B.)

Column A

1. enclave
2. Romance language
3. Transylvania
4. *trattoria*
5. *paella*

Column B

a. a restaurant in Italy
b. language used for love poems
c. small territory within a larger one
d. legendary home of Count Dracula
e. Spanish rice dish
f. language related to Latin

II. Understanding the Facts

In your notebook, copy the following sentences, filling in the blanks.

1. Iberia, the Italian "boot," and the Balkans are all _____ that protrude from the European continent.

2. The parts of Southern Europe that were once under the control of Islamic civilizations are _____ and _____.

3. The only major Southern European nation that is not a republic with an elected president is _____.

4. The nation of Southern Europe that has the highest standard of living is _____.

5. Three languages spoken in Spain are _____, _____, and _____.

III. Thinking It Through

In your notebook, write the letter of the word or phrase that best completes each of the following sentences.

1. One factor contributing to the poverty of southern Italy is that the region:
   a. gets less rain than the north.
   b. has no access to sea trade.
   c. has too few people to cultivate the land.
   d. has been devastated by volcanoes.

2. One reason for Italy's frequent changes of government is that:
   a. many Italians vote for the Communist party.
   b. Italy has no king or queen.
   c. more than a dozen political parties hold seats in parliament.
   d. elections are held at six-month intervals.

3. Many Italians have emigrated to other countries because:
   a. Italy has never had a democratic government.
   b. Italy has the lowest standard of living in Southern Europe.
   c. it is hard to make a living in southern Italy.
   d. there are too many floods and mudslides in Italy.

4. The fact that people in Italy and Spain use olive oil in their cooking probably reflects the fact that:
   a. they are too poor to afford butter.
   b. olives are easily grown in the Mediterranean climate.
   c. both countries were once under Turkish rule.
   d. Italy was colonized by Spain.

5. It was hard for Yugoslavia's republics to separate peacefully because:
   a. they all had weak and ineffective governments.
   b. outside powers became involved in the republics' internal quarrels.
   c. most Yugoslavs preferred to keep the Communist system.
   d. ethnic groups were intermingled rather than living in their own separate regions.

DEVELOPING CRITICAL THINKING SKILLS

1. Describe ways in which the geography of Southern Europe has hampered the development of modern industrial economies.

2. Why is Italy said to be a nation with "two cultures"? What recommendations would you make to Italy's government about ways to heal the split and unite the two cultures? Explain your reasoning.

3. In what ways can Spain and Portugal be described as "twins"? In what ways are they different from each other?

4. Why have the Balkans so often been a region of strife? In answering the question, refer both to the peninsula's geography and to its history.

ENRICHMENT AND EXPLORATION

1. Find out about an artist, writer, or composer from Southern Europe. Write a paper describing the person's life and telling how the person contributed to the world's cultural heritage.

2. Collect stories from newspapers and magazines about current events in one of the countries of Southern Europe. Present an oral report to the class, describing what you have learned.

3. Using library resources, discover what aspects of life in present-day Spain reflect Jewish and Moorish contributions from before 1492. Alternatively, learn how centuries of Turkish rule in the past have affected the Balkans of today. Make a classroom display showing how different cultures have interacted in Southern Europe.

4. Plan a trip that will take you to at least three locations in Southern Europe. Describe how you will get to each location and what you expect to see and do while you are there. Tell how such a visit would deepen your understanding of Southern European life and culture.

5. Read a book relating a writer's travels somewhere in Southern Europe, either in the past or in our own time. Alternatively, read a novel or play written by a Southern European writer. Write a book report describing what insights into Southern European life you have gained through your reading.

6. Collect information and pictures about bullfights in Spain. Stage a classroom debate on the pros and cons of bullfighting. Make a classroom display that incorporates students' comments about the practice.

EUROPE AND THE WORLD

1947–Today

1947	India and Pakistan become independent.
1948–1949	*Arab–Israeli War*
1950–1953	*Korean War*
1951	Iran nationalizes its oil fields.
1953	Military coup deposes Egyptian king.
1954	Battle of Dien Bien Phu
1956	Nasser nationalizes Suez Canal.
1957	Ghana becomes first sub-Saharan colony to be granted independence.
1958	Morocco and Tunisia become independent from France.
1960	African members of the French Community gain independent status.
1960	OPEC instituted in Baghdad.
1961	*Berlin Wall built.*
1962	Algeria becomes independent from France.
1964	*U.S. bombs North Vietnam and sends troops to South Vietnam.*
1979	Soviet troops airlifted into Afghanistan.
1980	Iraq invades Iran.
1985	*Mikhail Gorbachev becomes general secretary in USSR.*
1988	Soviets begin withdrawal from Afghanistan.
1991	The Persian Gulf War
	Breakup of Soviet Union and formation of the Commonwealth of Independent States
1992	Treaty of Maastricht

12 Europe and the World

The role of Europe in the world underwent a major change in the years following World War II. Great Britain, France, and Germany were no longer the economic and political giants they had been during the 1800s and early 1900s. Now, as they and their neighbors rebuilt their war-torn countries, they were confronted with independence movements throughout their colonial empires. As the century drew to a close, other world developments began to affect Europe.

THE END OF EMPIRES

One of the most important changes after World War II was the collapse of European empires throughout Asia, Africa, the Middle East, and the Caribbean. From 1945 to 1985, 96 new countries were born. One third of the world's people became citizens of newly independent countries.

Roots of Revolution.   World War II intensified the natural longing of the colonized peoples for freedom from foreign control. Many of them had fought for the Allies, an experience that gave them a stronger sense of their rights and abilities. At the same time, they came to realize that the colonial powers were not necessarily all-powerful. Moreover, as they heard and read Allied wartime propaganda about the forces of freedom pitted against the forces of oppression, they became more inspired to achieve their own freedom. All that was needed to transform these feelings into action was dynamic leadership. In many colonies, such leaders arose, most often from the educated minority who had studied at European or American universities. There they had learned the history of the United States' and Europe's revolutionary struggles. These inspired them to lead their own struggles against colonialism.

The roots of revolution could also be traced to Europe itself. The European colonial powers had won the war, but it had taken a tremendous toll. An exhausted Europe was in no mood to fight new wars. In addition, many Europeans now questioned the moral justification of colonialism.

One by one, peoples in Asia, Africa, the Middle East, and the Caribbean won their freedom. Each victory was different, depending on local conditions and the attitudes of the colonial powers. Three case studies—how the British left India, how the French lost Indochina, and how Britain lost control of the Suez Canal—illustrate this variety.

The British Leave India.   India was the first colony after the war to win its freedom. The British had long considered it the "jewel in the crown" of their empire. But many Indians held a different view of the relationship. Late in the 1800s, members of the Indian National Congress had begun to speak out against British domination and to urge resistance through strikes, boycotts, and other peaceful protests. The tactics of nonviolence were adopted before the war by an inspiring western-educated leader, Mohandas K. Gandhi (GAN-dee).

When war broke out in 1939, Britain declared that India was also at war, a decision that enraged many Indians. By 1942, Britain's fortunes were at a low point. With Japan on India's doorstep in neighboring Burma, and German troops advancing eastward across North Africa, Britain felt an urgent need to gain Indian support for the war. A member of the British cabinet, Sir Stafford Cripps, was sent to India with the message that if Indians would support the war effort, Britain would give them independence after victory was achieved.

Nationalist leaders rejected the Cripps offer and passed a "Quit India" resolution, demanding immediate freedom. The British response was to jail resistance leaders for the duration of the war. Although the move temporarily silenced the opposition, it created another problem. Because most of the silenced Congress leaders were Hindus, their imprisonment gave the large number of Muslims in India a chance to strengthen their political power. The Muslim League, under the leadership of Mohammed Ali Jinnah, began to demand not only independence from the British, but also independence from the Hindus—in other words, a separate Islamic state.

After the war, elections in Britain brought the Labor Party to power. Long opposed to colonialism, the Laborites set about fulfilling Cripps's promise. Admiral Lord Louis Mountbatten was sent to India as viceroy (governor) with instructions to arrange a peaceful transition to

*Lord Louis Mountbatten, the last British viceroy in
India, and his wife meet with Mohandas Gandhi, leader
of the independence movement in India, in April 1947.*

self-rule. Although Mountbatten and Indian leaders such as Gandhi
tried to bring the two religious groups together, little progress was made.
Eventually Mountbatten recommended division into a Hindu state and
a Muslim state. The British colony of India became two independent
nations, Hindu India and Islamic Pakistan.

The French Fight for Indochina. While the British adopted a fairly
flexible attitude toward the breakup of their empire, other colonial powers, such as the Dutch in Indonesia, the French in Indochina and North
Africa, and the Portuguese in southern Africa, made every effort to
reestablish a rigid control over their possessions after the war.

Parts of Indochina, for example, had been under French rule since
1862. This area, the present-day countries of Vietnam, Laos, and
Cambodia, had fallen into Japanese hands during the war, a takeover
made easier by strong anti-European sentiments among the people of
Indochina. Playing on these feelings, the Japanese occupiers called their
own empire the "Greater East Asia Co-Prosperity Sphere."

When the war ended in 1945, the French returned to reclaim their
colony. The Japanese were forced to withdraw, but only after giving

support and arms to a resistance movement called the Viet Minh (vee-et MIN), or League for the Independence of Vietnam. The Viet Minh was led by a Communist, Ho Chi Minh, who had lived and studied in Paris, Moscow, and China.

When the French refused to recognize the Viet Minh, fighting broke out. Laos and Cambodia soon fell to the French, but Ho Chi Minh's power base in Vietnam remained strong. For nine long years the struggle continued. France received help from the United States, which now saw the Viet Minh's activities as part of Communist expansion in the Cold War. Gradually the Viet Minh got the upper hand. The turning point for the French came in 1954, with France's stunning defeat at the battle of Dien Bien Phu (dyen-byen-FOO). The French withdrew from Indochina. The country was temporarily divided into a Communist North Vietnam and a non-Communist South Vietnam until elections could be held.

Britain Loses the Suez Canal.   Sometimes the postwar struggles focused more on economic than on political issues. Egypt, for example, had gained its freedom from British political domination in 1937. But the French held a 99-year lease on the Suez Canal, and the British owned the company that ran it. Each year, the canal earned British stockholders some $3 million in fees collected from trading vessels that used the canal as a shortcut between Europe and Asia. For the British, and the rest of Europe, however, the canal represented something far more important than transit fees. It was the quickest, most efficient way for tankers to transport oil from the Middle East and Southeast Asia to Europe. Industrial Europe, by the 1950s, needed oil even more desperately than Europe in the 1500s had needed spices.

But the times had changed. Europe could no longer dominate events as it had in the 1500s or the 1800s. A new Egyptian leader, Gamal Abdel Nasser (NAHS-uhr), challenged Europe's right to control a waterway running through his country. As a fiery nationalist, Nasser was intent on asserting full control over all of Egypt's territory, as well as uniting Arabs throughout the Middle East. He decided to defy the imperialist powers who had built the canal in the 1800s and who had controlled it ever since. In 1956, he **nationalized** the canal, placing it under government ownership and control.

Nasser's actions outraged both the French and the British. The recently founded state of Israel, still in conflict with Egypt after the Arab–Israeli war of 1948–1949, joined the French and British, and together they invaded Egypt.

The Suez Crisis was resolved only after pressure was brought to bear on the invaders by the United States, the Soviet Union, and the United Nations. In the face of such condemnation, the invaders withdrew, and Nasser completed his nationalization of the canal. As historian H. Stuart Hughes has noted, "The Suez Expedition was the last stand of old-fashioned imperialism. . . . Suez showed that never again could Europeans coerce 'natives' in the old manner."

POST-COLONIAL RELATIONSHIPS

The collapse of Europe's overseas empires had a tremendous impact on the former colonies and the former colonizers alike. Both groups experienced widespread social, economic, and political readjustments. Both, however, continued to be influenced by their former relationships.

Lingering Ties with Europe. Having won their independence, many of the former colonies maintained relations with their former rulers. European languages, customs, currencies, and political systems were still strong in the newly independent countries.

This cultural imprint could be seen quite clearly in those countries once ruled by Britain. In India, Pakistan, and new nations throughout Africa, English remained the language of educated people. Many British political institutions, such as the parliamentary system and English common law, also were continued.

In addition to these informal ties, most of Britain's former colonies became linked to each other and to their former ruler by membership in the **British Commonwealth of Nations**, later called simply the **Commonwealth of Nations**. This organization of Britain and most of its former colonies offered its members a chance to exchange views and to work together toward common goals. Originally, members of the Commonwealth were allowed special tax privileges on goods imported and sold in Britain. However, this policy had to be abandoned when Britain joined the Common Market in 1973. In its place, the European Community worked out a series of agreements in which products originating in many of the developing countries received tariff-free access to all the European Community markets.

France continued to play an important role in the nations of West Africa. In 1958, the 12 French colonies there were offered the option of complete independence or an "autonomous" (self-governing) status within the "French Community." Initially, only Guinea chose independence.

President Ahmadou Ahidjo of Cameroon, a former French colony in West Africa, meets with President de Gaulle in July 1960. Cameroon had gained its independence earlier that year.

Within two years, however, all the others made the same choice. Still, the French presence remained strong, perhaps even stronger than the British. The French government provided generous economic aid and sent a steady stream of civil servants to help administer the governments, run the banks, and develop the education systems. As a result, those African nations of "French expression," as they described themselves, remained more strongly influenced by their former ruler than were their English-speaking counterparts.

The Politics of Independence. Apart from their relationship with their former rulers, the newly independent states became caught up in new patterns of association, based first on Cold War politics.

In the long era of hostility between the two superpowers, many of the new nations were pressured into choosing sides, either that of the "First World" of the United States and Europe or the "Second World" of the Soviet Union and its satellites. Instead, many of the new "Third World" states declared themselves to be **nonaligned**, or uncommitted, nations.

With the end of the Cold War, another pattern of alignment seemed to be emerging. In this view, the world was divided not between

Communist and non-Communist, but between north and south. North of the Equator were most of the richer nations, including Europe, the United States, and Japan. Near the Equator or south of it were most of the poorer nations. Some people in the South argued that their poverty was due largely to past exploitation by the North. The North, they said, should take responsibility for a fairer distribution of wealth, food, and technology among all countries.

Post-Colonial Europe. Decolonization also affected those European countries that lost their empires. Tens of thousands of colonial administrators, merchants, and military people lost both their professions and their sense of worth. Even greater numbers of settlers lost the only homes they had ever known. Forced to relocate in Europe, they often became outspoken opponents of Asian and African nationalism.

For companies, the loss of empire meant the loss of investments and sources of income. For several years, an exception to the trend was the continuing influence of British and Dutch oil companies. Yet even here, conditions changed. When oil companies lowered their payments to oil-producing countries in the late 1950s, several Middle East countries joined with Venezuela to create the Organization of Petroleum Exporting Countries (OPEC) in an effort to increase their bargaining power with the companies.

However, the loss of their colonial empires had some advantages for the people of Europe. Even in the glory days of empire, wealth had gone only to investors, settlers, and colonial administrators. The vast majority of Europeans never profited from the colonies. Moreover, by the 1950s the colonies had begun to cost the European governments more money than they brought in. Economists pointed to the contrast between Germany and France. Germany, which had had no colonies since 1918, had enjoyed the most rapid economic growth of any nation in postwar Europe. France, which clung to its holdings in Southeast Asia and North Africa, had been slower to prosper.

Changing Population Patterns. Another major effect of decolonization was the change it produced in Europe's **demographic,** or population, profile. For nearly 500 years, Europeans had been leaving the continent to settle in colonies scattered around the world. But following World War II, populations from abroad began to immigrate to Europe, largely to take advantage of the economic boom that occurred during the 1960s and 1970s. By the 1990s, more than 13 million newcomers had settled in Europe.

CASE STUDY:

Migrants on the Move

As Alan B. Simmons explains, recent immigrants to Europe are part of a world-wide pattern of migrations. They are part of a worldwide flow not easily stopped.

> Efforts by Europe, North America, and other developed regions to shut the door on the rising tide of migrants from the Third World are not only questionable on ethical grounds but may also turn out to be impractical as well. Many migrants will find ways round all but the most costly, vigorous, and harsh control systems. This is because the very logic of social and economic change tends to create new avenues and opportunities for migrants. . . .
>
> Equally misguided is the argument that coordinated international development efforts and economic growth in the countries of out-migration will soon lead to a reduction in South-to-North migration. . . . In the short to medium term—over twenty to thirty years or even longer—development efforts will probably tend to increase South–North migration. This is because the mechanization and increased efficiency required to boost productivity [in Third World countries] will mean that large numbers of workers will lose their jobs. As unemployment rises, so too will the numbers of people seeking refuge elsewhere. . . .
>
> It is estimated that some 60 million people in the world are currently "on the move." . . .
>
> Potential migrants are heavily concentrated in the poor regions of the South—in the previously colonized nations of Africa, Asia, the Caribbean, and Latin America, and in the southern regions of the [former] Soviet Union. They not only move to neighboring countries within their own regions, but, more and more, they are seeking to move to industrially advanced regions such as Europe. . . .

Alan B. Simmons, "Sixty Million on the Move." *UNESCO Courier*, January, 1992.

1. Why does Simmons think that efforts to improve production in Third World countries will actually increase the number of migrants?

2. How many migrants does Simmons think there are in the world today?

3. Why do many migrants try to settle in Europe?

A sign in Turkish identifies a grocery store in Berlin, the capital of Germany. By 1992 there were 1.7 million Turks living in Germany, 135,000 in Berlin alone.

The immigrants were from many places. People from Suriname, a former Dutch colony in South America, came to the Netherlands. Algerians, Moroccans, and Tunisians came to France. Indians, Pakistanis, Nigerians, Kenyans, and Caribbean islanders came to Great Britain. Turks came to Germany. When the economy boomed, these immigrants found jobs and acceptance. But when the economy faltered and jobs were scarce, the foreigners often encountered discrimination and hostility.

A new immigration began after the collapse in 1989 of Europe's Communist governments. Many eastern Europeans, no longer kept home by the Iron Curtain, moved to the prosperous nations to the west.

Europe's governments found themselves ill-prepared to cope with ethnic problems. Unlike the United States, Europe had little experience with integrating immigrant groups into the fabric of society. Some countries, such as Austria, took steps to limit immigration. In France and Germany, new anti-immigrant political parties won enough votes to make their voices heard.

EUROPE AND THE GLOBAL ECONOMY

In the 1800s, the imperialist powers, especially Great Britain, dominated the world's economy. The years after the end of World War II witnessed the end of empires and the rise of two superpowers, the United States and the Soviet Union. In the last decade of the century, however, the collapse of the Soviet Union raised the possibility of a new economic order. This new order would be based on the revolutionary developments of the past half-century.

The Second Industrial Revolution.   Since 1945, so many changes have taken place in science, technology, agriculture, and industry that the era has become known as the **Second Industrial Revolution.**

The application of new technologies to agriculture created a **Green Revolution.** New hybrid varieties of plants, used with irrigation, fertilizers, and pesticides, resulted in much larger crop yields, which could be achieved on smaller plots of less fertile land by fewer farmers.

New forms of energy, especially nuclear energy, began to replace electricity and gas. However, concern over the safety of nuclear power remained strong, especially after a 1986 accident at a power plant at Chernobyl (chehr-NOH-buhl), Ukraine, left many people dead and a large area unsafe to live in.

Advances in science and technology created a wealth of new products and processes. These included computers and computer software, advanced telephone systems, and other electronic products. These products created a revolution in the way information was accumulated and distributed. It became possible for people at home, school, or work to be in instant touch with anyone else, or with the world's vast store of knowledge. Observers began to speak of the world as a "Global Village." Other new products included robots, used in facories, and products made possible by advances in biology, such as new medicines, growth hormones, and pesticides.

In the business world, a new type of organization came into existence, the **multinational** corporation. A "multinational" is a company that operates, as its name suggests, in many countries. It might have directors from different countries and stockholders from around the world. It might have factories in 12 different countries, depending on where labor was cheapest or where technical expertise was most plentiful. It might sell these products all over the world. So successful were the multinationals that they grew at a rate of 10 percent a year, in contrast to a 4 percent growth rate for traditional corporations.

New Rules of the Economic Game.   New economic rules evolved in reaction to these new developments. Under the old economic order, for example, countries became rich if they had an abundance of natural resources, such as coal, iron, or fertile farmland. Under the new order, natural resources did not necessarily give a nation a competitive advantage. Thanks to the Green Revolution, it was now possible for just a few farmers to grow more food on less land. New **synthetic** materials made it possible to produce products without having great quantities of the traditional raw materials. Synthetic materials are those produced by chemical processes, as opposed to those found in nature.

Under the old order, factories were usually built close to the natural resources that were used in production. But the major industries of the 1990s were "smart" industries, involved in the manufacture of high-technology products. "Smart" industries could be built anywhere. As a result, multinational corporations usually located such factories where the workforce had sufficient education and training to run the operation.

Economists in the 1990s asked what would give countries a competitive edge in the next century. Many economists focused on two factors. One would be control of a large market—in other words, a large population prepared to invest, produce, buy, and sell goods and services. The other would be the educational level of the population. To run the all-important high-technology industries, people with highly developed scientific, managerial, and technical skills would be needed, in addition to a large skilled labor force.

Europe's Role in the New Order. Politicians and economists tried to determine which country or group of countries had the potential to gain dominance in the new world order. Many believed that the three main contenders would be Japan, the United States, and the European Community. Some believed that in the long run, the competitive edge could belong to Europe. There were two main reasons for this belief.

First and foremost were the numbers. Taken singly, no European nation except Germany was a formidable economic power. At midnight on December 31, 1992, however, Europe was scheduled to become the largest market in the world, as 380 million people integrated their economies into a single unit, the European Community. Moreover, with the breakup of the Soviet Union, the potential market became even greater. If the countries of the former Soviet Union were able to develop strong free-market economies, they might eventually join an enlarged European Community. Then the number of potential investors, producers, sellers, and buyers could swell to as many as 850 or 900 million people.

Second, Europe already possessed the single most important resource of the new economic order: a well-educated population. Throughout Europe, including eastern Europe and the former Soviet Union, the people had reaped the benefits of some of the best educational systems in the world. Moreover, each European nation brought its own special talents to the Community. The Germans, for example, brought skills gleaned from their highly successful history of production and trade. The Italians provided a talent for design. The French brought a talent for improving the quality of almost anything. The English shared their expertise in finance and banking.

Hurdles to Success.   In spite of this great potential, no one could be sure of the eventual outcome. Everyone agreed that there would be major hurdles to overcome.

For one thing, this would be the first time in history that a group of sovereign nations had banded together in so close an association. Their members would speak many different languages and come from many different cultural traditions. Some would be former enemies. Would the economic "glue" be strong enough to bind together such different elements? Would the member states be willing to give up enough of their sovereignty to make the association work?

Another major hurdle would be the integration of the former Communist nations of eastern Europe and the Soviet Union. Never before had leaders tried to transform, virtually overnight, a group of centrally planned economies into free markets. Would the rest of Europe (and the United States and Japan, as well) be prepared to invest huge amounts of money to build the desperately needed roads, telephone systems, and other basic systems that a modern economy needs? Would they help to replace the outdated, heavily polluting factories with new, well-equipped, environmentally acceptable plants? Would the people of these countries be able to develop new attitudes about working hard, taking risks, and being competitive? Would they be able to suffer through the years of hardship that would inevitably accompany the birth of a new system?

The Big Gamble.   The leaders of the newly formed European Community knew that their grand experiment was a gamble, but they also believed that the stakes were worth it. If the sovereign nations of Europe could overcome the difficulties of integration, and if the ex-Communist regimes could quickly turn themselves into successful market economies, then Europe, along with Japan and the United States, would surely be a formidable competitor in the new world order. Just possibly, it would fulfill the prediction of the economist Lester Thurow that "future historians are likely to record that the 21st century belong[ed] to the House of Europe."

REVIEWING THE CHAPTER

I. Building Your Vocabulary

In your notebook, write the correct term that matches the definition.

synthetic	demographic	infrastructure
Third World	nonalignment	multinational

1. having to do with population figures
2. a corporation owned and operated in more than one country
3. the nonindustrialized countries of Asia, Africa, and Latin America
4. a policy of neutrality as regards the Communist and non-Communist blocs
5. made by chemical processes
6. the underlying support system for a nation's economic development

II. Understanding the Facts

In your notebook, write the numbers 1 to 4. Write the letter of the correct answer to each question next to its number.

1. Who favored the partition of India?
   a. Gandhi   b. Jinnah   c. Mountbatten
2. When did the French relinquish control of Indochina?
   a. 1954   b. 1973   c. 1975
3. What kind of resources are most important for the new "smart industries"?
   a. capital resources   b. natural resources   c. human resources
4. How many people became part of the European Community in 1992?
   a. 100 million   b. 380 million   c. 850 million

III. Thinking It Through

In your notebook, write the numbers from 1 to 5. After each number, write the number of the correct answer to the question.

1. Which of the following factors seems to have been the best preparation for leadership in the colonial independence movements?
   a. a longing for freedom
   b. European military service
   c. a Western education

2. As a result of decolonization:
   a. many African and Asian workers emigrated to Europe.
   b. many settlers and administrators lost their jobs.
   c. the former colonial powers suffered permanent economic losses.

3. Which of the following factors gives the European Community the greatest advantage in the new global economy?
   a. a large amount of accumulated wealth
   b. a large, well-educated population
   c. rich natural resources

4. Which of the following motives behind the French and British invasion of Egypt in 1956 was probably most important?
   a. protection of easy access to oil
   b. protection of legal ownership
   c. protection of transit fees

5. The French influence in Africa remained strong due to the fact that:
   a. many Africans emigrated to France.
   b. many French civil servants helped administer the new nations.
   c. many new nations joined the French Community.

DEVELOPING CRITICAL THINKING SKILLS

1. Explain why most of Europe's colonies gained their freedom after World War II.

2. Discuss the effects on European countries (a) of trying to maintain their colonial empires, and (b) of losing their colonial empires.

3. Discuss the economic advantage and political disadvantage of membership in the European Community.

ENRICHMENT AND EXPLORATION

1. Choose one of the European powers that established colonies in Africa and Asia. Make a time line beginning with the initial colonization effort and ending with the year of independence. Use appropriate library references to gather information.

2. Plan an independence day celebration for one of the nations that gained its freedom during the postwar years. Using library resources, find out the date of the holiday and some of the customs of the country. Then plan a parade, describing the floats, the costumes, and the national flag. Plan food booths that offer national specialties. Plan for musical groups and dancers that reflect the local culture. Write a short speech for the leader of the country to deliver.

3. As a class project, prepare a large chart giving comparative information about the European Community, the United States, and Japan. Using library resources such as almanacs and encyclopedias, include the most recent information regarding population sizes, literacy rates, monetary units, gross national products, per capita gross national products, and the rates of real economic growth.

4. Working in small groups, collect recent information about the European nations that were once Soviet satellites: East Germany, Poland, Czechoslovakia, Hungary, Romania, and Bulgaria. You may need to use the *Reader's Guide to Periodical Literature* or a computerized searching system if one is available. Find out how the nation is adjusting to a free market society, what problems it is encountering, what progress it is making, and what outside aid it is receiving. Each group should prepare an oral report for the rest of the class.

5. Make a list of appropriate subjects for postage stamps to be used in a centralized European Community postal system. For example, what historical figures best embody the ideal of a United Europe? What scenic views best convey an idea of Europe's variety? Students with artistic ability may translate some of these suggestions into designs.

Glossary

absolute: not limited by any person or governmental body (*p. 38*)

absolutism: a political system that concentrates power in the hands of one person (*p. 88*)

Allies: an alliance in World War I, including Great Britain, France, Russia, Serbia, Belgium, and the United States (*p. 125*); during World War II, the opponents of the Axis, including the United States, Britain, and the Soviet Union (*p. 146*)

alloy: a blend of two metals (*p. 17*)

anarchy: the complete absence of government (*p. 43*)

anti-Semitism: discrimination against Jews (*p. 60*)

apostle: a disciple of Jesus who spread his teachings (*p. 42*)

appeasement: conciliation, especially the attempts by European nations to avoid war by meeting Hitler's demands (*p. 144*)

archer: a foot-soldier wielding a longbow (*p. 68*)

aristocracy: hereditary nobility or upper class (*p. 29*)

astrolabe: a navigational tool that indicates direction (*p. 80*)

Axis: alliance of Germany, Italy, and Japan in the 1930s and 1940s (*p. 143*)

balance of power: a distribution of power that keeps any one nation from becoming dangerous to the others (*p. 109*)

Battle of Britain: German air attacks on London and other British cities during World War II (*p. 146*)

barter: a system in which goods and services are exchanged without money (*p. 44*)

Benelux: acronym for the neighboring nations of Belgium, the Netherlands, and Luxembourg; customs union of those nations (*p. 161*)

Black Death: an epidemic of bubonic plague that struck Europe in the 1340s and 1350s (*p. 67*)

Blitzkrieg: during World War II, the German style of lightning-quick attack (*p. 145*)

Bolshevik: a member of the radical socialist party that established a Communist government in Russia (*p. 119*)

British Commonwealth of Nations: former name of the Commonwealth of Nations (*p. 275*)

Bundesrat: upper house of the German parliament (*p. 231*)

Bundestag: lower house of the German parliament (*p. 231*)

Byzantine: having to do with the eastern Roman Empire that flourished from A.D. 330 to 1453 (*p. 45*)

canton: a state of the Swiss confederation (*p. 242*)

capitalism: economic system characterized by private ownership of natural resources and the means of production, and by economic decision-making by private investors *(p. 93)*

Carolingian Renaissance: the efforts during the reign of Charlemagne to foster education and to preserve and copy religious and classical texts *(p. 48)*

Cavalier: a supporter of the English monarchy during the civil war that began in 1642 *(p. 91)*

Central Powers: an alliance in World War I, including Germany, Austria-Hungary, the Ottoman Empire, and Bulgaria *(p. 125)*

centralize: to concentrate power in one person or place *(p. 44)*

chancellor: the German equivalent of prime minister *(p. 231)*

Christian humanism: a philosophy that applies the ideals of humanism to the church *(p. 73)*

Christos: the Greek word for *Messiah (p. 42)*

chivalry: the code of behavior for knights *(p. 57)*

Chunnel: a railroad tunnel under the English Channel, connecting England and France *(p. 200)*

circumnavigate: to sail completely around *(p. 83)*

city-state: a political unit composed of a town and the area surrounding it *(p. 28)*

classical: having to do with the culture of ancient Greece and Rome *(p. 41)*

classical liberalism: an economic and political theory emphasizing the laws of supply and demand rather than government regulation *(p. 117)*

coalition: an alliance of two or more political parties

code: a body of laws that have been organized and arranged for easy use *(p. 38)*

Cold War: a period of hostility between Communist nations, led by the Soviet Union, and western nations, led by the United States, that began immediately after World War II and ended with the collapse of the USSR in 1991 *(p. 153)*

collectively: as a group *(p. 118)*

Comecon: the Council for Mutual Economic Assistance, an economic association of the Soviet Union and its satellites *(p. 166)*

commercial agriculture: a type of agriculture in which one or two crops are grown and sold for cash *(p. 93)*

Common Law: a body of law developed in England, based primarily on judicial precedents *(p. 61)*

Common Market: the European Economic Community, an economic union of European nations founded in 1957 *(p. 162)*

Commonwealth: the English republic set up by Oliver Cromwell in 1649 *(p. 91)*

Commonwealth of Nations: an organization of Great Britain and most of its former colonies (*p. 275*)

communism: an internationalist, totalitarian system of government in which the means of production and distribution are owned by the state (*p. 119*)

compass: a navigational tool that indicates direction (*p. 80*)

concentration camp: a prison camp (*p. 141*)

Congress of Vienna: a meeting of European leaders in 1815 that attempted to restore Europe to the order that existed before the French Revolution (*p. 109*)

constitutional monarchy: a system of government in which a monarch possesses ceremonial powers but an elected government rules (*p. 93*)

continental: a climate with long, cold winters, hot summers, and moderate to scarce rainfall (*p. 11*)

cottage industry: an economic system of small-scale industry in which people work in their homes (*p. 93*)

Council for Mutual Economic Assistance (Comecon): an Eastern European trading bloc consisting of the Soviet Union and its satellites (*p. 166*)

Counter-Reformation: the response of the Roman Catholic Church to the establishment of Protestant churches (*p. 87*)

coup d'état: a sudden overthrow of a government (*p. 92*)

crusade: one of series of Christian military expeditions mounted to recover Jerusalem and the Holy Land from the Turks (*p. 65*)

cultural diffusion: the spread of knowledge or technology from one culture to another (*p. 25*)

customs union: an agreement among a group of nations to eliminate taxes or tariffs on goods moving from one member nation to another (*p. 161*)

D-Day: June 6, 1944; date of Allied invasion of Normandy, in northwestern France (*p. 148*)

demilitarization: the removal of all military forces from an area (*p. 130*)

democratic liberalism: a political philosophy stressing the government's role in protecting the welfare of all its citizens (*p. 118*)

democracy: government by all citizens (*p. 29*)

demographic: having to do with the statistical study of human population (*p. 277*)

devolution: the handing of power to a lower level of government (*p. 209*)

dictator: a ruler with absolute power (*p. 138*)

direct democracy: a system of government in which all eligible citizens, not elected representatives, make the laws (*p. 29*)

disciple: a follower or pupil of a teacher (*p. 42*)

divine right of kings: the theory advanced by absolute monarchs that they received their authority directly from God *(p. 88)*

economist: a social scientist who studies the production, distribution, and consumption of goods and services *(p. 117)*

edict: an order or decree *(p. 45)*

enclave: a small, separate territory within the borders of a larger nation *(p. 265)*

enclosure: the fencing in of common farmland for grazing sheep, put into effect between 1714 and 1820 *(p. 113)*

Enlightenment: ideas and attitudes of the 1700s in Europe, character- ized by a scientific outlook and an emphasis on the rights of the individual *(p. 95)*

entrepreneur: a private investor; one who assumes the risks of and orga- nizes a business venture *(p. 93)*

Estates-General: the prerevolutionary French national parliament *(p. 99)*

estuary: a wide part of a river at its mouth, where tides influence the river's current *(p. 9)*

ethnocentric: characterized by the belief that one's own nation or group is superior *(p. 121)*

Euratom: the European Atomic Energy Agency, formed to promote the joint development of peaceful atomic energy *(p. 162)*

European Coal and Steel Community (ECSC): an international authority established in 1953 to oversee the coal and steel industries of France, West Germany, Italy, and the Benelux countries *(p. 162)*

European Community (EC): an organization of European nations cre- ated to encourage free trade and economic and political unity among its members; sucessor to the Common Market *(p. 163)*

European Economic Area (EEA): an organization formed in 1991 by uniting the EC and the EFTA *(p. 172)*

European Free Trade Association (EFTA): a rival trade group to the European Community *(p. 163)*

excommunicate: to punish by officially depriving a person of the rights of church membership *(p. 55)*

Fascist: having to do with the political party in Italy founded by Benito Mussolini *(p. 137)*

fealty: a pledge of loyalty by a vassal to a lord *(p. 55)*

feudalism: a system of medieval political organization in which a vassal gave loyalty and service to a lord in exchange for protection and land *(p. 55)*

fief: an estate given by a lord to a vassal in exchange for service and loy- alty *(p. 55)*

Fifth Republic: the framework of government of France established by Charles de Gaulle in 1958 *(p. 215)*

Finlandization: the situation of a small nation that carefully avoids angering a larger neighbor (p. 190)

fossil fuel: an energy source, such as coal or oil, formed from the remains of plants and animals (p. 15)

Fourteen Points: Woodrow Wilson's plan to ensure a just and lasting peace after World War I (p. 129)

Franco-Prussian War: a conflict between France and Prussia in 1870 and 1871, leading to the unification of Germany (p. 111)

Führer: title taken by Hitler; the German word for *leader* (p. 140)

genocide: the murder of an entire nation or religious group (p. 151)

Gestapo: German secret police during the Nazi era (140)

Girondist: a member of a French radical group that favored war with countries that opposed the revolution (p. 100)

gladiator: a person engaged in a fight to the death for public entertainment (p. 41)

glasnost: a policy of openness in the government of the Soviet Union, introduced in the 1980s by Mikhail Gorbachev (p. 167)

Glorious Revolution: the bloodless *coup d'état* in England that replaced King James II with William and Mary (p. 92)

Gospel: in Christianity, the "good news" that Jesus came to earth to save all human beings (p. 42)

goulash communism: the Hungarian program of economic reforms begun in 1968 (p. 167)

grand duchy: a government headed by a grand duke or a grand duchess (p.217)

Greco-Roman: referring to the culture of ancient Rome, which incorporated most of the philosophy and art of ancient Greece (p. 41)

Green Revolution: the use of hybrid plants, irrigation, fertilizers, and pesticides to produce more abundant crop yields (p. 280)

Gulf Stream: a warm ocean current that flows north and east across the Atlantic Ocean (p. 3)

guild: a medieval trade association (p. 60)

Hellene: a Greek-speaking person in the anicent world (p. 28)

Hellenic: the civilization of ancient Greek-speaking peoples (p. 28)

Hellenistic: having to do with the period from 323 B.C. to 30 B.C. and with the blended Greek and eastern culture that resulted from the conquests of Alexander the Great (p. 36)

heretic: a person whose beliefs defy church authority (p. 85)

hierarchy: an organization into ranks, each of which is subordinate to the one above it (p. 55)

Holocaust: the mass murder of Jews by the Nazis (p. 151)

home front: civilian life during a war (p. 127)

homogeneous: made up of similar or identical individuals (p. 1701)

House of Commons: the democratically elected lower house of the British Parliament (p. 206)

House of Lords: the upper house of the British Parliament; its members are not elected (*p. 206*)

Huguenot: a French Protestant, specifically a follower of John Calvin (*p. 86*)

Hundred Years' War: a war between France and England that lasted from 1337 to 1453 (*p. 68*)

humanism: a philosophy, developed during the Renaissance, that established human beings rather than God as the central focus of all study and artistic expression; it emphasized the importance and dignity of the individual (*p. 71*)

humanities: the branches of learning concerned with humanistic studies (*p. 73*)

imperialism: the policy of building an empire by extending a nation's rule over other countries (*p. 119*)

indulgence: a pardon by the church releasing a sinner from some of the punishments he or she would face after death (*p. 85*)

Industrial Revolution: the period in the 1800s and 1900s during which a mechanized factory system developed (*p. 112*)

inflation: a rapid rise in prices caused by increase in the volume of money and/or credit without an increase in available goods (*p. 43*)

Jacobin: a member of a radical group of the French Revolution, opposed by the Girondists (*p. 100*)

Jacquerie: a revolt by French peasants in 1358 (*p. 69*)

Jesuit: a member of the Society of Jesus, an order of Roman Catholic priests founded in 1534 (*p. 87*)

jingoism: extreme nationalism, characterized by hatred and suspicion of other nations (*p. 122*)

Junker: a member of the Prussian landowning class (*p. 227*)

Kaiser: title assumed by William I of Germany in 1871; the German word for *emperor* (*p. 111*)

laissez-faire: French phrase expressing the idea that economic markets should operate without government regulation (*p. 97*)

landlocked: totally enclosed by land, without access to the sea (*p. 14*)

Latin Christendom: the countries of Europe that were Roman Catholic in the Middle Ages (*p. 57*)

Law of Nations: a system of laws in the Roman empire (*p. 41*)

legion: the principle unit of the Roman army (*p. 38*)

lend-lease: a U.S. program of aid to the Allies in World War II (*p. 146*)

lignite: a soft, brown coal (*p. 230*)

Loyalist: a member of the pro-government forces in the Spanish Civil War; also called *Republican* (*p. 142*)

Magna Carta: a document, signed by King John of England in 1215, guaranteeing basic civil rights and privileges (*p. 61*)

mandate: a territory administered but not owned by a member nation of the League of Nations or the United Nations (*p. 131*)

manorial system: the medieval economic system of self-sufficient life on large estates called manors *(p. 55)*

maritime: a climate with moderate temperatures and much rainfall in all seasons *(p. 11)*

Marshall Plan: a U.S. program of aid to Europe after World War II *(p. 153)*

Marxism: the political, economic, and social theories of Karl Marx, emphasizing the importance of economic forces and class struggle *(p. 118)*

Mediterranean: a climate with warm, dry summers and mild winters, during which most of the rainfall occurs *(p. 11)*

medieval: having to do with the Middle Ages *(p. 53)*

megalith: a giant stone monument erected in prehistoric times *(p. 26)*

mercenary: a hired foreign soldier *(p. 43)*

mercantilism: economic policies meant to increase national wealth and power and stressing a favorable balance of trade *(p. 93)*

Messiah: the savior promised by Hebrew prophets; Christians believe that Jesus was the Messiah *(p. 42)*

metallurgy: the knowledge and use of metals *(p. 27)*

Middle Ages: the period in European history from about A.D. 500 to about A.D. 1500 *(p. 53)*

middle class: the social class between peasants and nobles *(p. 60)*

mineral fuel: a fuel formed from the remains of plants and animals; a fossil fuel *(p. 15)*

mobilize: to prepare an army for war *(p. 124)*

monastery: a residence for people who have withdrawn from the world for religious reasons *(p. 59)*

mosaic: a design made by fitting together small pieces of stone and colored glass *(p. 36)*

multinational: a corporation owned and operated in more than one country *(p. 280)*

Munich: giving in to an aggressor, as in the Munich Agreement of 1938 *(p. 144)*

nation: a community of people with a distinctive culture and, usually, its own territory and language *(p. 107)*

nation-state: a government that takes in one nation only *(p. 107)*

National Assembly: the name taken by the Third Estate of France in 1789 when it broke away from the Estates-General *(p. 100)*

nationalism: intense loyalty to one's country above all others; fervent support for one's ethnic group and its independence *(p. 101)*

nationalist: glorifying the goals of one nation to the exclusion of others *(p. 138)*

Nationalist: a military insurgent during the Spanish Civil War *(p. 142)*

nationalize: to remove an industry from private ownership and place it under government control *(p. 274)*

natural resource: anything in the environment that people can use to improve their lives *(p. 11)*

navigation canal: an artificial waterway for use by ships and other vessels *(p. 10)*

Nazi: the short name for Hitler's National Socialist German Workers' Party *(p. 139)*

Neolithic: having to do with the New Stone Age, beginning about 8000 B.C. in Europe *(p. 25)*

Ninety-Five Theses: the document that Martin Luther posted on the door of the castle church in Wittenberg, Germany, in 1517, attacking the practice of selling indulgences; the beginning of the Protestant Reformation *(p. 85)*

nonaligned: following a policy of neutrality toward both Communist and western powers *(p. 276)*

North Atlantic Treaty Organization (NATO): a military alliance of the United States, Canada, and 14 European nations *(p. 154)*

North German Confederation: a federal government of 22 states, formed by Bismarck in 1866 *(p. 111)*

oligarchy: rule by a few wealthy citizens *(p. 29)*

ombudsman: a government official who receives and investigates complaints from citizens about the government *(p. 187)*

ostracism: an ancient Greek practice of banishing potential tyrants for ten years *(p. 29)*

Paleolithic: having to do with the Old Stone Age, the earliest part of human prehistory *(p. 25)*

papacy: the pope and the chief administrators of the Roman Catholic Church *(p. 56)*

Papal States: parts of Italy ruled by the pope *(p. 47)*

parlement: the king's court introduced in medieval France *(p. 62)*

patrician: wealthy aristocrat of ancient Rome *(p. 38)*

Pax Romana: the years between 27 B.C. and A.D. 180, a period of peace throughout the Roman empire *(p. 39)*

peasant: a member of a farm worker family *(p. 56)*

Peloponnesian War: a war between Athens and Sparta from 431 to 404 B.C. *(p. 31)*

peninsula: a land area largely surrounded by water *(p. 1)*

perestroika: the restructuring of Soviet economic life instituted by Mikhail Gorbachev *(p. 168)*

philosophe: any of the Enlightenment writers who fostered ideas of individual liberty and freedom from unreasonable authority *(p. 95)*

philosophy: the study of the nature of existence, knowledge, and the principles of human thought and behavior *(p. 33)*

plebeian: a common person of ancient Rome *(p. 38)*

plebiscite: an election in which citizens vote yes or no on an issue *(p. 140)*

polar: a climate with constant cold temperatures and scarce rainfall (*p. 11*)

pope: the bishop of Rome and the head of the Roman Catholic Church (*p. 56*)

Popular Front: in Spain, the combination of left-of-center political parties that won the 1936 election (*p. 142*)

Prague Spring: a brief period of reform in Czechoslovakia in 1968 (*p.156*)

prehistoric: having to do with the time before written records (*p. 26*)

premier: the French equivalent of prime minister (*p. 215*)

privatize: in formerly socialist or communist states, to sell government-held businesses and industries to private investors (*p. 238*)

principality: a state headed by a prince (*p. 224*)

proletariat: the term used by Karl Marx for the working classes (*p. 119*)

proportional representation: an electoral system that distributes seats in a legislature among political parties in proportion to their share of votes (*p. 187*)

protocol: a supplemental agreement to a pact or treaty (*p. 144*)

Puritan: a member of a Calvinist sect that wished to purify the Church of England by removing much of its ritual and changing its doctrine (*p. 91*)

rational: based on logical reasoning (*p. 31*)

Realpolitik: the German term for policies grounded in practical considerations rather than theoretical or ethical ideals (*p. 110*)

Reconquista: the recovery of Spanish lands from the Moors (*p. 259*)

Reformation: the religious movement in the 1500s that led to the establishment of Protestant churches (*p. 84*)

region: an area that shares certain characteristics (*p. 3*)

Reich: German word for *empire* (*p. 111*)

Reign of Terror: a period during the French Revolution of extreme violence, when approximately 17,000 people were put to death (*p. 101*)

Renaissance: the period in European history from about 1350 to 1600, beginning with a revival of interest in classical culture and marked by a new world outlook and great activity in the arts (*p. 70*)

reparations: payment for war damages by a defeated country (*p. 130*)

republic: a government in which citizens with the right to vote elect their leaders (*p. 37*)

Republican: an individual favoring the government during the Spanish Civil War; a Loyalist (*p. 142*)

Resistance: French underground movement in World War II (*p. 148*)

Restoration: the period in English history from 1660 to 1688, following the Commonwealth, when the monarchy was restored (*p. 92*)

Risorgimento: the drive for the unification of Italy (*p. 109*)

Romance language: a language derived from Latin (*p. 251*)

Rome-Berlin Axis: alliance between Germany and Italy signed in 1937 (*p. 143*)

Roundhead: a supporter of Parliament during the English civil war *(p. 91)*

sacrament: one of formal rituals of Christianity *(p. 58)*

salon: an informal gathering of writers and thinkers; popular during the Enlightenment *(p. 95)*

sanctions: penalties, usually an economic or military action, against one nation by several other nations acting together *(p. 143)*

satellite: a nation dominated by another nation, especially the nations of eastern Europe dominated by the Soviet Union during the Cold War *(p. 155)*

scapegoat: a person or group that is blamed for conditions caused by others *(43)*

scientific method: a method of gaining knowledge through observation, experimentation, and rational deduction *(p. 94)*

Scientific Revolution: the introduction of scientific reasoning in the 1600s and 1700s *(p. 94)*

Second Industrial Revolution: changes in science, technology, agriculture, and industry since 1945 *(p. 280)*

sect: a smaller group within a religious body *(p. 42)*

secular: nonchurch *(p. 56)*

Senate: the governing body of ancient Rome *(p. 38)*

serf: a peasant bound for life to a manor under the feudal system *(p. 56)*

sheriff: an English royal agent *(p. 61)*

Six, the: the members of the ECSC: France, West Germany, Italy, Belgium, the Netherlands, and Luxembourg *(p. 162)*

socialism: an economic theory emphasizing the welfare of the community *(p. 118)*

Socratic method: a manner of teaching that tries to arrive at the truth by asking questions *(p. 33)*

Solidarity: a Polish labor union that defied the Communist government and later became a successful political party *(p. 235)*

Sophist: one of a school of ancient Greek philosophers who used reason to understand the nature of people and their society *(p. 33)*

sovereignty: power of a nation to make all decisions for itself *(p. 163)*

Stoicism: a philosophy of the Hellenistic period that taught that people should accept what happens to them without complaining *(p. 37)*

strait: a narrow body of water connecting larger bodies of water *(p. 11)*

subarctic: a dry climate with short, cool summers and long, cold winters *(p. 11)*

subsistence farming: agriculture in which almost everything needed is raised locally and crops are not raised to sell *(p. 93)*

Sudetenland: areas of Czechoslovakia with large German populations, annexed by Germany in 1938 *(p. 144)*

superpower: either the United States or the Soviet Union during the Cold War *(p. 151)*

synthetic: not made of natural ingredients; manmade *(p. 281)*

systematize: to arrange existing knowledge into a system *(p. 37)*

technology: applying scientific principles in practical ways *(p. 114)*

Third Reich: Hitler's government of Germany, in power from 1933 to 1945 *(p. 140)*

tithe: a tax representing 10 percent of a person's income *(p. 56)*

Toleration Act: An act of Parliament of 1689 granting all Protestants in England the right to worship as they saw fit *(p. 92)*

topography: the shape of the surface area of a geographic region *(p. 3)*

total war: a conflict demanding an all-out commitment of human and material resources *(p. 125)*

totalitarian state: a government that monopolizes power, controls almost every aspect of life, and demands strict obedience from the people *(p. 138)*

tragedy: a type of drama in which a noble hero comes to grief through a fatal flaw *(p. 34)*

trattoria: an Italian restaurant *(p. 255)*

tribute: regular payments of money paid by a weak state to a more powerful state to ensure peace and protection *(p. 31)*

Triple Alliance: a mutual-defense agreement among Germany, Austria-Hungary, and Italy, made in 1901 **(p. 123)**

Triple Entente: an alliance among Britain, France, and Russia, made in 1904 *(p. 123)*

troubadour: a wandering poet and singer of the Middle Ages *(p. 57)*

tyrant: in ancient Greece, a ruler who seized control by force *(p. 29)*

U-boat: a German submarine *(p. 127)*

Ulster: another name for Northern Ireland *(p. 212)*

unicameral: having only one legislative house or chamber *(p. 187)*

Unionists: residents of Northern Ireland who wish to remain part of the United Kingdom *(p. 213)*

Utopian Socialist: a social reformer who envisioned ideal communities in which the means of production would be owned collectively *(p. 118)*

vassal: in the feudal system, a person under obligation to provide a lord with loyalty and service *(p. 55)*

Velvet Revolution: massive but peaceful demonstrations that brought down the Communist government of Czechoslovakia in 1989 *(p. 238)*

vernacular: the everyday spoken language of a people *(p. 71)*

Weimar Republic: the democratic government of Germany from 1919 to 1933 *(p. 139)*

welfare state: a government that assumes primary responsibility for the welfare of its citizens *(p. 118)*

Zealot: a member of a Jewish sect that urged armed revolt against the Roman emperor *(p. 42)*

Bibliography

Chapter 1

Adams, Simon, John Briquebee, and Ann Kramer. *Illustrated Atlas of World History*. New York: Random House, 1992.

DeBlij, H.J. and P.O. Muller. *Geography: Regions and Concepts*. 5th ed. New York: Wiley, 1988.

Lee, W. Robert, ed. *European Demography and Economic Growth*. New York: St. Martin's, 1985.

Moore, R. I., ed. *Atlas of World History*. Chicago: Rand McNally, 1987.

Turnock, David. *Eastern Europe: An Historical Geography, 1915-1945*. New York: Routledge, Chapman and Hall, 1988.

Chapter 2

Ferrill, Arther. *The Fall of the Roman Empire*. London: Thames & Hudson, 1986.

Caselli, Giovanni. *The Roman Empire and the Dark Ages*. New York: Harper & Row, 1989.

Grant, Michael. *The Founders of the Western World: A History of Greece and Rome*. New York: Scribner, 1991.

Hamilton, Edith. *The Greek Way*. New York: Norton, 1930.

Vickers, Michael J. *The Roman World*. New York: Peter Bedrick, 1989.

Chapter 3

Cardini, Franco. *Europe 1492: Portrait of a Continent Five Hundred Years Ago*. New York: Facts on File, 1989.

Caselli, Giovanni. *The Renaissance and the New World*. New York: Peter Bedrick, 1990.

Gies, Frances, and Joseph Gies. *Life in a Medieval Village*. New York: Harper & Row, 1990.

Hay, Denys, ed. *The Age of Renaissance*. New York: Bonanza Books, 1986.

Holmes, George. *The Oxford Illustrated History of Medieval Europe*. New York: Oxford University Press, 1988.

Chapter 4

Durant, Will, and Ariel Durant. *The Age of Napoleon*. New York: Simon and Schuster, 1975.

Jones, Colin. *Voices of the French Revolution*. Topsfield, MA: Salem House, 1988.

Ozment, Steven. *Protestants: The Birth of a Revolution*. New York: Doubleday, 1992.

Smith, Lacey B. *The Horizon Book of the Elizabethan World*. New York: American Heritage Publishing Company, Inc., 1967.

Chapter 5

Droz, Jacques. *Europe between the Revolutions, 1815-1848*. New York: Harper & Row, 1967.

Kennan, George F. *The Fateful Alliance: France, Russia, and the Coming of the First World War*. New York: Pantheon, 1984.

Mayer, Arno. *The Persistence of the Old Regime: Europe to the Great War*. New York: Pantheon, 1981.

Ward, Barbara. *Nationalism and Ideology*. New York: Norton, 1966.

Young, Brigadier Peter, ed. *The Marshall Cavendish Illustrated Encyclopedia of World War I*. New York: Marshall Cavendish, 1986.

Chapter 6

Commager, Henry Steele. *The Story of the Second World War*. New York: Brassey's (US), Inc., 1991.

De Grand, Alexander J. *Italian Fascism: Its Origin and Development*. Lincoln, NE: University of Nebraska Press, 1982.

Hogan, Michael J. *The Marshall Plan: America, Britain, and the Reconstruction of Western Europe, 1947-1952*. Cambridge: Cambridge University Press, 1987.

Noakes, J. and G. Pridham, eds. *Nazism: A History in Documents and Eyewitness Accounts, 1919-1945*. Vol. 1. New York: Schocken, 1983.

Willmott, H. P. *The Great Crusade: A New Complete History of the Second World War*. New York: The Free Press, 1990.

Walters, E. Garrison. *The Other Europe: Eastern Europe to 1945*. Syracuse, NY: Syracuse University Press, 1988.

Wyden, Peter. *The Passionate War: The Narrative History of the Spanish Civil War*. New York: Simon Schuster, 1983.

Chapter 7

Finan, William W., Jr., ed. "The New Europe." *Current History*, November, 1991.

Havinghurst, Alfred F. *Britain in Transition: Twentieth Century*. 4th ed. Chicago: University of Chicago Press, 1985.

Lippmann, Walter. *Western Unity and the Common Market*. Boston: Little, Brown, 1962.

Mayne, Richard. *The Recovery of Europe: From Devastation to Unity*. New York: Harper & Row, 1970.

Chapter 8

Cannery, Donald S. *The Scandinavians.* New York: Simon and Schuster, 1966.

Editors of Time-Life Books. *Scandinavia.* Alexandria, VA: Time-Life Books, 1987.

Lander, Patricia, and Claudette Charbonneau. *The Land and People of Finland.* New York: Lippincott, 1990.

Roberts, David. *Iceland: Land of the Sagas.* New York: Abrams, 1990.

Visiland, Priita J. "The Baltic Nations." *National Geographic,* November, 1990, pp. 2-37.

Chapter 9

Editors of Time-Life Books. *France.* Alexandria, VA: Time-Life Books, 1985.

Foster, R. F. *The Oxford Illustrated History of Ireland.* New York: Oxford University Press, 1989.

Harris, Jonathan. *The Land and People of France.* New York: Lippincott, 1989.

Thompson, Carol L., ed. "Europe: West." *Current History,* November, 1990.

Tourtellot, Johnathan B., ed. *Discovering Britain and Ireland.* Washington, D. C.: National Geographic Society, 1985.

Chapter 10

Burant, Stephen R., ed. *Hungary: a Country Study.* Washington, D.C.: U.S. Government Printing Office, 1990.

Fulbrook, Mary. *A Concise History of Germany.* New York: Cambridge University Press, 1990.

Garton Ash, Timothy. *The Uses of Adversity: Essays on the Fate of Central Europe.* New York: Random House, 1989.

Gawdiak, Ihor, ed. *Czechoslovakia: A Country Study.* Washington, DC: U.S. Government Printing Office, 1989.

Riodan, James. *Eastern Europe.* Englewood Cliffs, NJ: Silver Burdett, 1987.

Chapter 11

Editors of Time-Life Books. *Spain.* Amsterdam: Time-Life Books, 1986.

Harrison, Barbara. *Italian Days.* New York: Grove-Weidenfeld, 1989.

Murray, William. *The Last Italian: Portrait of a People.* New York: Prentice Hall, 1991.

Shinn, R.S., ed. *Italy: a Country Study*. Washington DC: U.S. Government Printing Office, 1985.

Solstein, Eric, ed. *Spain: a Country Study*. Washington DC: U.S. Government Printing Office, 1990.

Chapter 12

Laqueur, Walter. *Europe in Our Time: A History, 1945-1992*. New York: Viking, 1992.

Lewis, Flora. *Europe: A Tapestry of Nations*. New York: Simon and Schuster, 1987.

Treverton, Gregory F. "The New Europe." *Foreign Affairs*, Vol. 71, No. 1, 1992, pp. 94-112.

Wallace, William, ed. *The Dynamics of European Integration*. New York: Columbia University Press, 1991.

Index

304

306

Ural Mountains, 1, 146
Urban II (pope), 65
Utopian Socialists, 118

Vandals, 45
Vatican City, 138, 247, 248, 266
Velvet Revolution, 238
Venice, 10, 65, 66, 70, 79, 110, 253, 256
Versailles, 90, 129-130
    Treaty of, 130-131, 143
Vesuvius, 252
Vichy France, 145
Victor Emmanuel III (Italy), 137, 254
Vienna, 109, 112, 222, 223, 226, 242
    Congress of, 109, 110
Vietnam, 273
Vikings, 53-55, 205
Vilnius, 179, 182, 193
Visigoths, 44-45, 250
Vistula River, 9, 234
Volga River, 225
Voltaire, 95

Wagner, Richard, 229
Wales, 3, 13, 17, 201, 205, 208-209
Walesa, Lech, 235, 237
Wallonia, 203
Walter the Penniless, 65
War of the Spanish Succession, 90
Wars of the Roses, 91
Warsaw Pact, 154, 156, 169, 232
Warsaw, 223, 226, 234
Waterloo, battle of, 103

Watt, James, 114
Weimar Republic, 139-140
welfare states, 118, 119, 184-189, 210
Wellington, duke of, 103
Weser River, 9, 10, 229
West Germany, 154, 162, 168, 223, 230-
    231; see also Germany
West Indies, 98, 113
William I (Germany), 111
William of Normandy (the Conqueror),
    55, 61, 200
William of Orange, 92
Wilson, Woodrow, 128, 129-130
Winter War (1939-40), 145, 146, 190
Wollstonecraft, Mary, 96
women, 29, 35, 38, 56-57, 93, 95-96, 115,
    117, 127, 207, 208 233
World War I, 119, 122-131, 135, 137, 139,
    140, 141, 142, 218
    causes, 122-125, 260
    effects, 128-131, 222, 223, 254
World War II, 143-151, 169, 190, 218, 226,
    241, 262
    causes, 143-144
    effects of 152-153, 170, 192, 223, 225,
    226, 228, 233, 234, 277-279

Xerxes I (Persia), 30
Yalta Conference, 152
Yeltsin, Boris, 169
Yugoslavia, 9, 18, 130, 151, 155, 170-171,
    240-241, 247, 248, 250, 251, 261-263
Zagreb, 223, 241

Photo Acknowledgments: 2, Fridmar Damm/FPG; 5, Georgia Engelhard/FPG; 7, TWA Photograph; 12, Spencer Grant/FPG; 15, Steve Vidler/Leo de Wys; 20, Steve Vidler/FPG; 26, Arthur Hustwitt/Leo de Wys; 30, Bernard G. Silberstein/FPG; 33, FPG; 36, Bettmann Archive; 39, Art Resource; 46, Kerwin G. Roche/FPG; 54, Joachim Messerschmidt/Leo de Wys; 58, 63, 72, Bettmann Archive; 81, Art Resource; 86, From *Here I Stand: A Life of Martin Luther* by Roland H. Bainton (Abingdon Press, 1950); 89, Steve Vidler/Leo de Wys; 92, 99, 102, 111, 113, 116, 120, 125, 129, Bettmann Archive; 137, FPG; 141, 147, 149, 155, Bettmann Archive; 162, Leo de Wys; 169, Reuters/Bettmann; 180, Joachim Messer/FPG; 183, D and J/Stock Boston; 184, Nicholas Sapieha/Leo de Wys; 188, Dallas & John Heaton/Stock Boston; 191, Stacy Pick/Stock Boston; 193, Reuters/Bettmann; 203, British Information Service; 204, Henry Moore; 207, British Information Service; 213, UPI Bettmann; 216, Bettmann Archive; 224, Steve Vidler/Leo de Wys; 229, Lufthansa; 232, W. Hille/Leo de Wys; 235, 237, Reuters/Bettmann; 239, Van Phillips/Leo de Wys; 240, J. Rau/Leo de Wys; 249, Van Phillips/Leo de Wys; 251, Ulf Sjostedt/FPG; 253, UPI/Bettmann; 257, Richard Harrington/FPG; 262, Reuters/Bettmann; 266, 273, 276, FPG; 279, Jean Smolar.